AN ESSAY ON THE PRINCIPLE OF POPULATION AND OTHER WRITINGS

THOMAS ROBERT MALTHUS was the second son born into a relatively affluent Surrey family in 1766. He was privately schooled and then went to Jesus College, Cambridge, completing his degree in 1788. He went on to take an MA in 1791 and to become a fellow of the college in 1793. Malthus was also ordained as a minister of the Church of England in 1788. In 1798 Malthus anonymously published his *Essay on the Principle of Population*, unquestionably the most influential demographic treatise ever written and a pioneering work of social science. He went on to produce much expanded editions of the *Essay* throughout his life, the first appearing in 1803 and the last in 1826. Malthus married in 1804 and in the subsequent year he was appointed Professor of History and Political Economy at the East India College in Haileybury, the first professorial appointment in economics in Britain and one he would hold for the rest of his life. Malthus contributed pamphlets about the key political debates of the early nineteenth century such as the Poor Laws, the Corn Laws and the condition of Ireland and crystallized his ideas as an economist in *Principles of Political Economy* (1820). Malthus was a Fellow of the Royal Society, an Associate of the Royal Society of Literature and a founder member of both the Political Economy Club and the Statistical Society. He died in 1834.

ROBERT J. MAYHEW is Professor of Historical Geography and Intellectual History at the University of Bristol. He was educated at Hertford College, Oxford, and St John's College, Oxford, and held a Fellowship at Corpus Christi College, Cambridge. He is the author of *Malthus: The Life and Legacies of an Untimely Prophet* (2014).

THOMAS MALTHUS

An Essay on the Principle of Population and Other Writings

Introduction and Notes by
ROBERT J. MAYHEW

PENGUIN BOOKS

PENGUIN CLASSICS

UK | USA | Canada | Ireland | Australia
India | New Zealand | South Africa

Penguin Books is part of the Penguin Random House group of companies
whose addresses can be found at global.penguinrandomhouse.com

Penguin
Random House
UK

This edition first published in Penguin Classics 2015

Introduction and Notes copyright © Robert J. Mayhew, 2015
All rights reserved

Set in 10.25/12.25 pt Adobe Sabon
Typeset by Jouve (UK), Milton Keynes
Printed in Great Britain by Clays Ltd, St Ives plc

ISBN: 978-0-141-39282-0

www.greenpenguin.co.uk

Penguin Random House is committed to a
sustainable future for our business, our readers
and our planet. This book is made from Forest
Stewardship Council® certified paper.

Contents

Introduction   vii
Further Reading   xliii

An Essay on the Principle of
Population and Other Writings

An Essay on the Principle of Population
   (1798)   3

The Travel Diaries of Thomas Malthus:
   The Scandinavian Journal (1799)   165

An Investigation of the Cause of the
   Present High Price of Provisions
   (1800)   173

Two Selections from the 1803 Edition
   of the *Essay*   191

Observations on the Effects of the Corn
   Laws (1814)   213

Selections from Principles of Political
   Economy (1820)   241

Notes   285

Introduction

In January 2014, in their annual 'state of the globe' address entitled *3 Myths that Block Progress for the Poor*, Bill and Melinda Gates suggested that one great myth preventing global development is the idea that population growth makes advances in personal and societal wealth and happiness impossible. The Gateses focused on life in the present and visions for the future, but in addressing myths about population they honed in on the contributions of a man born 250 years earlier, Thomas Robert Malthus. They commented that 'going back at least to Thomas Malthus, who published his *An Essay on the Principle of Population* in 1798, people have worried about doomsday scenarios in which food supply can't keep up with population growth' and ascribed to him 'a laissez-faire approach to development – letting children die now so they don't starve later', before commenting that this 'doesn't actually work, thank goodness'.[1] It is not clear from these comments if the Gateses have actually read the works of Malthus (as this volume will allow you to!), but a good part of Malthus's historical power and importance rests precisely in the fact that people don't have to read him to invoke his name.

The Gateses are by no means alone in framing Malthus's work as something still to be jousted with in the present day. On the contrary, recent years have witnessed commentators see in Malthus a prophet, variously false or visionary, someone who can help us understand such global issues as the food price 'spike' of 2007–8, global economic depression in the credit crunch and impending environmental Armageddon.[2] Thus Malthus finds his way once again front and centre in political, environmental and economic discussions in a way not seen since the fears of a 'population bomb' that gripped policy makers in the 1960s and '70s.

Public commentators such as John Gray have suggested Malthus explains the future of global warfare in the twenty-first century far more effectively than discussions of the clash of political or religious ideals, while Niall Ferguson has told us in the context of both rising food prices and increased price volatility not to count Malthus out too soon.[3] They are not alone: more sober economists also see a need to return to Malthus to understand our present global situation. Paul Krugman and Joseph Stiglitz, for example, Nobel Laureates in economics both, have recently acknowledged that, whereas they could dismiss Malthusian fears about the balance between population and resources over the previous three decades, current statistical data leaves them less confident.[4] And behind these modest claims for Malthus's enduring importance are the more grandiose allegations made about him; over the decades Malthus has been seen as the progenitor of the Victorian workhouses of Dickensian legend, as the patron saint of the compulsory sterilization of tens of thousands of Americans in the twentieth century, as paving the high road to Hitler and, latterly, as intellectual ammunition for Islamic fundamentalism.[5] Given this hubbub of discussion around Malthus, this introduction will give insight into his early life and the ideas set out in *An Essay on the Principle of Population* of 1798, which forms the core of this edition, before moving on to address how his ideas evolved over the remaining thirty years of his life as excerpted in this volume. I will conclude by addressing the legacy of his ideas, the question of why Malthus's work has remained so perennially modern as to engage the attention of telecom tycoons and Nobel prizewinners alike.

MALTHUS'S LIFE AND
INFLUENCES UNTIL 1798

Thomas Robert Malthus, known universally as Robert or Bob, was born in 1766 into a family at the upper end of the 'middling sort' in Surrey.[6] As the second son, however, Malthus would have to work to earn his living, despite the comparative affluence of his origins. In many ways the manner in which Malthus was educated can help us to understand his achievement both in the *Essay* of 1798 and in his life's work more generally. Malthus's initial education was under the tutelage of the poet, cleric and writer Richard Graves in the village of Claverton, just outside the fashionable spa town of Bath. The curriculum there was the standard fare for its era, centred on the acquisition of ancient languages and literature, and yet Graves himself was anything but a run-of-the-mill teacher. On the contrary, he has some claim to being one of the finest satirists of his age, thanks to his authorship of *The Spiritual Quixote* (1773), a satire on the irrationalism and pomposity of the Methodism of John Wesley and George Whitefield written in implicit support of the Anglican Church of which Graves was an ordained minister. While one cannot draw direct lines of force between Graves's satire and Malthus's later writing, it is notable that the 1798 edition of the *Essay* is laced with satirical attacks on the enthusiastic advocates of French revolutionary ideals who saw the events of 1789 as ushering in a new age of perpetual improvement. Malthus took Graves's religious satire and transferred it to the realm of politics:

> A writer may tell me that he thinks man will ultimately become an ostrich. I cannot properly contradict him. But before he can expect to bring any reasonable person over to his opinion, he ought to show, that the necks of mankind have been gradually elongating; that the lips have grown harder, and more prominent; that the legs and feet are daily altering their shape; and that the hair is beginning to change into stubs of feathers. And till the probability of so

wonderful a conversion can be shown, it is surely lost time and
lost eloquence to expatiate on the happiness of man in such a
state, to describe his powers, both of running and flying (p. 15*).

Under Graves, Malthus's education was conventional, and yet
Malthus's father Daniel was anything but a provincial member
of the establishment, instead being a passionate advocate of the
emancipatory ideas of Jean-Jacques Rousseau. And it is this
paternal radicalism that probably explains why Malthus was
moved from Graves's school to the leading Dissenting school of
the age in Warrington in the early 1780s. In an age when pre-
ferment in the professions often required subscription to the
articles of faith of the Anglican Church, sending Malthus to a
Dissenting academy was a brave or, less charitably, foolhardy
move. Still Daniel clearly wanted his son to have a less restrict-
edly classical education. Warrington saw Malthus educated by
one of the great rationalist critics of church tradition of the age,
Gilbert Wakefield, and also saw him encounter at first hand the
traces of the emergent economy of coal and factories, about
whose impact on the balance of the British economy Malthus
would be enduringly ambivalent, an ambivalence that would
first be displayed in the sections of the 1798 *Essay* addressing
the ideas of Adam Smith (chapters Sixteen and Seventeen). And
yet it is Gilbert Wakefield's influence that is far more palpable
in the fabric of the *Essay* than that of Warrington, thanks to the
final two chapters (Eighteen and Nineteen), wherein Malthus
sets out a religious justification of the otherwise bleak consequences of his principle of population in terms of the need for
the human mind to come to know God through apprehension
of the laws by which he guides the universe. While a rational
approach to religion was common currency in Malthus's age,
the extent and starkness of his rationalism shocked many contemporary readers of the *Essay*, placing him uncomfortably
close to blasphemy for some, and leading Malthus to withdraw
these chapters in later editions.

* All future references to Malthus's writings in this introduction are by page
number to this edition unless otherwise stated.

Malthus's intellectual interests were strongly defined during his time at Jesus College, Cambridge, from 1784 to 1788. Cambridge was at the heart of rationalist Anglicanism thanks to William Paley and of pure mathematics thanks to the continued authority of its most influential alumnus of the past century, Isaac Newton. Both schools of thought would have a lasting effect on Malthus's outlook and life's work. And yet, as Malthus wrote to his father as an undergraduate, while mathematically able (he would come ninth overall in his year), pure mathematics did not fire his imagination: 'The plan of Mathematical & Philosophical reading pursued at Cambridge is perhaps too much confined to speculation.' He went on to reveal that his extracurricular reading had earned him a reputation as someone interested in applied mathematics, being 'rather remark'd in College for talking of what actually exists in nature, or may be put to real practical use'.[7] It was precisely this application of mathematics to the real world that would become Malthus's passion and expertise.

The decade between Malthus taking his degree in Cambridge and the publication of his *Essay* has left few documentary traces. We know that he was ordained in 1788 and became curate of Okewood in Surrey, returning to live under his parents' roof once more. We also know that he was made a fellow of Jesus College in 1793. Finally, we know thanks to a few preserved fragments only published after his death that Malthus sought to become an author, writing a political pamphlet entitled *The Crisis* in 1796. And yet, if Malthus is hard to track down personally, the decade after the French Revolution was one of manifest intellectual, political and social turmoil in England and it is this turmoil that helps to explain why and when Malthus turned to writing. There was a pitched ideological battle in England about the rights and wrongs of the French Revolution: was it a harbinger of collapse, as Edmund Burke most famously argued in *Reflections on the Revolution in France* (1790), or did it presage the triumph of the Enlightenment, the ushering in of what Burke's arch rival Thomas Paine dubbed the age of reason? The 1790s saw persistent food shortages and high levels of unemployment, which led to rioting and machine breaking across the country. Though such riots were a conventional part of what has been called the moral economy of the era,[8] they were seen differently in the highly charged atmosphere generated by the French Revolution. Taken together, the conjunction of rioting and intellectual ferment generated a frenzied tone of hysteria and anxiety.

If the 1790s saw the emergence of a 'paranoid style' in English politics, this peaked in 1798 for two related reasons. First, 1798 saw the eruption of the Irish Rebellion, itself in good part energized by the example of the French Revolution. English political life had long feared that its Irish empire/territory (depending on one's political point of view) would prove vulnerable to insurrection and that such insurrection would provide a strategic back door via which England herself could be destabilized. The speed and violence of the Irish Rebellion terrorized an England already riven by ideological and social tensions. And tied to this was the French threat. By 1798, Napoleon could marshal powerful forces that were at least a match for England. It was known that Napoleon's fleet had sailed from Toulon, the fear being either that it was heading to assist the Irish Rebellion or that it would try a direct landing on the British mainland, in South Wales or on the English side of the Severn Channel. Such fears led William Pitt's government to have its network of informants seek dubious foreign agents in that area, with the activities of Samuel Taylor Coleridge and William Wordsworth being closely monitored as they wandered the Quantock Hills, apparently just looking at the landscape. It was in this feverish context that Malthus tried for a second time to earn a reputation as an author.[9]

AN ESSAY ON THE PRINCIPLE
OF POPULATION

Published at the peak of the Irish Rebellion of 1798, *An Essay on the Principle of Population* might well, by its title page, have led readers to anticipate a radical tract supporting the French Revolution, emerging as it did both anonymously to conceal its author's identity and from the publishing house of

Joseph Johnson, the leading radical publisher of the age and a man who would be imprisoned for inciting sedition shortly thereafter. In fact, Malthus's authorship was soon widely known. Johnson probably published the *Essay* thanks to the good offices of Malthus's old teacher, Gilbert Wakefield, and the counter-revolutionary ambitions of the project become clear by the end of an opening chapter that advertises the achievement of the book as being an 'argument [that] is conclusive against the perfectibility of the mass of mankind' (p. 17). Malthus hoped the conclusiveness of his argument would come from its logical construction. True to his mathematical training in Cambridge, Malthus argued from a set of axioms, via empirical evidence, for what he saw as quasi-Newtonian 'laws of nature', to what he believed was an unavoidable conclusion whose acceptance would explode some of the more dizzying claims that the French Revolution was ushering in an age of reason and unending societal improvement.

Malthus's axioms are laid out in the opening chapter of the *Essay*: human beings need food to survive and 'the passion between the sexes is necessary, and will remain nearly in its present state' (p. 15). In fact, the second of these axioms was highly controversial because radical writers, most notably William Godwin who was Malthus's prime target in the *Essay*, had argued that sexual desire would wither with the progress of civilization. Godwin argued thus in his *Enquiry Concerning Political Justice*, but for Malthus this was a mere conjecture to be ignored as 'towards the extinction of the passion between the sexes, no progress whatever has hitherto been made' (p. 16). Taking Malthus's axioms as read, they do not in and of themselves create a social dilemma until the addition of a second set of arguments, namely the claim that population tends to grow at a faster rate than can the food supply: 'population, when unchecked, increases in a geometrical ratio. Subsistence increases only in an arithmetical ratio. A slight acquaintance with numbers will show the immensity of the first power in comparison of the second' (p. 16). If one accepts this imbalance between the rates of increase of population and of food supply, a societal dilemma has been uncovered, namely how to balance population growth and food resources.

Malthus acknowledged that his two ratios were as wholly unsubstantiated as Godwin's speculations at this point in his argument. For this reason he conducted a whistle-stop global tour in chapters Three to Seven of the *Essay* to show that, at each stage of social development that the modern world or the historical record offered to our scrutiny, one could find evidence of a need to control population increase to make it balance with available food resources. Malthus envisaged this balancing act in terms of what he called 'checks' and singled out two types of check. 'Positive' checks were natural forces that adjusted population growth downward and thereby brought it back in line with available food resources, these checks being famine, disease and warfare. 'Preventive' checks were human or social forces that achieved the same balancing act by less violent means. Malthus was aware that, with the progress of civilization down the ages, people had come to limit procreation by delaying marriage or by practising sexual restraint within marriage, each of which would reduce fertility levels. He was also aware that families could seek to balance family size against the standard of living, choosing to limit the numbers of children they had to ensure their relative affluence. In general, Malthus encoded in the first edition of the *Essay* the sense that over time preventive checks became more important and ensured that the aegis of positive checks was weakened. Thus, in chapter Three, which addressed primitive societies, there was a clear sense that for Malthus, aping Hobbes, life was nasty, brutish and short because there were only positive checks to population growth. Against his father's fondness for Rousseau, Malthus saw that in such societies 'the picture will not appear very free from the blot of misery' (p. 27). Modern societies still witness the power of positive checks, and yet they are mainly visited upon the poorer classes only and in all classes 'foresight of the difficulties attending the rearing of a family . . . acts as a preventive check' (p. 35).

It is foresight, not any putative decay in the passion between the sexes as for Godwin, that has eased the pressure created by human population growth. This mattered hugely to Malthus: if Godwin were right, the millennia of struggle to balance population and food supply would wither and ease of their own accord. For Malthus, that struggle had merely transmuted its form due to social advance: untrammelled by reason, soci-eties would see a recrudescence to war, famine and pestilence. Even allowing for social advance, the world of the Enlighten-ment that Malthus inhabited was one where years of poor harvests could lead to food riots of the variety that had wracked Britain in the 1790s, and where epidemics and 'sickly seasons' were still spasmodic reminders of the more than merely vestigial power of positive checks. As modern historical demography has shown, life expectancy in Malthus's time was still only just over forty years and a quarter of children did not survive the first five years of life.[10] Foresight had clipped the wings of Malthus's positive checks but by no means grounded them.

If Malthus had laid out his conceptual and historical case about the propensity of population to outstrip food resources to his satisfaction by the conclusion of chapter Seven, the rest of the *Essay* went on to plot the political, economic and reli-gious consequences of accepting his argument. We can identify four main lines of argument Malthus pursued. First, accepting the principle of population exposed the optimistic manifestos of radical personal and societal development that had been flowing from those enthused by the French Revolution as mere delusion. This was clearly a – if not the – key motivating force that spurred Malthus to put pen to paper, as the full title of his book made clear: *An Essay on the Principle of Population, as it Affects the Future Improvement of Society, with remarks on the Speculations of Mr Godwin, M. Condorcet and other writ-ers*. The Marquis de Condorcet, Jean Antoine Nicolas de Caritat, was a leading mathematician and savant who was at the heart of the revolutionary ferment in 1789 before being hounded to his death by Robespierre and the Terror in 1794. Condorcet had left a last philosophical testament in the form of his *Outlines of an Historical View of the Progress of the Human Mind* (1795), which predicted a future of infinite progress in which warfare would cease, disease would be conquered and 'the interval between the birth of man and his decay, will itself have no assignable limit'.[11] For Malthus, there was no evidence that the natural length of a human life, as opposed to our life expectancy, had changed over the course of history, such that to accept Condorcet's argument 'is at once an end of all human science. The whole train of reasonings from effects to causes will be destroyed. We may shut our eyes to the book of nature' (p. 72).

The other radical named in the *Essay*'s subtitle, William Godwin, was the most celebrated English radical writer after Thomas Paine, thanks to his *Enquiry Concerning Political Justice*, the third, 1797, edition of which had argued that population growth would not derail the progress of social advance as the passion between the sexes would wither. As Godwin put it, in due course humans 'will probably cease to propagate. The whole will be a people of men, and not of children. Generation will not succeed generation, nor truth have, in a certain degree, to recommence her career every thirty years . . . There will be no war, no administration of justice . . . no government. Beside this there will be neither disease, anguish, melancholy, nor resentment.'[12] As we have seen, Malthus sketched a reverse trajectory: the passion between the sexes being constant, social betterment came from controlling population (not the other way round as Godwin had it). Condorcet and Godwin, then, may sketch a dizzying vision of future advance that we may wish to believe – 'a kind of mental intoxication', as Malthus framed it (p. 73) – but following Newton's lead we should look for actual laws of nature, how nature does function rather than how we would like it to function. And in this realm Malthus felt he had shown the unavoidable empire of population increase over food supply and the resultant necessity for checks, personal and societal.

Switching from Enlightened rhapsodies to more prosaic political realities, Malthus also saw in his principle of population a key basis for scepticism about the ways in which poverty was alleviated by the state apparatus. For the better part of two centuries prior to the publication of the *Essay*, the Elizabethan Poor Laws had operated in England to relieve extreme distress. Functioning at the parish level, the Poor Laws ensured that, when the price of bread rose above a certain threshold, money was collected from the wealthier strata of society to cross subsidize those who could no longer ensure their subsistence. Malthus had two main objections to the Poor Laws. First, he argued that 'they may be said . . . in some measure to create the poor which they maintain' (p. 43). The Poor Laws separated the ability to have children from the ability to support them as the state would aid in extremis. Removing the necessity for foresight in determining when and whether to have children weakened the power of Malthus's preventive check. Reducing the power of the preventive check de facto increased the number of children people had and thereby for Malthus the Poor Laws created the very poor they supported.

Second, and in an anticipation of the modern concept of the poverty trap, Malthus noted that giving the poor more money to buy food could not in the short term increase food supply and would therefore lead to the price of foodstuffs increasing. Such increases would lead those who were just above the poverty line to be made reliant on the same poor relief: as such, for Malthus, the Poor Laws 'may have alleviated a little the intensity of individual misfortune, [but] they have spread the general evil over a much larger surface' (p. 40). For these reasons Malthus advocated the abolition of the Poor Laws and their replacement with a system of workhouses where the poor would have to work for their entitlement to food. He also argued that state incentives should be enacted to increase tillage and food production, not to redistribute the entitlement to food via state subsidy. Only an increase in actual food production could act to alleviate want rather than redistribute it.

The attention to food production as the core of economic wellbeing also explained the third consequence Malthus detected in his principle of population, the need to correct Adam Smith's definition of wealth. Malthus emerged in the generation following Smith's epochal economic treatise, *The Wealth of Nations* (1776), and was a lifelong supporter of and advocate for Smith's ideas. And yet for Malthus Smith's definition of wealth was misleading and problematic. Malthus was as keenly aware as Smith that he wrote at a time of massive change in the economic structure of British society, as agrarian production came to be far less dominant in the face of rapidly expanding commercial and manufacturing sectors of the sort Malthus had first witnessed as a schoolboy in Warrington. And yet for Malthus, far more than Smith, this diversification of the economy was not an unbridled good if it did not bolster food supply. For this reason, Malthus took polite issue with Smith in chapters Sixteen and Seventeen of the *Essay*. Just as the Poor Laws could not increase the quantity of food, only spread its shortage over a wider spectrum of society, so for Malthus trade-created monetary wealth could only lead to increased nominal wealth in the absence of increased food production. In taking this line, Malthus was in some ways drawing on the earlier economic ideas of the Physiocrats who saw land as the only basis of wealth, but he was more immediately drawing out a consequence of his own principle of population: if food is necessary for survival, only the production of more food can create the conditions in which more people can survive, in which the same number can survive in greater comfort or in which both processes can take place simultaneously. On this basis, Malthus disagreed with Smith's definition of wealth as 'the annual produce of ... land and labour' (p. 130) as some labour – that in manufacturing and trade – did not necessarily increase the produce of the land. As Malthus summarized his position: 'every accession to the food of a country, tends to the immediate benefit of the whole society; but the fortunes made in trade, tend, but in a remote and uncertain manner, to the same end, and in some respects have even a contrary tendency' (p. 141). Malthus, then, was qualified in his endorsement of the worth of the 'invisible hand' of free trade in determining economic priorities to a degree Smith was not. This ambivalence about the recentring of the English economy away from agriculture would prove a lifelong preoccupation for Malthus.

The fourth and final set of consequences Malthus drew from his principle of population related to religion, the topic addressed in the final two chapters of the *Essay*. For an ordained

clergyman to see in God's dispensation to humankind a system
of laws in which checks to population could, in Malthus's own
words, 'be fairly resolved into misery and vice' (p. 49) was to
pose a dilemma. How could the existence of a wise and good
Christian God be reconciled with the purported laws of population by which the world was allegedly governed? In a response
that teetered awkwardly between the heterodoxy of Gilbert
Wakefield and the orthodox rationalist Anglicanism of his
Cambridge education, Malthus argued that as 'the first great
awakeners of the mind seem to be the wants of the body'
(p. 149), so the principle of population in fact spurred the individual to greater efforts and societies in the aggregate to
civilizational advance. As such, the misery and vice detected as
the outcome of the principle of population 'produces much
partial evil; but a little reflection may, perhaps, satisfy us, that
it produces a great overbalance of good' (p. 151). The law-like
construction of the operation of the world allowed humans
to plan, prepare and produce, and it was such prudence
and diligence – qualities Malthus located predominantly in
the middle classes – that fuelled social advances. The human
ability to plan coupled to nature's niggardliness meant that for
Malthus a timeworn truism had new truth to it: 'necessity
has been with great truth called the mother of invention' (pp.
149–50).[13]

For all that Malthus then attacked what he saw as the
groundless conjectures of unending progress penned by Godwin and Condorcet, his was ultimately an equally Enlightened
picture of social advance, albeit one he saw as firmly moored in
an understanding of societal laws as the drivers of that progress. There is no evidence that the closing theological chapters
of the *Essay* were mere 'window dressing'. On the contrary,
they appear to have been a deeply felt emanation from the con-
tours of Malthus's education and beliefs, and yet he removed
them from all the later editions as they were received with great
nervousness on publication. Where the intention of the *Essay*
had been to oppose revolutionary fervour at the crisis point
that was 1798, the final two chapters smacked too strongly of
a similar radicalism in the eyes of many readers.

In sum, the *Essay* in its 1798 version was a medley of themes characteristic of what has been dubbed the 'English Enlightenment'.[14] Intellectually, Malthus displayed a Newtonian belief in laws and a desire to find such laws in the social as well as the natural realm. Socially, the *Essay* did not merely seek knowledge of such laws for their own sake, but in order to plan for improvement and progress, by tackling the Poor Laws, by advocating incentives to agrarian production and by analysing the balance between trade, manufactures and farming. And undergirding all of this was a Christian cosmology profoundly hostile to the brands of Enlightened secularism Malthus saw as characterizing the excesses of French revolutionary fervour.

MALTHUS'S LATER LIFE AND WRITINGS

The *Essay* made Malthus's name as a writer and yet he was clearly dissatisfied with it in some ways from the outset. One of the first traces we have of Malthus after the publication of the *Essay*, for example, is a letter to his father requesting a raft of books about demography and an array of travel writings.[15] No sooner was the *Essay* published than Malthus started working to deepen his knowledge and strengthen his arguments. And the trip Malthus took with friends to Scandinavia in 1799, while clearly recreational, also served a strong educative purpose. Malthus's travel diaries are peppered with comments on crop yields, food prices and manufacturing, and as such they betray the eye and the interests of the economist on the road. Malthus also showed himself keenly alert to the impact of weather on social and economic activity, travelling as he did in the wake of the exceptionally hard winter of 1798, the consequence of which had been to test preventive checks to the limit and even see a reversion to positive checks in some places. Above all, however, what is important about the Scandinavian travel diaries is that they witness a transition from Malthus the abstract philosopher of social laws to Malthus the empirical observer of the complex links between population, production and policy. The epitome of this transition is encoded at the most northerly point of Malthus's tour, in Trondheim in Norway, where he reflected on the ways in which the remoteness of the area necessitated a more conservative approach to food security, and that the exceptional fertility of the valleys in summer (given the near perpetual daylight afforded by their location adjacent to the Arctic Circle) made the area far more governed by preventive checks than its remoteness alone might suggest. Malthus went on to contrast this with the fishing cultures on the Norwegian littoral whose boom and bust food supply was entirely different from the continental interior and led to the near-perpetual threat of famine and the operation of positive checks.

Geographical, cultural and economic differentiation, then, created a complex mosaic of resource–population regimes. The diaries reflect the concern Malthus had expressed as early as 1785 with what really exists in nature in all its complexity; this attention to nuance would be an abiding characteristic of his published work from now on. It would also resurface in Malthus's periodic trips as a traveller – to France in 1802, 1820 and 1826, to Scotland in 1810 and 1826, to Ireland in 1817 and to Germany in 1825 – each of which resulted in manuscript travel notes attending to prices, population and polity, but none of which was as comprehensive as that for the Scandinavian trip.[16]

The first published product of Malthus's increasing preoccupation with the complex interactions of nature, politics and economic activity was a pamphlet, reprinted herein, on the heated debates about high food prices in the England to which Malthus returned from his continental sojourn. Politically, Malthus's *Investigation of the Causes of the Present High Price of Provisions* (1800) might seem a continuation of the anti-revolutionary rhetoric of the 1798 *Essay*, arguing as it does that high prices are not due to landowners or merchants storing food to cash in on high prices by artificially limiting supply. On the contrary, for Malthus 'the sole cause' (p. 177) of prices having been inflated so greatly relative to the dip in food supply is the impact of the Poor Laws artificially inflating the entitlements of the poor. And yet it is at this point that the more nuanced approach of the later Malthus is witnessed for the first time. For all his continued theoretical hostility to the Poor Laws – '[which] I certainly do most heartily condemn' (p. 184) – he is prepared to pragmatically accept their material value in the context of the dire food dearth of 1800:

> I am inclined to think that their operation in the present scarcity has been advantageous to the country. The principal benefit which they have produced, is exactly that which is most bitterly complained of – the high price of all the necessaries of life. The poor cry out loudly at this price; but, in so doing, they are very little aware of what they are about; for it has undoubtedly been owing to this price that a much greater number of them has not been starved. (pp. 184–5)

At the end of the *Investigation*, Malthus advertised the fact that he was working on a new edition of his *Essay* and that it would be made 'more worthy of the public attention, by applying the principle directly and exclusively to the existing state of society, and endeavouring to illustrate the power and universality of its operation from the best authenticated accounts that we have of the state of other countries' (p. 189). It would be three years later, and therefore almost exactly five years after its first iteration, that the second edition of the *Essay* emerged.

In a sense, Malthus somewhat misled his audience by retaining the title from 1798 for the 1803 *Essay*, for it was stretching credibility to see it merely as a new edition of an extant book. Yes, the topic remained the same, as did the central focus on the principle of population, its history and socio-economic ramifications, and yet the 1803 *Essay*, of which only very small fragments can be reprinted here, was about four times longer than its predecessor, being a massive tome of 200,000 words. And, despite this considerable expansion in size, Malthus also cut the theological sections from 1798 that had been such a key conceptual foundation. Taken as a whole, the changes took the *Essay* of 1803 in the direction of a detailed empirical investigation of the principle of population and away from being an abstract argument about Newtonian laws of social mechanics.

Malthus the economist and demographer emerged more strongly at the expense of Malthus the Enlightenment theorist. In truth, Malthus's advertisement of his intention to produce a new version of the *Essay* as quoted above from his 1800 *Investigation* was extremely fair in its foreshadowing of the new balance of that work, picking out as it did two key changes. First, just as Malthus asked his father for lots of new books of travel and demography in 1798 and as in 1800 he said he would use the best accounts, so Books I and II of the 1803 *Essay* conducted an exhaustive survey of the operation of the principle of population, both in 'the less civilised Parts of the World, and in Past Times' as the heading to Book I had it, and then in the 'different States of Modern Europe' in Book II, starting from Malthus's own experiences of Norway and Sweden before proceeding around the Continent and ending with Britain. These two books, far longer than the entirety of the 1798 *Essay*, replaced the short global tour of the first edition's chapters Three to Seven and evidenced a longstanding interest in historical and geographical writing that Malthus had first discussed while an undergraduate in Cambridge. Taken together, Books I and II were the illustration of the principle of population 'from authenticated accounts' that the *Investigation* had promised. The second key change for the 1803 *Essay* was its greater attention to the political and economic implications of the principle of population for modern societies. While the *Essay* still criticized Godwin and Condorcet, and thereby continued to betray its genesis in the tensions of 1798, the debate about schemes of perfectibility was overwhelmed by greatly expanded discussions of the definition of wealth (itself a continuation of Malthus's joustings with Adam Smith), of the impact – baleful or otherwise – of the Corn Laws on food supply, by a new and somewhat less astringent approach to the Poor Laws and, most importantly, by a more sanguine analysis of the power of the preventive check to population. On this last topic, Malthus conceded that he had been overly pessimistic in 1798; European demographic data showed the power of moral restraint and economically motivated forethought in checking fertility. While the power of population to outstrip food supply remained a basic predicate of Malthus's reasoning, he accepted that in modern European societies the preventive check was effective in staving off the imbalance of food and population on a long-term basis.

Malthus spent the rest of his life adjusting details of the 1803 edition of the *Essay*, with further editions emerging in 1806, 1807, 1817 and 1826. These editions were notably able to incorporate data from the first British censuses of 1801, 1811 and 1821, censuses whose very existence owed something to the interest in population as an object of political scrutiny that Malthus had sparked, but the structure of argument established in 1803 remained the foundation for all of these later amendments. If the 1798 *Essay* had made Malthus's name, in a sense the 1803 edition made his career and gave him financial security, leading as it did to his appointment as Professor of Political Economy at the East India College in Haileybury in 1805, a job he would retain for the rest of his life. And the year before, in 1804, Malthus had married Harriet Eckersall in what would prove a happy union that would produce three children (not, as a wonderfully persistent myth suggested, a very imprudently unchecked eleven!).[17] Year on year, Malthus taught intending colonial administrators a course in economics derived closely from Adam Smith,[18] and he increasingly engaged in public pamphlet commentary on the key economic issues of the first decades of the nineteenth century, each of them deriving from the interests he had first laid out as consequences of his *Essay* as long ago as 1798 – issues around bullion and whether Britain should go back on to the Gold Standard, the economic condition of Ireland and the likely impact of emigration on that condition, and the definition of value and the valuation of commodities.

In many ways the most highly charged issue Malthus addressed in these years was the worth of the Corn Laws, a topic about which he wrote two pamphlets, one of which is reproduced here. The Corn Laws were a system of state intervention in the operation of the market, and to that extent were akin to the Poor Laws, and yet Malthus was far more ambivalent about their worth than he was about the Poor Laws. The reason for this lay in his continued belief that the land and its

produce were the only true source of real as opposed to nominal wealth and that, therefore, systems that encouraged its
productivity increased that wealth. Where many liberal politi-
cians and economists, following what they saw as Adam
Smith's lead, argued that the Corn Laws were an expensive and
inefficient intervention in the operation of market forces, Malthus argued for their importance on two grounds. First, and as
he said in his 1814 pamphlet on the topic (reproduced here),
'security is of still more importance than wealth' (p. 229). The
maximization of nominal wealth was, for Malthus, meaning-
less if it endangered our ability to feed our population; political
embargoes, warfare and the increased wealth of corn-exporting
countries such as the USA and Russia could all block food supplies flowing to Britain and at that point the country would
face crippling food scarcities regardless of its ability to pay for
food. And resting behind this concern with what we might call
food security was the second reason to support the Corn Laws:
that without food security there could be no political security.
The turmoil of 1798 that had first led Malthus to pick up his
pen stayed with him as a concern throughout his life; as he put
it in the 1815 pamphlet not reprinted here, the labouring classes
are 'the foundation on which the whole [social] fabric rests'.[19]
And if those classes could not feed themselves – something that
both the increased price volatility of a free market in corn and
the increased vulnerability to political and economic changes
elsewhere in the market rendered more likely – then the maintenance of peace and prosperity could be endangered precisely
by the loosening of the protectionism that the Corn Laws
enshrined.

Malthus's interventions on the Corn Laws once again pointed
to his long established scepticism about the smooth functioning
of markets. And this scepticism was also a strong vein running
through his final great work and the second book-length project he put before the public, *Principles of Political Economy*
(1820), a few small sections of which are reproduced in this
volume. Malthus saw *Principles* as addressing many of the same
themes as the *Essay* from a different angle: he argued that the
Essay had 'endeavoured to trace the causes which practically

keep down the population of a country to the level of its actual supplies', while his *Principles* endeavoured to show 'what are the causes which chiefly influence these supplies, or call the powers of production forth into the shape of increasing wealth'.[20] At its simplest, then, Malthus depicted the *Essay* focusing on the demand side of the interrelationship between food and population whilst *Principles* attended to the questions posed by the supply side. While the *Principles* is Malthus's great engagement with the economists of his day, notably Smith and especially David Ricardo, what is most lastingly important about it is perhaps its claim to make Malthus one of the first great analysts of market failures. Emerging as it did after a long period of economic depression in the aftermath of the Napoleonic Wars, *Principles* was preoccupied with the fact that demand and supply could be sustainedly out of kilter. Emerging from Malthus's analysis of the Corn Laws and the Poor Laws was an awareness that a mere need for goods was not synonymous with an effective demand for them, this latter being a demand backed by the ability to pay for goods and thereby the entitlement to acquire them. And, likewise from the supply side, the mere existence of un- or under-utilized resources in terms of land or labour did not mean they would be used. Finally, and putting these two things together, one could have a need for goods alongside under-utilized resources, but a market would not put these two things together productively without the lubrication of effective demand. Malthus was not content to merely make these points in the abstract; true to his life-long interest in what really exists in nature he wanted to show how complex were the interrelations of supply and demand in real-world cases. This point was made theoretically in the summary of his mature approach to social scientific enquiry, which forms the introduction to the *Principles* and which is reproduced here. It is then exemplified in the two examples of market failure excerpted in this selection showing that in the New World large landowners had no incentive to produce more due to a lack of demand and therefore left land resources under-utilized, while in Ireland (which, as we have noted, Malthus visited in 1817) the subdivision of land meant that land was intensively utilized but could produce no goods for market exchange, the entire produce of the soil going to the subsistence needs of its cultivators, resulting in a small and stagnant economy.

The last decade or so of Malthus's life saw him propelled to public fame, to prestigious awards and to the role of a policy adviser. Thus Malthus was twice called to give evidence to parliamentary select committees, one concerning machinery and its impact on the labouring classes in 1824, and one concerning the likely efficacy of a scheme of Irish emigration on that country's economic prospects in 1827. In the same decade, Malthus was a founding member of the Political Economy Club, a dining society that has been seen as the first attempt to give some scholarly coherence to the study of economics; was elected as a Fellow of the Royal Society; and was given a stipendiary prize by the Royal Society of Literature. In the final year of his life, Malthus was also instrumental in the establishment of the Statistical Society of London (the forerunner of today's Royal Statistical Society). When Malthus died, probably of a heart attack, on 29 December 1834, he had cemented a place for himself in the national life of Britain, this being marked by the fact that *The Times*, not always a paper generous to him in life, ran a respectful obituary.

MALTHUS'S LEGACY: CRITICS, CHAMPIONS AND CONTEMPORARY CONVERSATIONS

Malthus was and is as important for the furore, critical and adulatory, that he has attracted as for his ideas in and of themselves. Only a brief tour of these controversies can be offered here. Long before his death, Malthus's ideas started to attract support and vilification in equal measure. Amongst his most important defenders was Harriet Martineau who in the year of Malthus's death published her *Illustrations of Political Economy* (1834). The *Illustrations* are twenty-four short stories where common people discourse on economics, and all, as Martineau put it in her *Autobiography*, 'to exemplify Malthus's doctrine'.[21] Martineau's tracts were remarkably popular in their own age, with each monthly instalment selling at least 10,000 copies. More popular still was the swingeing criticism directed at Malthus by the rural campaigner William Cobbett. Cobbett penned a rather lame play against Malthus, *Surplus Population*, which sold some 45,000 copies when it was reprinted after his death in 1835. This was just the last moment in a long history of vituperation, Cobbett having denounced 'the monster MALTHUS' in his most famous work, *Rural Rides* (1830), and also having penned an open letter to Malthus in 1819 that stated, 'I have, during my life, detested many men; but never any one so much as you.'[22] Charles Dickens's evocation of Malthus in *A Christmas Carol* (1843) was equally scathing albeit less acerbic. In the opening stave of the book, Scrooge is visited by two 'portly gentlemen, pleasant to behold', who ask him for a little Christian charity for the poor. Scrooge replies that he already pays towards the workhouse and that this is sufficient. When pressed that many would rather die than be consigned to the workhouse, Scrooge's infamous reply is couched in deliberately Malthusian terms: ' "If they would rather die", said Scrooge, "they had better do it, and decrease the surplus population." '[23]

Perhaps the most sophisticated and violent response to Malthus, which originated in his lifetime but ran on for decades afterwards, was that of the English Romantics. In 1798, as Malthus produced the *Essay*, Coleridge and Wordsworth published their *Lyrical Ballads*, a poetic manifesto for Romanticism that, in its celebration of the numinous and nutritive status of nature, was set on a collision course with the Malthusian image of nature as niggardly. It was the 1803 edition of Malthus's *Essay*, however, which witnessed that collision, Coleridge scribbling on a copy of 'the stupid Ignorance of the Man!' while his friend the poet Robert Southey added tersely that Malthus was a 'fool', an 'ass' and a 'booby'.[24] And, if Southey's comment in a letter that authorially Malthus was a 'voider of menstrual pollution' might be seen as a private excess, in a

published essay of 1812 he called Malthus's work 'a colliqua-
tive diarrhoea of the intellect'.[25]

Southey may have been the first Romantic to take up the
cudgels against Malthus publicly, but he was by no means the
last, with William Hazlitt penning a 400-page-long *Reply to
the Essay on Population* in 1807. The later generation of
Romantics shared this hostility to Malthus, Shelley dismissing
him as 'a priest of course, for his doctrines are those of a eunuch
and of a tyrant', and Byron targeting satirical flak at him in the
English cantos of *Don Juan*.[26] And, beyond the tradition of
the Romantics themselves, key social critics influenced by their
vision of nature and society took on a shared hostility to
Malthus. Thus Thomas Carlyle coined the denigration of economics as the 'dismal science' in direct reference to Malthus:
'the controversies on Malthus and the "Population Principle",
"Preventive check" and so forth, with which the public ear has
been deafened for a long while, are indeed sufficiently mourn-
ful. Dreary, stolid, dismal, without all hope for this world or
the next.'[27] In the generation after Carlyle, John Ruskin constructed a very similar criticism of Malthus. For Ruskin,
economics of the sort practised by Malthus was unchristian in
its failure to understand that 'THERE IS NO WEALTH BUT
LIFE'. The meaning of this in the Malthusian realm was that
'in all the ranges of human thought I know none so melancholy
as the speculations of political economists on the population
question'. If all wealth is life, the 'maximum of life can only be
reached by the maximum of virtue', this not necessarily being
equivalent as the Malthusians implied with merely maximizing
the number of beings clothed, fed and housed on the globe.
Thus for Ruskin the population question was 'not how much
habitable land is in the world, but how many beings ought to
be maintained on a given space of habitable land'.[28]

The force that tied the criticisms of Coleridge and Carlyle,
and of Hazlitt and Southey, was a Christian one that saw in
Malthus's vision of the inevitability of human suffering and
pain a fundamental impiety. As we have seen, such Christian
concerns had dogged Malthus from the first appearance of the
Essay in 1798. And yet the greatest secularizing project of the

nineteenth century, the political economy of Marx and Engels, shared a hostility of equal vigour towards Malthus. It was in the 1860s that Marx levelled his sights on Malthus's *Essay* in *Capital*, dismissing it as 'nothing more than a schoolboyish, superficial plagiary', the fame of which was 'due solely to party interest', Malthus's 'party' being that of his own class as a 'parson of the English State Church'. Where scholars have pointed out Engels's indebtedness to Malthusian ideas of population and Marx's indebtedness to his ideas of effective demand, Marx focused on his conflict with Malthus; there could be no universal law of population as Malthus had envisaged, each mode of production having its own 'special laws of population'. Malthus had correctly seen the 'disharmonies' capitalism created by its inevitable tendency to cycles of boom and bust, but by packaging this as a law of nature, he had mystified its social origins in defence of the interests of the landed aristocracy and the bourgeoisie. Engels, in a letter of 1881, looked forward to the day when communism arrived, feeling he was on its 'eve'. And, when it came, Europe would be 'certain to require a large increase in population'. But, once this had been achieved, the harmonious communist society it produced would be able to 'regulate the production of human beings . . . it will be precisely this society, and this society alone, which can carry this out without difficulty.'[29]

To the extent that this hostility towards Malthusian reasoning became embedded in the state socialisms of the twentieth-century world, it became important to the global population debate. This is particularly apparent in the case of China where Mao in 1949 dismissed the idea that 'food cannot keep up with increases in population' as 'the absurd argument of bourgeois Western economists like Malthus', preferring instead the slogan *'Ren Duo Liliang Da'* (with many people, strength is great). And, while the Great Chinese Famine of 1958–62 and its death toll of forty-five million or more cannot be directly attributed to this policy, it was certainly instrumental in the emergence of a far more stringently Malthusian policy of family limitation in the form of the one child policy thereafter.[30]

If Romantics and Marxists alike were hostile to Malthus, two other great strands of nineteenth-century thought were explicit in acknowledging their indebtedness to Malthus: Darwinism and economics. Commemorating the fiftieth anniversary of the publication of *On the Origin of Species*, Alfred Russel Wallace noted that he and Darwin shared three influences in their co-discovery of the idea of evolution by natural selection. Beetle collecting and travel were two of them, but a shared encounter with Malthus was the third, and Wallace claimed its influence 'was analogous to that of friction upon the specially prepared match, producing that flash of insight which led us immediately to the simple but universal law of the "survival of the fittest," as the long sought *effective* cause of the continuous modification and adaptations of living things'. Darwin made similar if more plain comments in his *Autobiography* about reading Malthus in 1838 'for amusement' but finding here 'a theory by which to work'.[31] That this was not a mere retrospective fabrication by Darwin and Wallace in their dotages is made clear by a perusal of Darwin's notebooks, which show that he did in fact read Malthus when he said, while Wallace's inspiration was always clear from his direct references to 'geometrical ratios' in his breakthrough essay, 'On the Tendencies of Varieties to Depart Indefinitely from the Original Type' of 1858.

Malthus is also directly referenced in *On the Origin of Species* (1859), the struggle for existence being styled as 'the doctrine of Malthus applied with manifold force to the whole animal and vegetable kingdoms'.[32] And yet how Malthus was to be read in evolutionary terms was the subject of great controversy, even between Wallace and Darwin. Darwin read Malthus's perpetual struggle between the power of population and the abilities of food to sustain it as still active in the human world as had Malthus himself, where Wallace argued that Malthus's ratios still applied in the natural world but had been superseded in the human world by the powers of our reasoning. In this Wallace was true to the Socialist utopianism he had imbibed as a child and points the way towards various 'non Malthusian' versions of evolution that circulated in the late nineteenth and early twentieth centuries, perhaps the most prominent of which was Pyotr Kropotkin's idea that nature worked cooperatively by means of 'mutual aid' between species, not by a vicious competition for resources as the Malthus-inspired vision of Darwin had it. Just as Marx had attacked Malthus, so there was a Marxist reworking of evolutionary ideas along anti-Malthusian lines.[33]

Darwin went on to extend his vision of natural selection to human beings more explicitly, notably in *The Descent of Man* (1871), and in this he was part of a far broader current of thinkers applying evolutionary ideas to mankind. This set of doctrines is often dubbed 'social Darwinism', and then and now Malthus has often been deemed its progenitor. Indeed, it has even been suggested that 'social Darwinism' is a misleading sobriquet, and that 'scientific Malthusianism' may more accurately encapsulate the efforts to apply evolutionary ideas to society.[34] It was, for example, Herbert Spencer who coined the term 'survival of the fittest' before Darwin had started writing, and he had in fact begun his career building a modified version of Malthus's theory of population in 1849. This application of Darwinian ideas back into the human world from which they had initially sprung in Malthus's thought led to two main currents of debate either side of 1900 that Malthus himself could not really have anticipated. First, there was the emergence of groups advocating contraception as a preventive check to ease the pressure of population growth that Darwin had viewed as still such an immediate concern for modern societies. These groups were often labelled 'Malthusian', the adjective coming to be a synonym for 'contraception' despite the fact that Malthus as an eighteenth-century clergyman had viewed such methods of birth control with horror, only ever alluding to them in print by an oblique reference to 'improper arts'.[35] The Malthusian League in Britain, for example, was founded in 1877 and was extraordinarily active, printing an estimated three million pamphlets between 1879 and 1921, publishing a regular journal, the *Malthusian*, and encouraging the formation of sister societies across the globe, an enumeration of 1911 suggesting that Malthusian Leagues now existed in

'Holland, Germany, France, Austria, Spain, Brazil, Belgium, Switzerland, Cuba and Portugal'.[36] It was no accident, then, that when Aldous Huxley imagined his dystopian future in *Brave New World* (1932), its mode of contraception was called a 'Malthusian belt'. It is one of history's terminological ironies that Malthus's name became a global brand in the service of a doctrine he would have abhorred.

The second set of ideas was at some odds with the doctrine of Malthusianism, arguing as it did that societies must encourage selective human breeding to ensure that evolutionarily favourable human traits were preserved. In the struggle to survive, only those who demonstrated advanced intelligence should be encouraged to breed. As such, the poor should be treated as Malthusian Leagues across the globe suggested, that is encouraged to use contraception or, in more extreme arguments, forcibly prevented from procreating by sterilization and the like,[37] but a different approach was needed for the rich and the intelligent, encouraging them to procreate. This doctrine, known as eugenics, was most clearly advocated by Darwin's cousin Francis Galton from the 1870s, and was hostile to Malthusianism, which it saw as recklessly indiscriminate in encouraging the more and less developed groups alike to limit their fertility. And yet eugenicists also claimed Malthus as their intellectual forbearer, notably on the basis of his comments on selective breeding in chapter Nine of the 1798 *Essay*, Galton calling him 'the rise of a morning star before a day of free social investigation', while in 1923 the first issue of the *Annals of Eugenics*, founded by Galton's pupil and successor Karl Pearson, featured a portrait of Malthus, whom it lauded as 'Strewer of the Seed which reached its Harvest in the Ideas of Charles Darwin and Francis Galton'.[38] Well into the twentieth century, then, whichever side of arguments about population control and social Darwinism one took, Malthus remained a key inspiration, striking the match as assuredly as he had done for Darwin himself.

Throughout this ferment of debates to which Malthus's ideas had been subjected in the century after his death, economists had unsurprisingly remained respectful of Malthus as one of the triptych of classical economists who had given shape to their discipline along with Smith and Ricardo. Indeed, the great nineteenth-century economists – John Stuart Mill, Stanley Jevons and Alfred Marshall – all made positive reference to Malthus's demographic work. And yet none saw Malthus as a vital interlocutor as had the Darwinians, Romantics and Marxists for all their mixed response to him. It was only with the emergence of John Maynard Keynes that Malthus was once again seen as vital. Malthus has been described by Keynes's biographer as his 'favourite economist', a judgement that was more wittily endorsed by Keynes's Cambridge undergraduates who nicknamed him 'Jeremiah Malthus'.[39] Above all, in two sharply separate engagements with Malthus in the aftermath of the First World War and then in the Depression of the late 1920s and early '30s, Keynes would make Malthus relevant to the modern era, reworking the meaning of Malthus's ideas to accord with the needs of the times as he perceived them. In 1919 in his *Economic Consequences of the Peace*, Keynes argued that the trauma of the First World War could be viewed in Malthusian terms as a struggle for scarce resources created by population pressure in Germany. And, in the throes of the Great Depression, Keynes turned again for understanding to Malthus, but this time to Malthus the economist rather than Malthus the demographer, arguing that Malthus had shown why economies fail to generate demand even when there is spare labour and under-utilized capital in his *Principles of Political Economy*. In 1933, Keynes passed a celebrated judgement that would be echoed closely in his *General Theory of Employment, Interest and Money* (1936), perhaps the most politically influential economic tract of the twentieth century: 'If only Malthus, instead of Ricardo, had been the parent stem from which nineteenth-century economics proceeded, what a much wiser and richer place the world would be today.' The core insight that Keynes offered to substantiate this claim was Malthus's discovery of the principle of effective demand, which would become the lynchpin of Keynes's *General Theory*.[40]

Keynes died in 1946, just as his ideas were becoming the founding tenets of government fiscal policies in the postwar period across the advanced world. Interest in Malthus remained undimmed, but shifted back at this time to Malthus the demographer from Malthus the economist. In particular, economists, scholars, novelists and ecologists started to speak of a parallel between the atomic bombs that had ended the Second World War and a 'population bomb' that needed to be defused. As the philosopher Bertrand Russell noted in 1964 in what was already becoming a hackneyed formula, there were 'two antithetical dangers', those of the H-bomb and of the population bomb, arguing that, though antithetical, they were in fact linked: 'Nothing is more likely to lead to an H-bomb war than the threat of universal destitution through over-population.'[41] Governments agreed. US presidencies from Truman's to Carter's poured money into population and development programmes, as did global agencies such as the United Nations. And behind all this action lay a shared fear of Malthusian catastrophe and a possible third world war in the global struggle for food and resources. Emerging from these fears was the so-called 'neo-Malthusianism' of the 1960s and '70s, a new ecological perspective arguing that the sheer proliferation of human beings on the planet would lead to the breakdown of the ecological systems on which life on earth was predicated, this being a new and ultimate form of positive check in the terms Malthus had pioneered in 1798. The most famous proponent of ideas of ecological neo-Malthusianism was (and is) Paul Ehrlich, whose 1968 book *The Population Bomb*, has been dubbed 'the most famous population treatise since Malthus'.[42]

All of the strands of postwar Malthusianism – development economics, global population policies, ecological doomsaying – remain active in our age. Thus Jared Diamond's controversial *Collapse* (2005) framed the Rwandan conflict as a Malthusian war of resource scarcity in the context of mushrooming population growth.[43] Similarly, with still rapid population growth in many parts of the world and a reverse demographic decline in many developed nations, scholars and political analysts have been quick to speak of 'new population bombs' ready to explode in our contemporary world, many ascribing political and religious fundamentalism and radicalization to this demographic juxtaposition in trying to explain the events of 9/11.[44] And yet Malthus's ideas are also being used in new ways today. In particular, recent years have seen the terms of debate shift to the question of whether both population increase and escalating per capita consumption will lead to Malthusian positive checks via climate change undermining the habitability of the earth as a home for humankind.

Perhaps the most high-profile instantiation of these ideas came in 2009 when the United Kingdom's Chief Scientific Adviser, Sir John Beddington, captured headlines around the world for his fears of 'a perfect storm of global events'. Beddington argued that food and water shortages, depletion of energy sources and climate change might act in a negative loop. In the speech in which Beddington first aired these ideas, he concluded: 'We have got to deal with increased demand for energy, increased demand for food, increased demand for water, and we've got to do that while mitigating and adapting to climate change. And we have but twenty-one years to do it.' And then Malthus came into his picture: 'Are we doomed? Is there any hope? Whenever I interview, people always mention Thomas Malthus and am I now a second Thomas Malthus? Not quite because I am reasonably optimistic.'[45] While Beddington's grasp of what Malthus actually said is as shaky as that demonstrated by Bill and Melinda Gates at the beginning of this introduction, that contemporary commentators feel drawn to position their views against those of a quiet country clergyman born a quarter of a millennium ago shows the remarkable clarity, intelligence and ongoing relevance of Malthus as we face new planetary predicaments.

Robert Mayhew, 2015

NOTES

1. Bill Gates and Melinda Gates, 2014 *Annual Gates Letter: 3 Myths that Block Progress for the Poor*, available at: http://annualletter.gatesfoundation.org/ (last accessed 7 March 2014).

2. For all of which see Robert J. Mayhew, *Malthus: The Life and Legacies of an Untimely Prophet* (Cambridge, MA: Harvard University Press, 2014), pp. 213–31.

3. John Gray, *Straw Dogs: Thoughts on Humans and Other Animals* (London: Granta, 2002) and John Gray, *Gray's Anatomy: Selected Writings* (London: Penguin, 2009). Niall Ferguson, 'Don't Count out Malthus', *Los Angeles Times*, 30 July 2007.

4. For Stiglitz, see Justin Lahart, Patrick Barta and Andrew Batson, 'New Limits to Growth Revive Malthusian Fears', *Wall Street Journal*, 24 March 2008; Paul Krugman, 'We Are Wrong to Overlook the Food Crisis' speech to Momagri (Mouvement Pour une Organisation Mondiale de L'Agriculture), 20 April 2009, which can be found at: www.momagri.org/UK/points-of-view/For-Paul-Krugman-We-Are-Wrong-to-Overlook-the-Food-Crisis_479.html.

5. For Malthus, eugenics and Hitler, see Allan Chase, *The Legacy of Malthus: The Social Costs of the New Scientific Racism* (New York: Knopf, 1977) and Robert Zubrin, *Merchants of Despair: Radical Environmentalists, Criminal Pseudo-Scientists, and the Fatal Cult of Antihumanism* (New York: Encounter, 2012). On Malthus and fundamentalism, see Harun Yahya, *The Social Weapon: Darwinism*, available at: http://books.harunyahya.com/read.php?id=3984. This is but one example of the vast internet debate with Malthus, much of it hysterical.

6. What follows is indebted to Patricia James, *Population Malthus: His Life and Times* (London: Routledge, 1979), to which readers are directed for a full and authoritative biography of Malthus.

7. John Pullen and Trevor Hughes Parry (eds), *T. R. Malthus: The Unpublished Papers in the Collection of Kanto Gakuen University* (Cambridge: Cambridge University Press, 1997–2004), 1: 39 and 41.

8. E. P. Thompson, 'The Moral Economy of the English Crowd in the Eighteenth Century,' *Past & Present*, 50 (1971), pp. 76–136.

9. Nicholas Roe, *Wordsworth and Coleridge: The Radical Years* (Oxford: Clarendon Press, 1988), pp. 248–62.

10. See E. A. Wrigley, R. S. Davies, J. E. Oeppen and R. S. Schofield, *English Population History from Family Reconstruction, 1580–1837* (Cambridge: Cambridge University Press, 1997).

11. Jean Antoine Nicolas de Caritat, *Outlines of an Historical View of the Progress of the Human Mind* (London: J. Johnson, 1795), p. 410.

12. William Godwin, *Enquiry Concerning Political Justice,* ed. Isaac Kramnick (Harmondsworth: Penguin, 1976), pp. 776–7.

13. School children and students are still routinely taught of a contrast between the pessimism of Malthus's demography with its negative feedback loop between population and wealth and the optimism of Ester Boserup's view that population growth spurs inventiveness, breaking such a cycle (see Ester Boserup, *The Conditions of Agricultural Growth: The Economic Consequences of Agrarian Change under Population Pressure* [Chicago: Aldine, 1965]). That Malthus himself pre-empted Boserup shows that we should beware simple binaries, however attractive they may be pedagogically. We should also read Malthus if we want to know what he said!

14. See J. G. A. Pocock, *Barbarism and Religion, Vol. 1: The Enlightenments of Edward Gibbon, 1737–1764* (Cambridge: Cambridge University Press, 1999).

15. Pullen and Parry, *Unpublished Papers,* 1: 63–5.

16. For which see Patricia James (ed.), *The Travel Diaries of T. R. Malthus* (Cambridge: Cambridge University Press for the Royal Economic Society, 1966), pp. 152–64 on Trondheim. See also James, *Travel Diaries,* pp. 226–72, and Pullen and Parry, *Unpublished Papers,* 2: 25–55 and 2: 212–41, for Malthus's other trips. The importance of Malthus's Trondheim writings to his development is emphasized in Mayhew, *Malthus,* pp. 107–9.

17. A myth still pedalled by Michael P. Fogarty in his introduction to the 1958 Everyman edition of the 1803 *Essay,* p. vi.

18. For Malthus's economics teaching, we have manuscript notes made by students: see John Pullen, 'Notes from Malthus: the Inverarity Manuscript', *History of Political Economy,* 13 (1981), pp. 794–811. For his other teaching of historical material, see Pullen and Parry, *Unpublished Papers,* 2: 166–211.

19. E. A. Wrigley and David Souden (eds), *The Works of Thomas Robert Malthus* (London: Pickering and Chatto, 1986), 7: 162.

20. T. Robert Malthus, *Principles of Political Economy,* ed. John Pullen (Cambridge: Cambridge University Press for the Royal Economic Society, 1989), p. 344.

21. See James P. Huzel, *The Popularization of Malthus in Early Nineteenth-Century England: Martineau, Cobbett and the Pauper Press* (Aldershot: Ashgate, 2006), pp. 55 and 57.

22. William Cobbett, *Rural Rides,* ed. George Woodcock (Harmondsworth: Penguin, 1985), 298. For the open letter, see Huzel, *Popularization of Malthus,* p. 105.

23. Charles Dickens, *A Christmas Carol and Other Christmas Writings,* ed. Michael Slater (Harmondsworth: Penguin, 2003), pp. 38–9.

24. Coleridge and Southey's reactions to the 1803 edition are contained in H. J. Jackson and George Whalley (eds), *The Collected Works of Samuel Taylor Coleridge, Marginalia Volume III: Irving to Oxlee* (Princeton: Princeton University Press, 1992), pp. 805– 9.

25. Kenneth Curry (ed.), *New Letters of Robert Southey* (New York: Columbia University Press, 1965), 1: 357. I quote Southey's 1812 *Quarterly Review* essay from Robert Southey, *Essays, Moral and Political* (London: John Murray, 1832), 1:246.

26. Percy Shelley, *A Philosophical View of Reform,* ed. T. W. Rolleston (1914; repr., Honolulu: University of Hawaii Press, 2004), p. 51.

27. Thomas Carlyle, 'Chartism' (1839), in *Selected Writings,* ed. Alan Shelston (Harmondsworth: Penguin, 1971), p. 229.

28. John Ruskin, *Unto This Last and Other Writings,* ed. Clive Wilmer (London: Penguin, 1997), pp. 207–9 and 222–6.

29. All these comments can be found in Ronald L. Meek (ed.), *Marx and Engels on Malthus* (London: Lawrence and Wishart, 1953). For Marx and Engels's veiled indebtedness to Malthus, see John M. Sherwood, 'Engels, Marx, Malthus and the Machine', *American Historical Review* 90 (1985), pp. 837–65.

30. For the attack on Malthus, see Judith Shapiro, *Mao's War against Nature: Politics and the Environment in Revolutionary China* (Cambridge: Cambridge University Press, 2001), pp. 21–48, whence Mao is cited (p. 31). Estimates of death tolls in the Great Chinese Famine are from Frank Dikötter, *Mao's Great Famine: The History of China's Most Devastating Catastrophe, 1958–62* (New York: Walker, 2010).

31. Andrew Berry (ed.), *Infinite Tropics: An Alfred Russel Wallace Anthology* (London: Verso, 2003), pp. 68–9; Charles Darwin, *Autobiographies,* ed. Michael Neve and Sharon Messenger (Harmondsworth: Penguin, 2002), p. 72.

32. Charles Darwin, *The Origin of Species,* ed. Jim Endersby, (Cambridge: Cambridge University Press, 2009), p. 58.

33. For these debates in England, see Piers Hale, *Political Descent: Malthus, Mutualism and the Politics of Evolution in Victorian England* (Chicago: University of Chicago Press, 2014). For the Russian strand to the same debate, see Daniel Todes, *Darwin without Malthus: The Struggle for Existence in Russian Evolutionary Thought* (New York: Oxford University Press, 1989).

34. For social Darwinism as scientific Malthusianism, see Gregory Claeys, 'The "Survival of the Fittest" and the Origins of Social Darwinism', *Journal of the History of Ideas* 61 (2000): pp. 223–40.

35. Malthus's reference to improper arts is from the 1803 edition of the *Essay*: see Patricia James (ed.), *An Essay on the Principle of Population* (Cambridge: Cambridge University Press, 1989), 2: 97.

36. See Rosanna Ledbetter, *A History of the Malthusian League, 1877–1927* (Columbus: Ohio State University Press, 1976).

37. On which topic see Matthew Connelly, *Fatal Mis-Conception: The Struggle to Control the World's Population* (Cambridge MA: Harvard University Press, 2008).

38. For Galton on Malthusianism and Malthus, see Richard Soloway, *Demography and Degeneration: Eugenics and the Declining Birthrate in Twentieth-Century Britain* (Chapel Hill: University of North Carolina Press, 1990), pp. 92–3. For the *Annals of Eugenics*, see Chase, *Legacy of Malthus*, pp. 82–3.

39. Robert Skidelsky, *John Maynard Keynes: The Economist as Saviour, 1920–1937* (London: Macmillan, 1992), p. 416; and John Toye, *Keynes on Population* (Oxford: Oxford University Press, 2000), p. 205.

40. John Maynard Keynes, 'Thomas Robert Malthus: The First of the Cambridge Economists' (1933), in *The Collected Writings of John Maynard Keynes*, vol. 10: *Essays in Biography* (London: Macmillan, 1972), 71–103. Keynes's judgement of the relative merits of Ricardo and Malthus was rehearsed again in John Maynard Keynes, *The General Theory of Employment, Interest and Money* (London: Macmillan, 1936), p. 32.

41. Bertrand Russell, 'Population Pressure and War', in Stuart Mudd (ed.), *The Population Crisis and the Use of World Resources* (The Hague: W. Junk, 1964), p. 1.

42. See Derek S. Hoff, *The State and the Stork: The Population Debate and Policy Making in US History* (Chicago: University of Chicago Press, 2012), p. 165.

43. Jared Diamond, *Collapse: How Societies Choose to Fail or Survive* (London: Penguin, 2005), the chapter being entitled 'Malthus in Africa: Rwanda's Genocide'.

44. Jack Goldstone, 'The New Population Bomb: The Four Megatrends That Will Change the World,' *Foreign Affairs* 89 (2010), pp. 31–43.

45. Beddington's speech is quoted from the online version, which can be accessed at: www.govnet.co.uk/news/govnet/professor-sir-john-beddingtons-speech-at-sduk-09. A formalized version of his argument was offered in John Beddington, 'Food, Energy, Water and the Climate: A Perfect Storm of Global Events?', which can be accessed at: www.bis.gov.uk/assets/goscience/docs/p/perfect-storm-paper.pdf.

Further Reading

MALTHUS'S WORKS

The Works of Thomas Robert Malthus were edited in eight volumes by E. A. Wrigley and David Souden (London: Pickering, 1986). The best edition of the 1803 *Essay*, however, which also includes all the editorial changes Malthus made in subsequence editions, is that edited by Patricia James (Cambridge: Cambridge University Press for the Royal Economic Society, 1989). An abridged version of this text is also available, edited by Donald Winch (Cambridge: Cambridge University Press, 1992). Likewise, the best available edition of *Principles of Political Economy* is that edited by John Pullen (Cambridge: Cambridge University Press for the Royal Economic Society, 1989). Portions of Malthus's correspondence, travel accounts, sermons, lecture notes and other miscellanea are contained in John Pullen and Trevor Hughes Parry (eds) *T. R. Malthus: The Unpublished Papers in the Collection of Kanto Gakuen University* (2 vols, Cambridge: Cambridge University Press, 1997–2004). For Malthus's important Scandinavian travel diaries, see Patricia James (ed.), *The Travel Diaries of T. R. Malthus* (Cambridge: Cambridge University Press, 1966).

MALTHUS'S LIFE AND IDEAS

The only reliable full modern biography of Malthus is Patricia James, *Population Malthus: His Life and Times* (London: Routledge, 1979). A readable and reliable short summary of

Malthus's life and ideas is Donald Winch, *Malthus: A Very Short Introduction* (Oxford: Oxford University Press, 2013). Robert J. Mayhew, *Malthus: The Life and Legacies of an Untimely Prophet* (Cambridge, MA: Harvard University Press, 2014) canvasses Malthus's life, ideas and the reception of his ideas down to the present. General collections of essays about Malthus's ideas and their legacy are: J. Dupâquier (ed.), *Malthus: Past and Present* (London: Academic Press, 1983), Michael Turner (ed.) *Malthus and his Time* (Basingstoke: Macmillan, 1986), and Brian Dolan (ed.), *Malthus, Medicine and Morality: 'Malthusianism' after 1798* (Amsterdam: Rodopi, 2000).

For more detail on Malthus as a political economist set in the context of his times, see Donald Winch, *Riches and Poverty: An Intellectual History of Political Economy in Britain, 1750–1834* (Cambridge: Cambridge University Press, 1996). For a mammoth assessment of Malthus's economics from the vantage point of modern economics, see Samuel Hollander, *The Economics of Thomas Robert Malthus* (Toronto: University of Toronto Press, 1997). For Malthus's religious ideas and their role in his work see A. M.C. Waterman, *Revolution, Economics and Religion: Christian Political Economy, 1798-1833* (Cambridge: Cambridge University Press, 1991).

MALTHUS'S LEGACY

For an overview of the reception of Malthus's ideas, see Mayhew, *Malthus*. More detailed studies of the reception of Malthus's ideas include James Huzel, *The Popularization of Malthus in Early Nineteenth-Century England: Martineau, Cobbett and the Pauper Press* (Aldershot: Ashgate, 2006), and Kenneth Smith, *The Malthusian Controversy* (London: Routledge, 1951) for the early nineteenth century. For the later nineteenth century, see Piers Hale, *Political Descent: Malthus, Mutualism and the Politics of Evolution in Victorian England* (Chicago: University of Chicago Press, 2014) on evolutionary debates. Ronald L. Meek (ed.), *Marx and Engels on Malthus* (London: Lawrence and Wishart, 1953) usefully gathers together

Marx and Engels's responses to Malthus. Keynes's writings on Malthus are usefully reprinted with exhaustive commentary in John Toye, *Keynes on Population* (Oxford: Oxford University Press, 2000).

For twentieth-century responses to Malthus from a demographic perspective, see Alison Bashford, *Global Population: History, Geopolitics, and Life on Earth* (New York: Columbia University Press, 2014), and Matthew Connelly, *Fatal Mis-Conception: The Struggle to Control World Population* (Cambridge, MA: Harvard University Press, 2008). For Malthus and the politics of development, see Ronald W. Greene, *Malthusian Worlds: U.S. Leadership and the Governing of the Population Crisis* (Boulder, CO: Westview Press, 1999) and Derek S. Hoff, *The State and the Stork: The Population Debate and Policy Making in US History* (Chicago: University of Chicago Press, 2012). For the later twentieth-century connection of Malthus with debates about ecology and the environment, see Björn-Ola Linnér, *The Return of Malthus: Environmentalism and Post-War Population-resource Crises* (Isle of Harris: White Horse Press, 2003), and Thomas Robertson, *The Malthusian Moment: Global Population Growth and the Birth of American Environmentalism* (New Brunswick, NJ: Rutgers University Press, 2012).

AN ESSAY ON THE PRINCIPLE OF POPULATION AND OTHER WRITINGS

PREFACE

The following essay owes its origin to a conversation with a friend,[1] on the subject of Mr Godwin's[2] essay on avarice and profusion, in his *Enquirer*. The discussion, started the general question of the future improvement of society; and the author at first sat down with an intention of merely stating his thoughts to his friend upon paper, in a clearer manner than he thought he could do in conversation. But as the subject opened upon him, some ideas occurred, which he did not recollect to have met with before; and as he conceived, that every, the least light, on a topic so generally interesting, might be received with candour, he determined to put his thoughts in a form for publication.

The essay might, undoubtedly, have been rendered much more complete by a collection of a greater number of facts in elucidation of the general argument.[3] But a long and almost total interruption, from very particular business, joined to a desire (perhaps imprudent) of not delaying the publication much beyond the time that he originally proposed, prevented the author from giving to the subject an undivided attention. He presumes, however, that the facts which he has adduced, will be found to form no inconsiderable evidence for the truth of his opinion, respecting the future improvement of mankind. As the author contemplates this opinion at present, little more appears to him to be necessary than a plain statement, in addition to the most cursory view of society, to establish it.

It is an obvious truth, which has been taken notice of by many writers, that population must always be kept down to the level of the means of subsistence; but no writer, that the author recollects, has inquired particularly into the means by which this level is effected: and it is a view of these means which forms, to his mind, the strongest obstacle in the way to any very great future improvement of society. He hopes it will appear that, in the discussion of this interesting subject, he is actuated solely by a love of truth; and not by any prejudices against any particular set of men, or of opinions. He professes to have read some of the speculations on the future improvement of society, in a temper very different from a wish to find them visionary; but he has not acquired that command over his understanding which would enable him to believe what he wishes, without evidence, or to refuse his assent to what might be unpleasing, when accompanied with evidence.

The view which he has given of human life has a melancholy hue; but he feels conscious that he has drawn these dark tints, from a conviction that they are really in the picture, and not from a jaundiced eye, or an inherent spleen of disposition. The theory of mind which he has sketched in the two last chapters accounts to his own understanding, in a satisfactory manner, for the existence of most of the evils of life; but whether it will have the same effect upon others, must be left to the judgement of his readers.

If he should succeed in drawing the attention of more able men to what he conceives to be the principal difficulty in the way to the improvement of society, and should, in consequence, see this difficulty removed, even in theory, he will gladly retract his present opinions, and rejoice in a conviction of his error.

7 June 1798[4]

CONTENTS

PREFACE   3

ONE

Question stated – Little prospect of a determination of it, from the enmity of the opposing parties – The principal argument against the perfectibility of man and of society has never been fairly answered – Nature of the difficulty arising from population – Outline of the principal argument of the essay   12

TWO

The different rations in which population and food increase – The necessary effects of these different ratios of increase – Oscillation produced by them in the condition of the lower classes of society – Reasons why this oscillation has not been so much observed as might be expected – Three propositions on which the general argument of the essay depends – The different states in which mankind have been known to exist proposed to be examined with reference to these three propositions   18

THREE

The savage or hunter state shortly reviewed – The shepherd state, or the tribes of barbarians that overran the Roman

Empire – The superiority of the power of population to the means of subsistence – The cause of the great tide of northern emigration   26

FOUR

State of civilized nations – Probability that Europe is much more populous now than in the time of Julius Caesar – Best criterion of population – Probable error of Hume in one of the criterions that he proposes as assisting in an estimate of population – Slow increase of population at present in most of the states of Europe – The two principal checks to population – The first, or preventive check examined with regard to England   32

FIVE

The second, or positive check to population examined, in England – The true cause why the immense sum collected in England for the poor does not better their condition – The powerful tendency of the poor laws to defeat their own purpose – Palliative of the distresses of the poor proposed – The absolute impossibility from the fixed laws of our nature, that the pressure of want can ever be completely removed from the lower classes of society – All the checks to population may be resolved into misery or vice   39

SIX

New colonies – Reasons of their rapid increase – North American colonies – Extraordinary instance of increase in the back settlements – Rapidity with which even old states recover the ravages of war, pestilence, famine, or the convulsions of nature   50

SEVEN

A probable cause of epidemics – Extracts from Mr Süssmilch's tables – Periodical returns of sickly seasons to be expected in certain cases – Proportion of births to burials for short periods in any country an inadequate criterion of the real average increase of population – Best criterion of a permanent increase of population – Great frugality of living one of the causes of the famines of China and Hindustan – Evil tendency of one of the clauses in Mr Pitt's Poor Bill – Only one proper way of encouraging population – Causes of the happiness of nations – Famine, the last and most dreadful mode by which nature represses a redundant population – The three propositions considered as established 55

EIGHT

Mr Wallace – Error of supposing that the difficulty arising from population is at a great distance – Mr Condorcet's sketch of the progress of the human mind – Period when the oscillation, mentioned by Mr Condorcet, ought to be applied to the human race 66

NINE

Mr Condorcet's conjecture concerning the organic perfectibility of man, and the indefinite prolongation of human life – Fallacy of the argument, which infers an unlimited progress from a partial improvement, the limit of which cannot be ascertained, illustrated in the breeding of animals, and the cultivation of plants 71

TEN

Mr Godwin's system of equality – Error of attributing all the vices of mankind to human institutions – Mr Godwin's first answer to the difficulty arising from population totally insufficient – Mr Godwin's beautiful system of equality supposed to be realized – Its utter destruction simply from the principle of population in so short a time as thirty years   78

ELEVEN

Mr Godwin's conjecture concerning the future extinction of the passion between the sexes – Little apparent grounds for such a conjecture – Passion of love not inconsistent either with reason or virtue   92

TWELVE

Mr Godwin's conjecture concerning the indefinite prolongation of human life – Improper inference drawn from the effects of mental stimulants on the human frame, illustrated in various instances – Conjectures not founded on any indications in the past, not to be considered as philosophical conjectures – Mr Godwin's and Mr Condorcet's conjecture respecting the approach of man towards immortality on earth, a curious instance of the inconsistency of scepticism   96

THIRTEEN

Error of Mr Godwin in considering man too much in the light of a being merely rational – In the compound being, man, the passions will always act as disturbing forces in the decisions of the understanding – Reasonings of Mr Godwin on the subject of coercion – Some truths of a nature not to be communicated from one man to another 108

FOURTEEN

Mr Godwin's five propositions respecting political truth, on which his whole work hinges, not established – Reasons we have for supposing from the distress occasioned by the principle of population, that the vices, and moral weakness of man can never be wholly eradicated – Perfectibility, in the sense in which Mr Godwin uses the term, not applicable to man – Nature of the real perfectibility of man illustrated 114

FIFTEEN

Models too perfect, may sometimes rather impede than promote improvement – Mr Godwin's essay on avarice and profusion – Impossibility of dividing the necessary labour of a society amicably among all – Invectives against labour may produce present evil, with little or no chance of producing future good – An accession to the mass of agricultural labour must always be an advantage to the labourer 120

SIXTEEN

Probable error of Dr Adam Smith in representing every increase of the revenue or stock of a society as an increase in the funds for the maintenance of labour – Instances where an increase of wealth can have no tendency to better the condition of the labouring poor – England has increased in riches without a proportional increase in the funds for the maintenance of labour – The state of the poor in China would not be improved by an increase of wealth from manufactures 129

SEVENTEEN

Question of the proper definition of the wealth of a state –
Reason given by the French economists for considering all
manufacturers as unproductive labourers, not the true reason –
The labour of artificers and manufacturers sufficiently
productive to individuals, though not to the state – A remarkable passage in Dr Price's two volumes of observations – Error
of Dr Price in attributing the happiness and rapid population of
America, chiefly, to its peculiar state of civilization – No advantage can be expected from shutting our eyes to the difficulties
in the way to the improvement of society   138

EIGHTEEN

The constant pressure of distress on man, from the principle of
population, seems to direct our hopes to the future – State of
trial inconsistent with our ideas of the foreknowledge of God –
The world, probably, a mighty process for awakening matter
into mind – Theory of the formation of mind – Excitements
from the wants of the body – Excitements from the operation
of general laws – Excitements from the difficulties of life arising
from the principle of population   146

NINETEEN

The sorrows of life necessary to soften and humanize the
heart – The excitements of social sympathy often produce
characters of a higher order than the mere possessors of
talents – Moral evil probably necessary to the production of
moral excellence – Excitements from intellectual wants continually kept up by the infinite variety of nature, and the
obscurity that involves metaphysical subjects – The difficulties
in revelation to be accounted for upon this principle – The

degree of evidence which the scriptures contain probably best suited to the improvement of the human faculties and the moral amelioration of mankind – The idea that mind is created by excitements, seems to account for the existence of natural and moral evil   155

ONE

Question stated – Little prospects of a determination of it, from the enmity of the opposing parties – The principal argument against the perfectibility of man and of society has never been fairly answered – Nature of the difficulty arising from population – Outline of the principal argument of the essay.

The great and unlooked-for discoveries that have taken place of late years in natural philosophy; the increasing diffusion of general knowledge from the extension of the art of printing; the ardent and unshackled spirit of inquiry that prevails throughout the lettered, and even unlettered world; the new and extraordinary lights that have been thrown on political subjects, which dazzle, and astonish the understanding; and particularly that tremendous phenomenon in the political horizon the French revolution, which, like a blazing comet, seems destined either to inspire with fresh life and vigour, or to scorch up and destroy the shrinking inhabitants of the earth, have all concurred to lead many able men into the opinion, that we were touching on a period big with the most important changes, changes that would in some measure be decisive of the future fate of mankind.

It has been said, that the great question is now at issue, whether man shall henceforth start forwards with accelerated velocity towards illimitable, and hitherto unconceived improvement; or be condemned to a perpetual oscillation between happiness and misery, and after every effort remain still at an immeasurable distance from the wished-for goal.

Yet, anxiously as every friend of mankind must look forwards to the termination of this painful suspense; and, eagerly as the inquiring mind would hail every ray of light that might assist its view into futurity, it is much to be lamented, that the writers on each side of this momentous question still keep far aloof from each other. Their mutual arguments do not meet with a candid examination. The question is not brought to rest on fewer points; and even in theory scarcely seems to be approaching to a decision.

The advocate for the present order of things, is apt to treat the sect of speculative philosophers, either as a set of artful[5] and designing knaves, who preach up ardent benevolence, and draw captivating pictures of a happier state of society, only the better to enable them to destroy the present establishments, and to forward their own deep-laid schemes of ambition; or, as wild and mad-headed enthusiasts,[6] whose silly speculations, and absurd paradoxes, are not worthy the attention of any reasonable man.

The advocate for the perfectibility of man, and of society, retorts[7] on the defender of establishments a more than equal contempt. He brands him as the slave of the most miserable, and narrow prejudices; or, as the defender of the abuses of civil society, only because he profits by them. He paints him either as a character who prostitutes his understanding to his interest; or as one whose powers of mind are not of a size to grasp anything great and noble; who cannot see above five yards before him; and who must therefore be utterly unable to take in the views of the enlightened benefactor of mankind.

In this unamicable contest, the cause of truth cannot but suffer. The really good arguments on each side of the question are not allowed to have their proper weight. Each pursues his own theory, little solicitous to correct, or improve it, by an attention to what is advanced by his opponents.

The friend of the present order of things condemns all political speculations in the gross. He will not even condescend to examine the grounds from which the perfectibility of society is inferred. Much less will he give himself the trouble in a fair and candid manner to attempt an exposition of their fallacy.

The speculative philosopher equally offends against the cause of truth. With eyes fixed on a happier state of society, the blessings of which he paints in the most captivating colours, he allows himself to indulge in the most bitter invectives against every present establishment, without applying his talents to consider the best and fastest means of removing abuses, and without seeming to be aware of the tremendous obstacles that threaten, even in theory, to oppose the progress of man towards perfection.

It is an acknowledged truth in philosophy,[8] that a just theory will always be confirmed by experiment. Yet so much friction, and so many minute circumstances occur in practice, which it is next to impossible for the most enlarged and penetrating mind to foresee, that on few subjects can any theory be pronounced just, that has not stood the test of experience. But an untried theory cannot fairly be advanced as probable, much less as just, till all the arguments against it, have been maturely weighed, and clearly and consistently refuted.

I have read some of the speculations on the perfectibility of man and of society, with great pleasure. I have been warmed and delighted with the enchanting picture which they hold forth. I ardently wish for such happy improvements. But I see great, and, to my understanding, unconquerable difficulties in the way to them. These difficulties it is my present purpose to state; declaring, at the same time, that so far from exulting in them, as a cause of triumph over the friends of innovation, nothing would give me greater pleasure than to see them completely removed.

The most important argument that I shall adduce is certainly not new. The principles on which it depends have been explained in part by Hume,[9] and more at large by Dr Adam Smith.[10] It has been advanced and applied to the present subject, though not with its proper weight, or in the most forcible point of view, by Mr Wallace:[11] and it may probably have been stated by many writers that I have never met with. I should certainly therefore not think of advancing it again, though I mean to place it in a point of view in some degree different from any that I have hitherto seen, if it had ever been fairly and satisfactorily answered.

The cause of this neglect on the part of the advocates for the perfectibility of mankind, is not easily accounted for. I cannot doubt the talents of such men as Godwin and Condorcet.[12] I am unwilling to doubt their candour. To my understanding, and probably to that of most others, the difficulty appears insurmountable. Yet these men of acknowledged ability and penetration;[13] scarcely deign to notice it, and hold on their course in such speculations, with unabated ardour, and undiminished confidence. I have certainly no right to say that they purposely shut their eyes to such arguments. I ought rather to doubt the validity of them, when neglected by such men, however forcibly their truth may strike my own mind. Yet in this respect it must be acknowledged that we are all of us too prone to err. If I saw a glass of wine repeatedly presented to a man, and he took no notice of it, I should be apt to think that he was blind or uncivil. A juster philosophy might teach me rather to think that my eyes deceived me, and that the offer was not really what I conceived it to be.

In entering upon the argument I must premise that I put out of the question, at present, all mere conjectures; that is, all suppositions, the probable realization of which cannot be inferred upon any just philosophical grounds. A writer may tell me that he thinks man will ultimately become an ostrich. I cannot properly contradict him. But before he can expect to bring any reasonable person over to his opinion, he ought to show, that the necks of mankind have been gradually elongating; that the lips have grown harder, and more prominent; that the legs and feet are daily altering their shape; and that the hair is beginning to change into stubs of feathers. And till the probability of so wonderful a conversion can be shown, it is surely lost time and lost eloquence to expatiate on the happiness of man in such a state; to describe his powers, both of running and flying; to paint him in a condition where all narrow luxuries would be condemned; where he would be employed only in collecting the necessaries of life; and where, consequently, each man's share of labour would be light, and his portion of leisure ample.

I think I may fairly make two postulata.[14]

First, that food is necessary to the existence of man.

Secondly, that the passion between the sexes is necessary, and will remain nearly in its present state.

These two laws ever since we have had any knowledge of mankind, appear to have been fixed laws of our nature; and, as we have not hitherto seen any alteration in them, we have no right to conclude that they will ever cease to be what they now are, without an immediate act of power in that Being who first arranged the system of the universe; and for the advantage of his creatures, still executes, according to fixed laws, all its various operations.

I do not know that any writer has supposed that on this earth man will ultimately be able to live without food. But Mr Godwin has conjectured that the passion between the sexes may in time be extinguished. As, however, he calls this part of his work, a deviation into the land of conjecture, I will not dwell longer upon it at present, than to say, that the best arguments for the perfectibility of man, are drawn from a contemplation of the great progress that he has already made from the savage state, and the difficulty of saying where he is to stop.[15] But towards the extinction of the passion between the sexes, no progress whatever has hitherto been made. It appears to exist in as much force at present as it did two thousand, or four thousand years ago. There are individual exceptions now as there always have been. But, as these exceptions do not appear to increase in number, it would surely be a very unphilosophical mode of arguing, to infer merely from the existence of an exception, that the exception would, in time, become the rule, and the rule the exception.

Assuming then, my postulata as granted, I say, that the power of population is indefinitely greater than the power in the earth to produce subsistence for man.

Population, when unchecked, increases in a geometrical ratio. Subsistence increases only in an arithmetical ratio.[16] A slight acquaintance with numbers will show the immensity of the first power in comparison of the second.

By that law of our nature which makes food necessary to the life of man, the effects of these two unequal powers must be kept equal.

This implies a strong and constantly operating check on population from the difficulty of subsistence. This difficulty must fall somewhere; and must necessarily be severely felt by a large portion of mankind.

Through the animal and vegetable kingdoms, nature has scattered the seeds of life abroad with the most profuse and liberal hand. She has been comparatively sparing in the room, and the nourishment necessary to rear them. The germs of existence contained in this spot of earth, with ample food, and ample room to expand in, would fill millions of worlds in the course of a few thousand years. Necessity, that imperious all-pervading law of nature, restrains them within the prescribed bounds. The race of plants, and the race of animals shrink under this great restrictive law. And the race of man cannot, by any efforts of reason, escape from it. Among plants and animals its effects are waste of seed, sickness, and premature death. Among mankind, misery and vice. The former, misery, is an absolutely necessary consequence of it. Vice is a highly probable consequence, and we therefore see it abundantly prevail; but it ought not, perhaps, to be called an absolutely necessary consequence. The ordeal of virtue is to resist all temptation to evil.

This natural inequality of the two powers of population, and of production in the earth, and that great law of our nature which must constantly keep their effects equal, form the great difficulty that to me appears insurmountable in the way to the perfectibility of society. All other arguments are of slight and subordinate consideration in comparison of this. I see no way by which man can escape from the weight of this law which pervades all animated nature. No fancied equality, no agrarian regulations in their utmost extent, could remove the pressure of it even for a single century. And it appears, therefore, to be decisive against the possible existence of a society, all the members of which, should live in ease, happiness, and comparative leisure; and feel no anxiety about providing the means of subsistence for themselves and families.

Consequently, if the premises are just, the argument is conclusive against the perfectibility of the mass of mankind.

I have thus sketched the general outline of the argument; but I will examine it more particularly; and I think it will be found that experience, the true source and foundation of all knowledge, invariably confirms its truth.

TWO

The different ratios in which population and food increase – The necessary effects of these different ratios of increase – Oscillation produced by them in the condition of the lower classes of society – Reasons why this oscillation has not been so much observed as might be expected – Three propositions on which the general argument of the essay depends – The different states in which mankind have been known to exist proposed to be examined with reference to these three propositions.

I said that population, when unchecked, increased in a geometrical ratio; and subsistence for man in an arithmetical ratio.

Let us examine whether this position be just.

I think it will be allowed, that no state has hitherto existed (at least that we have any account of) where the manners were so pure and simple, and the means of subsistence so abundant, that no check whatever has existed to early marriages; among the lower classes, from a fear of not providing well for their families; or among the higher classes, from a fear of lowering their condition in life. Consequently in no state that we have yet known, has the power of population been left to exert itself with perfect freedom.

Whether the law of marriage be instituted, or not, the dictate of nature and virtue, seems to be an early attachment to one woman. Supposing a liberty of changing in the case of an unfortunate choice, this liberty would not affect population till it arose to a height greatly vicious; and we are now supposing the existence of a society where vice is scarcely known.

In a state therefore of great equality and virtue, where pure and simple manners prevailed, and where the means of subsistence were so abundant, that no part of the society could have any fears about providing amply for a family, the power of population being left to exert itself unchecked, the increase of the human species would evidently be much greater than any increase that has been hitherto known.

In the United States of America, where the means of subsistence have been more ample, the manners of the people more pure, and consequently the checks to early marriages fewer, than in any of the modern states of Europe, the population has been found to double itself in twenty five years.[17]

This ratio of increase, though short of the utmost power of population, yet as the result of actual experience, we will take as our rule; and say, that population, when unchecked, goes on doubling itself every twenty five years, or increases in a geometrical ratio.

Let us now take any spot of earth, this island for instance, and see in what ratio the subsistence it affords can be supposed to increase. We will begin with it under its present state of cultivation.

If I allow that by the best possible policy, by breaking up more land, and by great encouragements to agriculture, the produce of this island may be doubled in the first twenty five years, I think it will be allowing as much as any person can well demand.

In the next twenty five years, it is impossible to suppose that the produce could be quadrupled. It would be contrary to all our knowledge of the qualities of land. The very utmost that we can conceive, is, that the increase in the second twenty five years might equal the present produce. Let us then take this for our rule, though certainly far beyond the truth; and allow that by great exertion, the whole produce of the island might be increased every twenty five years, by a quantity of subsistence equal to what it at present produces. The most enthusiastic speculator cannot suppose a greater increase than this. In a few centuries it would make every acre of land in the island like a garden.

Yet this ratio of increase is evidently arithmetical.

It may be fairly said, therefore, that the means of subsistence increase in an arithmetical ratio.

Let us now bring the effects of these two ratios together.

The population of the island is computed to be about 7 millions; and we will suppose the present produce equal to the support of such a number. In the first twenty five years the population would be 14 millions; and the food being also doubled, the means of subsistence would be equal to this increase. In the next twenty five years the population would be 28 millions; and the means of subsistence only equal to the support of 21 millions. In the next period, the population would be 56 millions, and the means of subsistence just sufficient for half that number. And at the conclusion of the first century, the population would be 112 millions, and the means of subsistence only equal to the support of 35 millions; which would leave a population of 77 millions totally unprovided for.

A great emigration necessarily implies unhappiness of some kind or other in the country that is deserted. For few persons will leave their families, connections, friends, and native land, to seek a settlement in untried foreign climes, without some strong subsisting causes of uneasiness where they are, or the hope of some great advantages in the place to which they are going.

But to make the argument more general, and less interrupted by the partial views of emigration, let us take the whole earth, instead of one spot, and suppose that the restraints to population were universally removed. If the subsistence for man that the earth affords was to be increased every twenty five years by a quantity equal to what the whole world at present produces; this would allow the power of production in the earth to be absolutely unlimited, and its ratio of increase much greater than we can conceive that any possible exertions of mankind could make it.

Taking the population of the world at any number, a thousand millions, for instance, the human species would increase in the ratio of 1, 2, 4, 8, 16, 32, 64, 128, 256, 512, etc. and subsistence as 1, 2, 3, 4, 5, 6, 7, 8, 9, 10, etc. In two centuries and a quarter, the population would be to the means of subsistence as 512 to 10: in three centuries as 4096 to 13; and in two thousand years the difference would be almost incalculable, though the produce in that time would have increased to an immense extent.

No limits whatever are placed to the productions of the earth; they may increase for ever and be greater than any assignable quantity; yet still the power of population being a power of a superior order, the increase of the human species can only be kept commensurate to the increase of the means of subsistence, by the constant operation of the strong law of necessity acting as a check upon the greater power.

The effects of this check remain now to be considered.

Among plants and animals the view of the subject is simple. They are all impelled by a powerful instinct to the increase of their species; and this instinct is interrupted by no reasoning, or doubts about providing for their offspring. Wherever therefore there is liberty, the power of increase is exerted; and the super-abundant effects are repressed afterwards by want of room and nourishment, which is common to animals and plants; and among animals, by becoming the prey of others.

The effects of this check on man are more complicated.

Impelled to the increase of his species by an equally power-ful instinct, reason interrupts his career,[18] and asks him whether he may not bring beings into the world, for whom he cannot provide the means of subsistence. In a state of equality, this would be the simple question. In the present state of society, other considerations occur. Will he not lower his rank in life? Will he not subject himself to greater difficulties than he at present feels? Will he not be obliged to labour harder? And if he has a large family, will his utmost exertions enable him to support them? May he not see his offspring in rags and misery, and clamouring for bread that he cannot give them? And may he not be reduced to the grating necessity of forfeiting his inde-pendence, and of being obliged to the sparing hand of charity for support?

These considerations are calculated to prevent, and certainly do prevent, a very great number in all civilized nations from pursuing the dictate of nature in an early attachment to one woman. And this restraint almost necessarily, though not abso-lutely so, produces vice. Yet in all societies, even those that are most vicious, the tendency to a virtuous attachment is so strong, that there is a constant effort towards an increase of population. This constant effort as constantly tends to subject the lower classes of the society to distress, and to prevent any great permanent amelioration of their condition.

The way in which these effects are produced seems to be this.

We will suppose the means of subsistence in any country just equal to the easy support of its inhabitants. The constant effort towards population, which is found to act even in the most vicious societies, increases the number of people before the means of subsistence are increased. The food therefore which before supported seven millions, must now be divided among seven millions and a half or eight millions. The poor consequently must live much worse, and many of them be reduced to severe distress. The number of labourers also being above the proportion of the work in the market, the price of labour must tend toward a decrease; while the price of provisions would at the same time tend to rise. The labourer therefore must work harder to earn the same as he did before. During this season of distress, the discouragements to marriage, and the difficulty of rearing a family are so great, that population is at a stand. In the meantime the cheapness of labour, the plenty of labourers, and the necessity of an increased industry amongst them, encourage cultivators to employ more labour upon their land; to turn up fresh soil, and to manure and improve more completely what is already in tillage; till ultimately the means of subsistence become in the same proportion to the population as at the period from which we set out. The situation of the labourer being then again tolerably comfortable, the restraints to population are in some degree loosened; and the same retrograde and progressive movements with respect to happiness are repeated.

This sort of oscillation will not be remarked by superficial observers; and it may be difficult even for the most penetrating mind to calculate its periods. Yet that in all old states some such vibration does exist; though from various transverse[19] causes, in a much less marked, and in a much more irregular manner than I have described it, no reflecting man who considers the subject deeply can well doubt.

Many reasons occur why this oscillation has been less obvious, and less decidedly confirmed by experience, than might naturally be expected.

One principal reason is, that the histories of mankind that we possess, are histories only of the higher classes. We have but few accounts that can be depended upon of the manners and customs of that part of mankind, where these retrograde and progressive movements chiefly take place. A satisfactory history of this kind, of one people, and of one period, would require the constant and minute attention of an observing mind during a long life. Some of the objects of inquiry would be, in what proportion to the number of adults was the number of marriages; to what extent vicious customs prevailed in consequence of the restraints upon matrimony; what was the comparative mortality among the children of the most distressed part of the community, and those who lived rather more at their ease; what were the variations in the real price of labour; and what were the observable differences in the state of the lower classes of society, with respect to ease and happiness, at different times during a certain period.

Such a history would tend greatly to elucidate the manner in which the constant check upon population acts; and would probably prove the existence of the retrograde and progressive movements that have been mentioned; though the times of their vibration must necessarily be rendered irregular, from the operation of many interrupting causes; such as, the introduction or failure of certain manufactures; a greater or less prevalent spirit of agricultural enterprise; years of plenty, or years of scarcity; wars and pestilence; poor laws; the invention of processes for shortening labour without the proportional extension of the market for the commodity; and, particularly, the difference between the nominal and real price of labour; a circumstance, which has perhaps more than any other, contributed to conceal this oscillation from common view.

It very rarely happens that the nominal price of labour universally falls; but we well know that it frequently remains the same, while the nominal price of provisions has been gradually increasing. This is, in effect, a real fall in the price of labour;

and during this period, the condition of the lower orders of the community must gradually grow worse and worse. But the farmers and capitalists are growing rich from the real cheapness of labour.[20] Their increased capitals enable them to employ a greater number of men. Work therefore may be plentiful; and the price of labour would consequently rise. But the want of freedom in the market of labour, which occurs more or less in all communities, either from parish laws, or the more general cause of the facility of combination[21] among the rich, and its difficulty among the poor, operates to prevent the price of labour from rising at the natural period, and keeps it down some time longer; perhaps, till a year of scarcity, when the clamour is too loud, and the necessity too apparent to be resisted.

The true cause of the advance in the price of labour is thus concealed; and the rich affect to grant it as an act of compassion and favour to the poor, in consideration of a year of scarcity; and when plenty returns, indulge themselves in the most unreasonable of all complaints, that the price does not again fall; when a little reflection would show them, that it must have risen long before, but from an unjust conspiracy of their own.

But though the rich by unfair combinations, contribute frequently to prolong a season of distress among the poor; yet no possible form of society could prevent the almost constant action of misery, upon a great part of mankind, if in a state of inequality, and upon all, if all were equal.

The theory, on which the truth of this position depends, appears to me so extremely clear; that I feel at a loss to conjecture what part of it can be denied.

That population cannot increase without the means of subsistence, is a proposition so evident, that it needs no illustration.

That population does invariably increase, where there are the means of subsistence, the history of every people that have ever existed will abundantly prove.

And, that the superior power of population cannot be checked, without producing misery or vice, the ample portion of these too bitter ingredients in the cup of human life, and the continuance of the physical causes that seem to have produced them, bear too convincing a testimony.

But in order more fully to ascertain the validity of these three propositions, let us examine the different states in which mankind have been known to exist. Even a cursory review will, I think, be sufficient to convince us, that these propositions are incontrovertible truths.

THREE

The savage or hunter state shortly reviewed – The shepherd state, or the tribes of barbarians that overran the Roman Empire – The superiority of the power of population to the means of subsistence – the cause of the great tide of northern emigration.

In the rudest[22] state of mankind, in which hunting is the principal occupation, and the only mode of acquiring food; the means of subsistence being scattered over a large extent of territory, the comparative population must necessarily be thin. It is said, that the passion between the sexes is less ardent among the North American Indians, than among any other race of men. Yet notwithstanding this apathy, the effort towards population, even in this people, seems to be always greater than the means to support it. This appears, from the comparatively rapid population that takes place, whenever any of the tribes happen to settle in some fertile spot, and to draw nourishment from more fruitful sources than that of hunting; and it has been frequently remarked, that when an Indian family has taken up its abode near any European settlement, and adopted a more easy and civilized mode of life, that one woman has reared five or six, or more children; though in the savage state, it rarely happens, that above one or two in a family grow up to maturity. The same observation has been made with regard to the Hottentots near the Cape.[23] These facts prove the superior power of population to the means of subsistence in nations of hunters; and that this power always shows itself the moment it is left to act with freedom. -

It remains to inquire, whether this power can be checked, and its effects kept equal to the means of subsistence, without vice, or misery.

The North American Indians, considered as a people, cannot justly be called free and equal. In all the accounts we have of them, and, indeed, of most other savage nations, the women are represented as much more completely in a state of slavery to the men, than the poor are to the rich in civilized countries. One half of the nation appears to act as helots[24] to the other half: and the misery that checks population falls chiefly, as it always must do, upon that part whose condition is lowest in the scale of society. The infancy of man in the simplest state requires considerable attention; but this necessary attention the women cannot give, condemned as they are, to the inconveniences and hardships of frequent change of place, and to the constant and unremitting drudgery of preparing everything for the reception of their tyrannic lords. These exertions, sometimes, during pregnancy, or with children at their backs, must occasion frequent miscarriages, and prevent any but the most robust infants from growing to maturity. Add to these hardships of the women, the constant war that prevails among savages, and the necessity which they frequently labour under of exposing their aged and helpless parents, and of thus violating the first feelings of nature; and the picture will not appear very free from the blot of misery. In estimating the happiness of a savage nation, we must not fix our eyes only on the warrior in the prime of life: he is one of a hundred; he is the gentleman, the man of fortune, the chances have been in his favour; and many efforts have failed ere this fortunate being was produced, whose guardian genius should preserve him through the numberless dangers with which he would be surrounded from infancy to manhood. The true points of comparison between two nations, seem to be, the ranks in each which appear nearest to answer to each other. And in this view, I should compare the warriors in the prime of life, with the gentlemen; and the women, children, and aged, with the lower classes of the community in civilized states.

May we not then fairly infer from this short review, or, rather, from the accounts that may be referred to of nations of hunters, that their population is thin from the scarcity of food; that it would immediately increase if food was in greater plenty;

and that, putting vice out of the question among savages, misery is the check that represses the superior power of population, and keeps its effects equal to the means of subsistence. Actual observation and experience, tell us that this check, with a few local and temporary exceptions, is constantly acting now upon all savage nations; and the theory indicates, that it probably acted with nearly equal strength a thousand years ago, and it may not be much greater a thousand years hence.

On the manners and habits that prevail among nations of shepherds, the next state of mankind, we are even more ignorant than of the savage state. But that these nations could not escape the general lot of misery arising from the want of subsistence, Europe, and all the fairest countries in the world, bear ample testimony. Want was the goad that drove the Scythian shepherds from their native haunts, like so many famished wolves in search of prey.[25] Set in motion by this all-powerful cause, clouds of barbarians seemed to collect from all points of the northern hemisphere. Gathering fresh darkness, and terror, as they rolled on, the congregated bodies at length obscured the sun of Italy, and sunk the whole world in universal night. These tremendous[26] effects, so long and so deeply felt throughout the fairest portions of the earth, may be traced to the simple cause of the superior power of population, to the means of subsistence.

It is well known, that a country in pasture cannot support so many inhabitants as a country in tillage; but what renders nations of shepherds so formidable, is, the power which they possess of moving all together, and the necessity they frequently feel of exerting this power in search of fresh pasture for their herds. A tribe that was rich in cattle, had an immediate plenty of food. Even the parent flock might be devoured in a case of absolute necessity. The women lived in greater ease than among nations of hunters. The men bold in their united strength, and confiding in their power of procuring pasture for their cattle by change of place, felt, probably, but few fears about providing for a family. These combined causes soon produced their natural and invariable effect, an extended population. A more frequent and rapid change of place became then necessary. A wider and more extensive territory was successively occupied. A broader desolation extended all around them. Want pinched the less fortunate members of the society; and, at length, the impossibility of supporting such a number together became too evident to be resisted. Young scions were then pushed out from the parent flock, and instructed to explore fresh regions, and to gain happier seats for themselves by their swords. 'The world was all before them where to choose.'[27] Restless from present distress; flushed with the hope of fairer prospects; and animated with the spirit of hardy enterprise, these daring adventurers were likely to become formidable adversaries to all who opposed them. The peaceful inhabitants of the countries on which they rushed, could not long withstand the energy of men acting under such powerful motives of exertion. And when they fell in with any tribes like their own, the contest was a struggle for existence; and they fought with a desperate courage, inspired by the reflection, that death was the punishment of defeat, and life the prize of victory.

In these savage contests many tribes must have been utterly exterminated. Some, probably, perished by hardship and famine. Others, whose leading star had given them a happier direction, became great and powerful tribes; and, in their turns, sent off fresh adventurers in search of still more fertile seats. The prodigious waste of human life occasioned by this perpetual struggle for room and food, was more than supplied by the mighty power of population, acting, in some degree, unshackled, from the constant habit of emigration. The tribes that migrated towards the south, though they won these more fruitful regions by continual battles, rapidly increased in number and power from the increased means of subsistence. Till, at length, the whole territory, from the confines of China to the shores of the Baltic, was peopled by a various race of barbarians, brave, robust, and enterprising; inured to hardship, and delighting in war. Some tribes maintained their independence. Others ranged themselves under the standard of some barbaric chieftain, who led them to victory after victory; and what was of more importance, to regions abounding in corn, wine and oil, the long wished for consummation, and great reward of their labours. An Alaric, an Attila or a Genghis Khan,[28] and the chiefs around them, might fight for glory, for the fame of extensive conquests; but the true cause that set in motion the great tide of northern emigration, and that continued to propel it till it rolled at different periods, against China, Persia, Italy, and even Egypt, was a scarcity of food, a population extended beyond the means of supporting it.

The absolute population at any one period, in proportion to the extent of territory, could never be great, on account of the unproductive nature of some of the regions occupied; but there appears to have been a most rapid succession of human beings; and as fast as some were mowed down by the scythe of war, or of famine, others rose in increased numbers to supply their place. Among these bold and improvident barbarians, population was probably but little checked, as in modern states, from a fear of future difficulties. A prevailing hope of bettering their condition by change of place; a constant expectation of plunder; a power even, if distressed, of selling their children as slaves, added to the natural carelessness of the barbaric character, all conspired to raise a population which remained to be repressed afterwards by famine or war.

Where there is any inequality of conditions, and among nations of shepherds this soon takes place, the distress arising from a scarcity of provisions, must fall hardest upon the least fortunate members of the society. This distress also must frequently have been felt by the women, exposed to casual plunder in the absence of their husbands, and subject to continual disappointments in their expected return.

But without knowing enough of the minute and intimate history of these people, to point out precisely on what part the distress for want of food chiefly fell; and to what extent it was generally felt; I think we may fairly say, from all the accounts that we have of nations of shepherds, that population invariably increased among them, whenever, by emigration, or any other cause, the means of subsistence were increased; and, that a further population was checked, and the actual population kept equal to the means of subsistence by misery and vice.

For, independently of any vicious customs that might have prevailed amongst them with regard to women, which always operate as checks to population, it must be acknowledged, I think, that the commission of war is vice, and the effect of it, misery; and none can doubt the misery of want of food.

FOUR

State of civilized nations – Probability that Europe is much more populous now than in the time of Julius Caesar – Best criterion of population – Probable error of Hume in one of the criterions that he proposes as assisting in an estimate of population – Slow increase of population at present in most of the states of Europe – The two principal checks to population – The first or preventive check examined with regard to England.

In examining the next state of mankind with relation to the question before us, the state of mixed pasture and tillage, in which, with some variation in the proportions, the most civilized nations must always remain; we shall be assisted in our review by what we daily see around us, by actual experience, by facts that come within the scope of every man's observation.

Notwithstanding the exaggerations of some old historians, there can remain no doubt in the mind of any thinking man, that the population of the principal countries of Europe, France, England, Germany, Russia, Poland, Sweden, and Denmark, is much greater than ever it was in former times. The obvious reason of these exaggerations, is, the formidable aspect that even a thinly peopled nation must have, when collected together, and moving all at once in search of fresh seats. If to this tremendous appearance be added a succession at certain intervals of similar emigrations, we shall not be much surprised that the fears of the timid nations of the south, represented the north as a region absolutely swarming with human beings. A nearer and juster view of the subject at present, enables us to see, that the inference was as absurd, as if a man in this country, who was continually meeting on the road droves of cattle from Wales and the north, was immediately to conclude that these countries were the most productive of all the parts of the kingdom.[29]

The reason that the greater part of Europe is more populous now than it was in former times, is, that the industry of the inhabitants has made these countries produce a greater quantity of human subsistence. For, I conceive, that it may be laid down as a position not to be controverted, that, taking a sufficient extent of territory to include within it exportation and importation; and allowing some variation for the prevalence of luxury, or of frugal habits; that population constantly bears a regular proportion to the food that the earth is made to produce. In the controversy concerning the populousness of ancient and modern nations, could it be clearly ascertained that the average produce of the countries in question taken altogether, is greater now than it was in the times of Julius Caesar, the dispute would be at once determined.

When we are assured that China is the most fertile country in the world; that almost all the land is in tillage; and that a great part of it bears two crops every year; and further, that the people live very frugally, we may infer with certainty, that the population must be immense, without busying ourselves in inquiries into the manners and habits of the lower classes, and the encouragements to early marriages. But these inquiries are of the utmost importance, and a minute history of the customs of the lower Chinese would be of the greatest use in ascertaining in what manner the checks to a further population operate; what are the vices, and what are the distresses that prevent an increase of numbers beyond the ability of the country to support.

Hume, in his essay on the populousness of ancient and modern nations,[30] when he intermingles, as he says, an inquiry concerning causes, with that concerning facts, does not seem to see with his usual penetration, how very little some of the causes he alludes to could enable him to form any judgement of the actual population of ancient nations. If any inference can be drawn from them, perhaps it should be directly the reverse of what Hume draws, though I certainly ought to speak with great diffidence in dissenting from a man, who of all others on such subjects was the least likely to be deceived by first appearances. If I find that at a certain period in ancient history, the encouragements to have a family were great, that early marriages were consequently very prevalent, and that few persons remained single, I should infer with certainty that population was rapidly increasing, but by no means that it was then actually very great; rather, indeed, the contrary, that it was then thin, and that there was room and food for a much greater number. On the other hand, if I find that at this period the difficulties attending a family were very great; that, consequently, few early marriages took place, and that a great number of both sexes remained single, I infer with certainty that population was at a stand; and, probably, because the actual population was very great in proportion to the fertility of the land, and that there was scarcely room and food for more. The number of footmen, housemaids, and other persons remaining unmarried in modern states, Hume allows to be rather an argument against their population. I should rather draw a contrary inference, and consider it an argument of their fullness; though this inference is not certain, because there are many thinly inhabited states that are yet stationary in their population. To speak, therefore, correctly, perhaps it may be said, that the number of unmarried persons in proportion to the whole number, existing at different periods, in the same, or different states, will enable us to judge whether population at these periods, was increasing, stationary, or decreasing, but will form no criterion by which we can determine the actual population.

There is, however, a circumstance taken notice of in most of the accounts we have of China, that it seems difficult to reconcile with this reasoning. It is said, that early marriages very generally prevail through all the ranks of the Chinese. Yet Dr Adam Smith supposes that population in China is stationary.[31] These two circumstances appear to be irreconcilable. It certainly seems very little probable that the population of China is fast increasing. Every acre of land has been so long in cultivation that we can hardly conceive there is any great yearly addition to the average produce. The fact, perhaps, of the universality of early marriages may not be sufficiently ascertained. If it be supposed true, the only way of accounting for the difficulty, with our present knowledge of the subject, appears to be, that the redundant population, necessarily occasioned by the prevalence of early marriages, must be repressed by occasional famines, and by the custom of exposing children, which, in times of distress, is probably more frequent than is ever acknowledged to Europeans. Relative to this barbarous practice, it is difficult to avoid remarking, that there cannot be a stronger proof of the distresses that have been felt by mankind for want of food, than the existence of a custom that thus violates the most natural principle of the human heart. It appears to have been very general among ancient nations, and certainly tended rather to increase population.

In examining the principal states of modern Europe, we shall find, that though they have increased very considerably in population since they were nations of shepherds, yet that, at present, their progress is but slow; and instead of doubling their numbers every twenty five years, they require three or four hundred years, or more, for that purpose. Some, indeed, may be absolutely stationary, and others even retrograde. The cause of this slow progress in population cannot be traced to a decay of the passion between the sexes. We have sufficient reason to think that this natural propensity exists still in undiminished vigour. Why then do not its effects appear in a rapid increase of the human species? An intimate[32] view of the state of society in any one country in Europe, which may serve equally for all, will enable us to answer this question, and to say, that a foresight of the difficulties attending the rearing of a family, acts as a preventive check; and the actual distresses of some of the lower classes, by which they are disabled from giving the proper food and attention to their children, acts as a positive check, to the natural increase of population.

England, as one of the most flourishing states of Europe, may be fairly taken for an example, and the observations made, will apply with but little variation to any other country where the population increases slowly.

The preventive check appears to operate in some degree through all the ranks of society in England. There are some men, even in the highest rank, who are prevented from marrying by the idea of the expenses that they must retrench, and the fancied pleasures that they must deprive themselves of, on the supposition of having a family. These considerations are certainly trivial; but a preventive foresight of this kind has objects of much greater weight for its contemplation as we go lower.

A man of liberal education, but with an income only just sufficient to enable him to associate in the rank of gentlemen, must feel absolutely certain, that if he marries and has a family, he shall be obliged, if he mixed at all in society, to rank himself with moderate farmers, and the lower class of tradesmen. The woman that a man of education would naturally make the object of his choice, would be one brought up in the same tastes and sentiments with himself, and used to the familiar intercourse[33] of a society totally different from that to which she must be reduced by marriage. Can a man consent to place the object of his affection in a situation so discordant, probably, to her tastes and inclinations? Two or three steps of descent in society, particularly at this round of the ladder, where education ends, and ignorance begins, will not be considered by the generality of people, as a fancied and chimerical, but a real and essential evil. If society be held desirable, it surely must be free, equal, and reciprocal society, where benefits are conferred as well as received; and not such as the dependant finds with his patron, or the poor with the rich.

These considerations undoubtedly prevent a great number in this rank of life from following the bent of their inclinations in an early attachment. Others, guided either by a stronger passion, or a weaker judgement, break through these restraints; and it would be hard indeed, if the gratification of so delightful a passion as virtuous love, did not, sometimes, more than counterbalance all its attendant evils. But I fear it must be owned, that the more general consequences of such marriages, are rather calculated to justify, than to repress, the forebodings of the prudent.

The sons of tradesmen and farmers are exhorted not to marry, and generally find it necessary to pursue this advice, till they are settled in some business, or farm, that may enable them to support a family. These events may not, perhaps, occur till they are far advanced in life. The scarcity of farms is a very general complaint in England. And the competition in every kind of business is so great, that it is not possible that all should be successful.

The labourer who earns eighteen pence a day, and lives with some degree of comfort as a single man, will hesitate a little before he divides that pittance among four or five, which seems to be but just sufficient for one. Harder fare and harder labour he would submit to, for the sake of living with the woman that he loves; but he must feel conscious, if he thinks at all, that, should he have a large family, and any ill luck whatever, no degree of frugality, no possible exertion of his manual strength, could preserve him from the heart-rending sensation of seeing his children starve, or of forfeiting his independence, and being obliged to the parish for their support.[34] The love of independence is a sentiment that surely none would wish to be erased from the breast of man: though the parish law of England, it must be confessed, is a system of all others the most calculated gradually to weaken this sentiment, and in the end, may eradicate it completely.

The servants who live in gentlemen's families, have restraints that are yet stronger to break through, in venturing upon marriage. They possess the necessaries, and even the comforts of life, almost in as great plenty as their masters. Their work is easy, and their food luxurious, compared with the class of labourers. And their sense of dependence is weakened by the conscious power of changing their masters, if they feel themselves offended. Thus comfortably situated at present, what are their prospects in marrying? Without knowledge or capital, either for business, or farming and unused, and therefore unable to earn a subsistence by daily labour, their only refuge seems to be a miserable alehouse, which certainly offers no very enchanting prospect of a happy evening to their lives. By much the greater part, therefore, deterred by this uninviting view of their future situation, content themselves with remaining single where they are.

If this sketch of the state of society in England be near the truth, and I do not conceive that it is exaggerated, it will be allowed, that the preventive check to population in this country operates, though with varied force, through all the classes of the community. The same observation will hold true with regard to all old states. The effects, indeed, of these restraints upon marriage are but too conspicuous in the consequent vices that are produced in almost every part of the world; vices, that are continually involving both sexes in inextricable unhappiness.

FIVE

The second, or positive check to population examined, in England – The true cause why the immense sum collected in England for the poor does not better their condition – The powerful tendency of the poor laws to defeat their own purpose – Palliative of the distresses of the poor proposed – The absolute impossibility from the fixed laws of our nature, that the pressure of want can ever be completely removed from the lower classes of society – All the checks to population may be resolved into misery or vice.

The positive check to population, by which I mean, the check that represses an increase which is already begun, is confined chiefly, though not perhaps solely, to the lowest orders of society. This check is not so obvious to common view as the other I have mentioned; and, to prove distinctly the force and extent of its operation, would require, perhaps, more data than we are in possession of. But I believe it has been very generally remarked by those who have attended to bills of mortality,[35] that of the number of children who die annually, much too great a proportion belongs to those, who may be supposed unable to give their offspring proper food and attention; exposed as they are occasionally to severe distress, and confined, perhaps, to unwholesome habitations and hard labour. This mortality among the children of the poor has been constantly taken notice of in all towns. It certainly does not prevail in an equal degree in the country; but the subject has not hitherto received sufficient attention to enable anyone to say, that there are not more deaths in proportion, among the children of the poor, even in the country, than among those of the middling and higher classes. Indeed, it seems difficult to suppose that a labourer's wife who has six children, and who is sometimes in absolute want of bread, should be able always to give them the food and attention necessary to support life. The sons and daughters of peasants will not be found such rosy cherubs in real life, as they are described to be in romances.[36] It cannot fail to be remarked by those who live much in the country, that the sons of labourers are very apt to be stunted in their growth, and are a long while arriving at maturity. Boys that you would guess to be fourteen or fifteen, are upon inquiry, frequently found to be eighteen or nineteen. And the lads who drive plough, which must certainly be a healthy exercise, are very rarely seen with any appearance of calves to their legs; a circumstance, which can only be attributed to a want either of proper, or of sufficient nourishment.

To remedy the frequent distresses of the common people, the poor laws of England have been instituted; but it is to be feared, that though they may have alleviated a little the intensity of individual misfortune, they have spread the general evil over a much larger surface. It is a subject often started in conversation, and mentioned always as a matter of great surprise, that notwithstanding the immense sum that is annually collected for the poor in England, there is still so much distress among them. Some think that the money must be embezzled; others that the churchwardens and overseers consume the greater part of it in dinners. All agree that somehow or other it must be very ill-managed. In short the fact, that nearly three millions are collected annually for the poor, and yet that their distresses are not removed, is the subject of continual astonishment. But a man who sees a little below the surface of things, would be very much more astonished, if the fact were otherwise than it is observed to be, or even if a collection universally of eighteen shillings in the pound instead of four, were materially to alter it. I will state a case which I hope will elucidate my meaning.

Suppose, that by a subscription of the rich, the eighteen pence a day which men earn now, was made up five shillings, it might be imagined, perhaps, that they would then be able to live comfortably, and have a piece of meat every day for their dinners. But this would be a very false conclusion. The transfer of three shillings and sixpence a day to every labourer, would not increase the quantity of meat in the country. There is not at present enough for all to have a decent share. What would then be the consequence? The competition among the buyers in the market of meat, would rapidly raise the price from six pence or seven pence, to two or three shillings in the pound; and the commodity would not be divided among many more than it is at present. When an article is scarce, and cannot be distributed to all, he that can show the most valid patent,[37] that is, he that offers most money becomes the possessor. If we can suppose the competition among the buyers of meat to continue long enough for a greater number of cattle to be reared annually, this could only be done at the expense of the corn, which would be a very disadvantageous exchange; for it is well known that the country could not then support the same population; and when subsistence is scarce in proportion to the number of people, it is of little consequence whether the lowest members of the society possess eighteen pence or five shillings. They must at all events be reduced to live upon the hardest fare, and in the smallest quantity.

It will be said, perhaps, that the increased number of purchasers in every article, would give a spur to productive industry, and that the whole produce of the island would be increased. This might in some degree be the case. But the spur that these fancied riches would give to population, would more than counterbalance it, and the increased produce would be to be divided among a more than proportionably increased number of people. All this time I am supposing that the same quantity of work would be done as before. But this would not really take place. The receipt of five shillings a day, instead of eighteen pence, would make every man fancy himself comparatively rich, and able to indulge himself in many hours or days of leisure. This would give a strong and immediate check to productive industry; and in a short time, not only the nation would be poorer, but the lower classes themselves would be much more distressed than when they received only eighteen pence a day.

A collection from the rich of eighteen shillings in the pound, even if distributed in the most judicious manner, would have a

little the same effect as that resulting from the supposition
I have just made; and no possible contributions or sacrifices
of the rich, particularly in money, could for any time prevent
the recurrence of distress among the lower members of society whoever they were. Great changes might, indeed, be made.
The rich might become poor, and some of the poor rich: but a
part of the society must necessarily feel a difficulty of living;
and this difficulty will naturally fall on the least fortunate
members.

It may at first appear strange, but I believe it is true, that I
cannot by means of money raise a poor man, and enable him to
live much better than he did before, without proportionably
depressing others in the same class. If I retrench the quantity of
food consumed in my house, and give him what I have cut off,
I then benefit him, without depressing any but myself and family, who, perhaps, may be well able to bear it. If I turn up a
piece of uncultivated land, and give him the produce, I then
benefit both him, and all the members of the society, because
what he before consumed is thrown into the common stock,
and probably some of the new produce with it. But if I only
give him money, supposing the produce of the country to
remain the same, I give him a title to a larger share of that produce than formerly, which share he cannot receive without
diminishing the shares of others. It is evident that this effect, in
individual instances, must be so small as to be totally imper-
ceptible; but still it must exist, as many other effects do, which
like some of the insects that people the air, elude our grosser
perceptions.

Supposing the quantity of food in any country to remain the
same for many years together; it is evident that this food must
be divided according to the value of each man's patent,* or the
sum of money that he can afford to spend in this commodity so
universally in request. It is a demonstrative truth therefore, that
the patents of one set of men could not be increased in value,

* Mr Godwin calls the wealth that a man receives from his ancestors a mouldy
patent. It may, I think, very properly be termed a patent; but I hardly see the
propriety of calling it a mouldy one, as it is an article in such constant use.

without diminishing the value of the patents of some other set of men. If the rich were to subscribe, and give five shillings a day to five hundred thousand men without retrenching their own tables, no doubt can exist, that as these men would naturally live more at their ease, and consume a greater quantity of provisions, there would be less food remaining to divide among the rest; and consequently each man's patent would be diminished in value, or the same number of pieces of silver would purchase a smaller quantity of subsistence.

An increase of population without a proportional increase of food, will evidently have the same effect in lowering the value of each man's patent. The food must necessarily be distributed in smaller quantities, and consequently a day's labour will purchase a smaller quantity of provisions. An increase in the price of provisions would arise, either from an increase of population faster than the means of subsistence; or from a different distribution of the money of the society. The food of a country that has been long occupied, if it be increasing, increases slowly and regularly, and cannot be made to answer any sudden demands; but variations in the distribution of the money of a society are not infrequently occurring, and are undoubtedly among the causes that occasion the continual variations which we observe in the price of provisions.

The poor laws of England tend to depress the general condition of the poor in these two ways. Their first obvious tendency is to increase population without increasing the food for its support. A poor man may marry with little or no prospect of being able to support a family in independence. They may be said therefore in some measure to create the poor which they maintain; and as the provisions of the country must, in consequence of the increased population, be distributed to every man in smaller proportions, it is evident that the labour of those who are not supported by parish assistance, will purchase a smaller quantity of provisions than before, and consequently, more of them must be driven to ask for support.

Secondly, the quantity of provisions consumed in workhouses upon a part of the society, that cannot in general be considered as the most valuable part, diminishes the shares that would otherwise belong to more industrious, and more worthy members; and thus in the same manner forces more to become dependent. If the poor in the workhouses were to live better than they now do, this new distribution of the money of the society would tend more conspicuously to depress the condition of those out of the workhouses, by occasioning a rise in the price of provisions.

Fortunately for England, a spirit of independence still remains among the peasantry. The poor laws are strongly calculated to eradicate this spirit. They have succeeded in part; but had they succeeded as completely as might have been expected, their pernicious tendency would not have been so long concealed.

Hard as it may appear in individual instances, dependent poverty ought to be held disgraceful. Such a stimulus seems to be absolutely necessary to promote the happiness of the great mass of mankind; and every general attempt to weaken this stimulus, however benevolent its apparent intention, will always defeat its own purpose. If men are induced to marry from a prospect of parish provision, with little or no chance of maintaining their families in independence, they are not only unjustly tempted to bring unhappiness and dependence upon themselves and children; but they are tempted, without knowing it, to injure all in the same class with themselves. A labourer who marries without being able to support a family, may in some respects be considered as an enemy to all his fellow labourers.

I feel no doubt whatever, that the parish laws of England have contributed to raise the price of provisions, and to lower the real price of labour. They have therefore contributed to impoverish that class of people whose only possession is their labour. It is also difficult to suppose that they have not powerfully contributed to generate that carelessness, and want of frugality observable among the poor, so contrary to the disposition frequently to be remarked among petty tradesmen and small farmers. The labouring poor, to use a vulgar expression, seem always to live from hand to mouth. Their present wants employ their whole attention, and they seldom think of the future. Even when they have an opportunity of saving they seldom exercise it; but all that is beyond their present necessities goes, generally speaking, to the alehouse. The poor laws of England may therefore be said to diminish both the power and the will to save, among the common people, and thus to weaken one of the strongest incentives to sobriety and industry, and consequently to happiness.

It is a general complaint among master manufacturers, that high wages ruin all their workmen; but it is difficult to conceive that these men would not save a part of their high wages for the future support of their families, instead of spending it in drunkenness and dissipation, if they did not rely on parish assistance for support in case of accidents. And that the poor employed in manufactures consider this assistance as a reason why they may spend all the wages they earn, and enjoy themselves while they can, appears to be evident from the number of families that, upon the failure of any great manufactory,[38] immediately fall upon the parish; when perhaps the wages earned in this manufactory, while it flourished, were sufficiently above the price of common country labour, to have allowed them to save enough for their support, till they could find some other channel for their industry.

A man who might not be deterred from going to the alehouse, from the consideration that on his death, or sickness, he should leave his wife and family upon the parish, might yet hesitate in thus dissipating his earnings, if he were assured that, in either of these cases, his family must starve, or be left to the support of casual bounty. In China, where the real as well as nominal price of labour is very low, sons are yet obliged by law to support their aged and helpless parents. Whether such a law would be advisable in this country, I will not pretend to determine. But it seems at any rate highly improper, by positive institutions, which render dependent poverty so general, to weaken that disgrace, which for the best and most humane reasons ought to attach to it.

The mass of happiness among the common people cannot but be diminished, when one of the strongest checks to idleness and dissipation is thus removed; and when men are thus allured to marry with little or no prospect of being able to maintain a family in independence. Every obstacle in the way of marriage must undoubtedly be considered as a species of unhappiness. But as from the laws of our nature some check to population must exist, it is better that it should be checked from a foresight of the difficulties attending a family, and the fear of dependent poverty, than that it should be encouraged, only to be repressed afterwards by want and sickness.

It should be remembered always, that there is an essential difference between food, and those wrought commodities, the raw materials of which are in great plenty. A demand for these last will not fail to create them in as great a quantity as they are wanted. The demand for food has by no means the same creative power. In a country where all the fertile spots have been seized, high offers are necessary to encourage the farmer to lay his dressing on land, from which he cannot expect a profitable return for some years. And before the prospect of advantage is sufficiently great to encourage this sort of agricultural enterprise, and while the new produce is rising, great distresses may be suffered from the want of it. The demand for an increased quantity of subsistence is, with few exceptions, constant everywhere, yet we see how slowly it is answered in all those countries that have been long occupied.

The poor laws of England were undoubtedly instituted for the most benevolent purpose; but there is great reason to think that they have not succeeded in their intention. They certainly mitigate some cases of very severe distress which might otherwise occur; yet the state of the poor who are supported by parishes, considered in all its circumstances, is very far from being free from misery. But one of the principal objections to them is, that for this assistance which some of the poor receive, in itself almost a doubtful blessing, the whole class of the common people of England, is subjected to a set of grating, inconvenient, and tyrannical laws, totally inconsistent with the genuine spirit of the constitution. The whole business of settlements, even in its present amended state, is utterly contradictory to all ideas of freedom.[39] The parish persecution of men whose families are likely to become chargeable, and of poor women who are near lying-in, is a most disgraceful and disgusting tyranny. And the obstructions continually occasioned in the market of labour by these laws, have a constant tendency to add to the difficulties of those who are struggling to support themselves without assistance.

These evils attendant on the poor laws, are in some degree irremediable. If assistance be to be distributed to a certain class of people, a power must be given somewhere of discriminating the proper objects, and of managing the concerns of the institutions that are necessary; but any great interference with the affairs of other people, is a species of tyranny; and in the common course of things, the exercise of this power may be expected to become grating to those who are driven to ask for support. The tyranny of justices, churchwardens, and overseers, is a common complaint among the poor: but the fault does not lie so much in these persons, who probably before they were in power, were not worse than other people; but in the nature of all such institutions.

The evil is perhaps gone too far to be remedied; but I feel little doubt in my own mind, that if the poor laws had never existed, though there might have been a few more instances of very severe distress, yet that the aggregate mass of happiness among the common people would have been much greater than it is at present.

Mr Pitt's Poor Bill[40] has the appearance of being framed with benevolent intentions, and the clamour raised against it was in many respects ill directed, and unreasonable. But it must be confessed that it possesses in a high degree the great and radical defect of all systems of the kind, that of tending to increase population without increasing the means for its support, and thus to depress the condition of those that are not supported by parishes, and, consequently, to create more poor.

To remove the wants of the lower classes of society, is indeed an arduous task. The truth is, that the pressure of distress on this part of a community is an evil so deeply seated, that no human ingenuity can reach it. Were I to propose a palliative,[41] and palliatives are all that the nature of the case will admit, it should be, in the first place, the total abolition of all the present parish laws. This would at any rate give liberty and freedom of action to the peasantry of England, which they can hardly be said to possess at present. They would then be able to settle without interruption, wherever there was a prospect of a greater plenty of work, and a higher price for labour. The market of labour would then be free, and those obstacles removed, which as things are now, often for a considerable time prevent the price from rising according to the demand.[42]

Secondly, premiums might be given for turning up fresh land, and all possible encouragements held out to agriculture above manufactures, and to tillage above grazing. Every endeavour should be used to weaken and destroy all those institutions relating to corporations, apprenticeships, etc.[43] which cause the labours of agriculture to be worse paid than the labours of trade and manufactures. For a country can never produce its proper quantity of food while these distinctions remain in favour of artisans. Such encouragements to agriculture would tend to furnish the market with an increasing quantity of healthy work, and at the same time, by augmenting the produce of the country, would raise the comparative price of labour, and ameliorate the condition of the labourer. Being now in better circumstances, and seeing no prospect of parish assistance, he would be more able, as well as more inclined, to enter into associations for providing against the sickness of himself or family.

Lastly, for cases of extreme distress, county workhouses might be established, supported by rates upon the whole kingdom, and free for persons of all counties, and indeed of all nations. The fare should be hard, and those that were able obliged to work. It would be desirable, that they should not be considered as comfortable asylums in all difficulties; but merely as places where severe distress might find some alleviation. A part of these houses might be separated, or others built for a most beneficial purpose, which has not been infrequently taken notice of, that of providing a place, where any person, whether native or foreigner, might do a day's work at all times, and receive the market price for it. Many cases would undoubtedly be left for the exertion of individual benevolence.

A plan of this kind, the preliminary of which, should be an abolition of all the present parish laws, seems to be the best calculated to increase the mass of happiness among the common people of England. To prevent the recurrence of misery, is, alas! beyond the power of man. In the vain endeavour to attain what in the nature of things is impossible, we now sacrifice not only possible, but certain benefits. We tell the common people, that if they will submit to a code of tyrannical regulations, they shall never be in want. They do submit to these regulations. They perform their part of the contract: but we do not, nay cannot, perform ours: and thus the poor sacrifice the valuable blessing of liberty, and receive nothing that can be called an equivalent in return.

Notwithstanding then, the institution of the poor laws in England, I think it will be allowed, that considering the state of the lower classes altogether, both in the towns and in the country, the distresses which they suffer from the want of proper and sufficient food, from hard labour and unwholesome habitations, must operate as a constant check to incipient population.

To these two great checks to population, in all long occupied countries, which I have called the preventive and the positive checks, may be added, vicious customs with respect to women, great cities, unwholesome manufactures, luxury, pestilence, and war.

All these checks may be fairly resolved into misery and vice.

And that these are the true causes of the slow increase of population in all the states of modern Europe, will appear sufficiently evident, from the comparatively rapid increase that has invariably taken place, whenever these causes have been in any considerable degree removed.

SIX

New colonies – Reasons of their rapid increase – North American colonies – Extraordinary instances of increase in the back settlements – Rapidity with which even old states recover the ravages of war, pestilence, famine, or the convulsions of nature.

It has been universally remarked, that all new colonies settled in healthy countries, where there was plenty of room and food, have constantly increased with astonishing rapidity in their population. Some of the colonies from ancient Greece, in no very long period, more than equalled their parent states in numbers and strength. And not to dwell on remote instances, the European settlements in the new world bear ample testimony to the truth of a remark, which, indeed, has never, that I know of, been doubted. A plenty of rich land, to be had for little or nothing, is so powerful a cause of population, as to overcome all other obstacles. No settlements could well have been worse managed than those of Spain in Mexico, Peru, and Quito. The tyranny, superstition, and vices, of the mother country, were introduced in ample quantities among her children.[44] Exorbitant taxes were exacted by the crown. The most arbitrary restrictions were imposed on their trade. And the governors were not behindhand in rapacity and extortion for themselves as well as their master. Yet, under all these difficulties, the colonies made a quick progress in population. The city of Lima, founded since the conquest, is represented by Ulloa[45] as containing fifty thousand inhabitants near fifty years ago. Quito, which had been but a hamlet of Indians, is represented by the same author as in his time equally populous. Mexico is said to contain a hundred thousand inhabitants, which, notwithstanding the exaggerations of the Spanish writers, is supposed to be five times greater than what it contained in the time of Montezuma.

In the Portuguese colony of Brazil, governed with almost equal tyranny, there were supposed to be, thirty years since, six hundred thousand inhabitants of European extraction.

The Dutch and French colonies, though under the government of exclusive companies of merchants, which, as Dr Adam Smith says very justly, is the worst of all possible governments, still persisted in thriving under every disadvantage.[46]

But the English North American colonies, now the powerful people of the United States of America, made by far the most rapid progress. To the plenty of good land which they possessed in common with the Spanish and Portuguese settlements, they added a greater degree of liberty and equality. Though not without some restrictions on their foreign commerce, they were allowed a perfect liberty of managing their own internal affairs. The political institutions that prevailed were favourable to the alienation and division of property. Lands that were not cultivated by the proprietor within a limited time, were declared grantable to any other person. In Pennsylvania there was no right of primogeniture;[47] and in the provinces of New England, the eldest had only a double share. There were no tithes in any of the states, and scarcely any taxes. And on account of the extreme cheapness of good land, a capital could not be more advantageously employed than in agriculture, which at the same time that it supplies the greatest quantity of healthy work, affords much the most valuable produce to the society.

The consequence of these favourable circumstances united, was a rapidity of increase, probably without parallel in history. Throughout all the northern colonies, the population was found to double itself in 25 years. The original number of persons who had settled in the four provinces of New England in 1643, was 21,200.* Afterwards it is supposed, that more left them, than went to them. In the year 1760, they were increased to half a million. They had therefore all along doubled their

---

* I take these facts from Dr Price's two volumes of *Observations*, not having Dr Styles's pamphlet, from which he quotes, by me.[48]

own number in 25 years. In New Jersey the period of doubling appeared to be 22 years; and in Rhode Island still less. In the back settlements, where the inhabitants applied themselves solely to agriculture, and luxury was not known, they were found to double their own number in 15 years, a most extraordinary instance of increase.* Along the sea coast, which would naturally be first inhabited, the period of doubling was about 35 years; and in some of the maritime towns, the population was absolutely at a stand.

These facts seem to show that population increases exactly in the proportion, that the two great checks to it, misery and vice, are removed; and that there is not a truer criterion of the happiness and innocence of a people, than the rapidity of their increase. The unwholesomeness of towns, to which some persons are necessarily driven, from the nature of their trades, must be considered as a species of misery; and even the slightest check to marriage, from a prospect of the difficulty of maintaining a family, may be fairly classed under the same head. In short, it is difficult to conceive any check to population, which does not come under the description of some species of misery or vice.[49]

The population of the thirteen American states before the war, was reckoned at about three millions. Nobody imagines,

---

* In instances of this kind, the powers of the earth appear to be fully equal to answer all the demands for food that can be made upon it by man. But we should be led into an error, if we were thence to suppose that population and food ever really increase in the same ratio. The one is still a geometrical and the other an arithmetical ratio, that is, one increases by multiplication, and the other by addition. Where there are few people, and a great quantity of fertile land, the power of the earth to afford a yearly increase of food may be compared to a great reservoir of water, supplied by a moderate stream. The faster population increases, the more help will be got to draw off the water, and consequently an increasing quantity will be taken every year. But the sooner, undoubtedly, will the reservoir be exhausted, and the streams only remain. When acre has been added to acre, till all the fertile land is occupied, the yearly increase of food will depend upon the amelioration of the land already in possession; and even this moderate stream will be gradually diminishing. But population, could it be supplied with food, would go on with unexhausted vigour, and the increase of one period would furnish the power of a greater increase the next, and this without any limit.

that Great Britain is less populous at present for the emigration of the small parent stock that produced these numbers. On the contrary, a certain degree of emigration, is known to be favourable to the population of the mother country. It has been particularly remarked, that the two Spanish provinces from which the greatest number of people emigrated to America, became in consequence more populous. Whatever was the original number of British emigrants that increased so fast in the North American colonies; let us ask, why does not an equal number produce an equal increase, in the same time, in Great Britain? The great and obvious cause to be assigned, is, the want of room and food, or, in other words, misery; and that this is a much more powerful cause even than vice, appears sufficiently evident from the rapidity with which even old states recover the desolations of war, pestilence, or the accidents of nature. They are then for a short time placed a little in the situation of new states; and the effect is always answerable to what might be expected. If the industry of the inhabitants be not destroyed by fear or tyranny, subsistence will soon increase beyond the wants of the reduced numbers; and the invariable consequence will be, that population which before, perhaps, was nearly stationary, will begin immediately to increase.

The fertile province of Flanders,[50] which has been so often the seat of the most destructive wars, after a respite of a few years, has appeared always as fruitful and as populous as ever. Even the Palatinate[51] lifted up its head again after the execrable ravages of Louis XIV. The effects of the dreadful plague in London in 1666, were not perceptible 15 or 20 years afterwards.[52] The traces of the most destructive famines in China and Hindustan, are by all accounts very soon obliterated. It may even be doubted whether Turkey and Egypt are upon an average much less populous, for the plagues that periodically lay them waste. If the number of people which they contain be less now than formerly, it is, probably, rather to be attributed to the tyranny and oppression of the government under which they groan, and the consequent discouragements to agriculture, than to the loss which they sustain by the plague. The most tremendous convulsions of nature, such as volcanic eruptions and earthquakes, if they do not happen so frequently as to drive away the inhabitants, or to destroy their spirit of industry, have but a trifling effect on the average population of any state. Naples, and the country under Vesuvius, are still very populous, notwithstanding the repeated eruptions of that mountain. And Lisbon and Lima[53] are now, probably, nearly in the same state with regard to population, as they were before the last earthquakes.

SEVEN

A probable cause of epidemics – Extracts from Mr Süssmilch's tables – Periodical returns of sickly seasons to be expected in certain cases – Proportion of births to burials for short periods in any country an inadequate criterion of the real average increase of population – Best criterion of a permanent increase of population – Great frugality of living one of the causes of the famines of China and Hindustan – Evil tendency of one of the clauses of Mr Pitt's Poor Bill – Only one proper way of encouraging population – Causes of the happiness of nations – Famine, the last and most dreadful mode by which nature represses a redundant population – The three propositions considered as established.

By great attention to cleanliness, the plague seems at length to be completely expelled from London. But it is not improbable, that among the secondary causes that produce even sickly seasons and epidemics, ought to be ranked, a crowded population and unwholesome and insufficient food. I have been led to this remark, by looking over some of the tables of Mr Süssmilch,[54] which Dr Price has extracted in one of his notes to the postscript on the controversy respecting the population of England and Wales. They are considered as very correct; and if such tables were general, they would throw great light on the different ways by which population is repressed, and prevented from increasing beyond the means of subsistence in any country. I will extract a part of the tables, with Dr Price's remarks.

In the Kingdom of Prussia, and Dukedom of Lithuania

Annual average	Births	Burials	Marriages	Proportion of births to marriages	Proportion of births to burials
10 yrs to 1702	21,963	14,718	5,928	37:10	150:100
5 yrs to 1716	21,602	11,984	4,968	37:10	180:100
5 yrs to 1756	28,392	19,154	5,599	50:10	148:100

'N.B. In 1709 and 1710, a pestilence carried off 247,733 of the inhabitants of this country, and in 1736 and 1737, epidemics prevailed, which again checked its increase.'

It may be remarked, that the greatest proportion of births to burials, was in the five years after the great pestilence.

Duchy of Pomerania

Annual average	Births	Burials	Marriages	Proportion of births to marriages	Proportion of births to burials
6 yrs to 1702	6,540	4,647	1,810	36:10	140:100
6 yrs to 1708	7,455	4,208	1,875	39:10	177:100
6 yrs to 1726	8,432	5,627	2,131	39:10	150:100
4 yrs to 1756	12,767	9,281	2,957	43:10	137:100

'In this instance the inhabitants appear to have been almost doubled in 56 years, no very bad epidemics having once interrupted the increase, but the three years immediately following the last period (to 1759), were years so sickly that the births were sunk to 10,229, and the burials raised to 15,068.'

Is it not probable, that in this case, the number of inhabitants had increased faster than the food and the accommodations necessary to preserve them in health? The mass of the people would, upon this supposition, be obliged to live harder, and a greater number would be crowded together in one house; and it is not surely improbable, that these were among the natural causes that produced the three sickly years. These causes may produce such an effect, though the country, absolutely considered, may not be extremely crowded and populous. In a country even thinly inhabited, if an increase of population take place, before more food is raised, and more houses are built, the inhabitants must be distressed in some degree for room and subsistence. Were the marriages in England, for the next eight or ten years, to be more prolific than usual, or even were a greater number of marriages than usual to take place, supposing the number of houses to remain the same; instead of five or six to a cottage, there must be seven or eight; and this, added to the necessity of harder living, would probably have a very unfavourable effect on the health of the common people.

Neumark of Brandenburg

Annual average	Births	Burials	Marriages	Proportion of births to marriages	Proportion of births to burials
5 yrs to 1701	5,433	3,483	1,436	37:10	155:100
5 yrs to 1726	7,012	4,254	1,713	40:10	164:100
5 yrs to 1756	7,978	5,567	1,891	42:10	143:100

'Epidemics prevailed for six years, from 1736, to 1741, which checked the increase.'

Dukedom of Magdeburg

Annual average	Births	Burials	Marriages	Proportion of births to marriages	Proportion of births to burials
5 yrs to 1702	6,431	4,103	1,681	38:10	156:100
5 yrs to 1717	7,590	5,335	2,076	36:10	142:100
5 yrs to 1756	8,850	8,069	2,193	40:10	109:100

'The years 1738, 1740, 1750, and 1751, were particularly sickly.'

For further information on this subject, I refer the reader to Mr Süssmilch's tables. The extracts that I have made are sufficient to show the periodical, though irregular returns of sickly seasons; and it seems highly probable, that a scantiness of room and food was one of the principal causes that occasioned them.

It appears from the tables, that these countries were increasing rather fast for old states, notwithstanding the occasional sickly seasons that prevailed. Cultivation must have been improving, and marriages, consequently, encouraged. For the checks to population appear to have been rather of the positive, than of the preventive kind. When from a prospect of increasing plenty in any country, the weight that represses population is in some degree removed; it is highly probable that the motion will be continued beyond the operation of the cause that first impelled it. Or, to be more particular, when the increasing produce of a country, and the increasing demand for labour, so far ameliorate the condition of the labourer, as greatly to encourage marriage, it is probable that the custom of early marriages will continue, till the population of the country has gone beyond the increased produce: and sickly seasons appear to be the natural and necessary consequence. I should expect, therefore, that those countries where subsistence was increasing sufficiently at times to encourage population, but not to answer all its demands, would be more subject to periodical epidemics than those where the population could more completely accommodate itself to the average produce.

An observation the converse of this will probably also be found true. In those countries that are subject to periodical sicknesses, the increase of population, or the excess of births above the burials, will be greater in the intervals of these periods, than is usual, *ceteris paribus*, in the countries not so much subject to such disorders. If Turkey and Egypt have been nearly stationary in their average population for the last century, in the intervals of their periodical plagues, the births must have exceeded the burials in a greater proportion than in such countries as France and England.

The average proportion of births to burials in any country for a period of five or ten years, will hence appear to be a very inadequate criterion by which to judge of its real progress in population. This proportion certainly shows the rate of increase during those five or ten years; but we can by no means thence infer, what had been the increase for the twenty years before, or what would be the increase for the twenty years after. Dr Price observes, that Sweden, Norway, Russia, and the kingdom of Naples, are increasing fast; but the extracts from registers that he has given, are not for periods of sufficient extent to establish the fact. It is highly probable, however, that Sweden, Norway, and Russia, are really increasing in their population, though not at the rate that the proportion of births to burials for the short periods that Dr Price takes would seem to show.* For five years, ending in 1777, the proportion of births to burials in the kingdom of Naples, was 144 to 100; but there is reason to suppose, that this proportion would indicate an increase much greater than would be really found to have taken place in that kingdom during a period of a hundred years.

Dr Short[55] compared the registers of many villages and market towns in England for two periods; the first, from Queen Elizabeth to the middle of the last century, and the second, from different years at the end of the last century, to the middle of the present. And from a comparison of these extracts, it appears, that in the former period the births exceeded the burials in the proportion of 124 to 100; but in the latter, only in the proportion of 111 to 100. Dr Price thinks that the registers in the former period are not to be depended upon; but, probably, in this instance, they do not give incorrect proportions. At least, there are many reasons for expecting to find a greater excess of births above the burials in the former period than in the latter. In the natural progress of the population of any country, more good land will, *ceteris paribus*,[†] be taken into cultivation in the earlier stages of it than in the later. And a greater proportional yearly increase of produce, will almost invariably be followed by a greater proportional increase of population. But, besides this great cause, which would naturally give the excess of births above the burials greater at the end of Queen Elizabeth's reign, than in the middle of the present century, I cannot help thinking that the occasional ravages of

---

* See R. Price, *Observations on reversionary payments*, 4th ed., 2 vols (1783). Postscript to the controversy on the population of England and Wales.

† I say *ceteris paribus*, because the increase of the produce of any country will always very greatly depend on the spirit of industry that prevails, and the way in which it is directed. The knowledge and habits of the people, and other temporary causes, particularly the degree of civil liberty and equality existing at the time, must always have great influence in exciting and directing this spirit.

the plague in the former period, must have had some tendency to increase this proportion. If an average of ten years had been taken in the intervals of the returns of this dreadful disorder; or if the years of plague had been rejected as accidental, the registers would certainly give the proportion of births to burials too high for the real average increase of the population. For some few years after the great plague in 1666, it is probable that there was a more than usual excess of births above burials, particularly if Dr Price's opinion be founded, that England was more populous at the Revolution (which happened only twenty two years afterwards) than it is at present.[56]

Mr King,[57] in 1693, stated the proportion of the births to the burials throughout the kingdom, exclusive of London, as 115 to 100. Dr Short makes it, in the middle of the present century, 111 to 100, including London. The proportion in France for five years, ending in 1774, was 117 to 100. If these statements are near the truth, and if there are no very great variations at particular periods in the proportions, it would appear, that the population of France and England has accommodated itself very nearly to the average produce of each country. The discouragements to marriage, the consequent vicious habits, war, luxury, the silent though certain depopulation of large towns, and the close habitations, and insufficient food of many of the poor, prevent population from increasing beyond the means of subsistence; and, if I may use an expression which certainly at first appears strange, supersede the necessity of great and ravaging epidemics to repress what is redundant. Were a wasting plague to sweep off two millions in England, and six millions in France, there can be no doubt whatever, that after the inhabitants had recovered from the dreadful shock, the proportion of births to burials would be much above what it is in either country at present.

In New Jersey, the proportion of births to deaths on an average of seven years, ending in 1743, was as 300 to 100. In France and England, taking the highest proportion, it is as 117 to 100. Great and astonishing as this difference is, we ought not to be so wonder-struck at it, as to attribute it to the miraculous interposition of heaven. The causes of it are not remote, latent and mysterious; but near us, round about us, and open to the investigation of every inquiring mind. It accords with the most liberal spirit of philosophy, to suppose that not a stone can fall, or a plant rise, without the immediate agency of divine power. But we know from experience, that these operations of what we call nature have been conducted almost invariably according to fixed laws. And since the world began, the causes of population and depopulation have probably been as constant as any of the laws of nature with which we are acquainted.[58]

The passion between the sexes has appeared in every age to be so nearly the same, that it may always be considered, in algebraic language, as a given quantity. The great law of necessity which prevents population from increasing in any country beyond the food which it can either produce or acquire, is a law, so open to our view, so obvious and evident to our understandings, and so completely confirmed by the experience of every age, that we cannot for a moment doubt it. The different modes which nature takes to prevent, or repress a redundant population, do not appear, indeed, to us so certain and regular; but, though we cannot always predict the mode, we may with certainty predict the fact. If the proportion of births to deaths for a few years, indicate an increase of numbers much beyond the proportional increased or acquired produce of the country, we may be perfectly certain, that unless an emigration takes place, the deaths will shortly exceed the births; and that the increase that had taken place for a few years cannot be the real average increase of the population of the country. Were there no other depopulating causes, every country would, without doubt, be subject to periodical pestilences or famines.

The only true criterion of a real and permanent increase in the population of any country, is the increase of the means of subsistence. But even this criterion is subject to some slight variations, which are, however, completely open to our view and observations. In some countries population appears to have been forced; that is, the people have been habituated by degrees to live almost upon the smallest possible quantity of food. There must have been periods in such countries when population increased permanently, without an increase in the means of subsistence. China seems to answer to this description. If the accounts we have of it are to be trusted,[59] the lower classes of people are in the habit of living almost upon the smallest possible quantity of food, and are glad to get any putrid offals that European labourers would rather starve than eat. The law in China which permits parents to expose their children, has tended principally thus to force the population. A nation in this state must necessarily be subject to famines. Where a country is so populous in proportion to the means of subsistence, that the average produce of it is but barely sufficient to support the lives of the inhabitants, any deficiency from the badness of seasons must be fatal. It is probable that the very frugal manner in which the Hindus are in the habit of living, contributes in some degree to the famines of Hindustan.[60]

In America, where the reward of labour is at present so liberal, the lower classes might retrench very considerably in a year of scarcity, without materially distressing themselves. A famine therefore seems to be almost impossible. It may be expected, that in the progress of the population of America, the labourers will in time be much less liberally rewarded. The numbers will in this case permanently increase, without a proportional increase in the means of subsistence.

In the different states of Europe there must be some variations in the proportion between the number of inhabitants, and the quantity of food consumed, arising from the different habits of living that prevail in each state. The labourers of the south of England are so accustomed to eat fine wheaten bread, that they will suffer themselves to be half starved, before they will submit to live like the Scottish peasants. They might perhaps in time, by the constant operation of the hard law of necessity, be reduced to live even like the lower Chinese: and the country would then, with the same quantity of food, support a greater population. But to effect this must always be a most difficult, and every friend to humanity will hope, an abortive attempt. Nothing is so common as to hear of encouragements that ought to be given to population. If the tendency of mankind to increase be so great as I have represented it to be, it may appear strange that this increase does not come when it is thus repeatedly called for. The true reason is, that the demand for a greater population is made without preparing the funds necessary to support it. Increase the demand for agricultural labour by promoting cultivation, and with it consequently increase the produce of the country, and ameliorate the condition of the labourer, and no apprehensions whatever need be entertained of the proportional increase of population. An attempt to effect this purpose in any other way is vicious, cruel, and tyrannical, and in any state of tolerable freedom cannot therefore succeed. It may appear to be the interest of the rulers, and the rich of a state, to force population, and thereby lower the price of labour, and consequently the expense of fleets and armies, and the cost of manufactures for foreign sale: but every attempt of the kind should be carefully watched and strenuously resisted by the friends of the poor, particularly when it comes under the deceitful garb of benevolence, and is likely, on that account, to be cheerfully, and cordially received by the common people.

I entirely acquit Mr Pitt of any sinister intention in that clause of his Poor Bill which allows a shilling a week to every labourer for each child he has above three.[61] I confess, that before the bill was brought into Parliament, and for some time after, I thought that such a regulation would be highly beneficial; but further reflection on the subject has convinced me, that if its object be to better the condition of the poor, it is calculated to defeat the very purpose which it has in view. It has no tendency that I can discover to increase the produce of the country; and if it tend to increase population, without increasing the produce, the necessary and inevitable consequence appears to be, that the same produce must be divided among a greater number, and consequently that a day's labour will purchase a smaller quantity of provisions, and the poor therefore in general must be more distressed.

I have mentioned some cases, where population may permanently increase, without a proportional increase in the means of subsistence. But it is evident that the variation in different states, between the food and the numbers supported by it, is restricted to a limit beyond which it cannot pass. In every country, the population of which is not absolutely decreasing, the food must be necessarily sufficient to support, and to continue, the race of labourers.

Other circumstances being the same, it may be affirmed, that countries are populous, according to the quantity of human food which they produce; and happy, according to the liberality with which that food is divided, or the quantity which a day's labour will purchase. Corn countries are more populous than pasture countries; and rice countries more populous than corn countries. The lands in England are not suited to rice, but they would all bear potatoes: and Dr Adam Smith observes, that if potatoes were to become the favourite vegetable food of the common people, and if the same quantity of land was employed in their culture, as is now employed in the culture of corn, the country would be able to support a much greater population; and would consequently in a very short time have it.[62]

The happiness of a country does not depend, absolutely, upon its poverty, or its riches, upon its youth, or its age, upon its being thinly, or fully inhabited, but upon the rapidity with which it is increasing, upon the degree in which the yearly increase of food approaches to the yearly increase of an unrestricted population. This approximation is always the nearest in new colonies, where the knowledge and industry of an old state, operate on the fertile unappropriated land of a new one. In other cases, the youth or the age of a state is not in this respect of very great importance. It is probable, that the food of Great Britain is divided in as great plenty to the inhabitants, at the present period, as it was two thousand, three thousand, or four thousand years ago. And there is reason to believe that the poor and thinly inhabited tracts of the Scottish Highlands, are as much distressed by an overcharged population as the rich and populous province of Flanders.

Were a country never to be overrun by a people more advanced in arts, but left to its own natural progress in civilization, from the time that its produce might be considered as an unit, to the time that it might be considered as a million, during the lapse of many hundred years, there would not be a single period, when the mass of the people could be said to be free from distress, either directly or indirectly, for want of food. In every state in Europe, since we have first had accounts of it, millions and millions of human existences have been repressed from this simple cause; though perhaps in some of these states, an absolute famine has never been known.

Famine seems to be the last, the most dreadful resource of nature. The power of population is so superior to the power in the earth to produce subsistence for man, that premature death must in some shape or other visit the human race. The vices of mankind are active and able ministers of depopulation. They are the precursors in the great army of destruction; and often finish the dreadful work themselves. But should they fail in this war of extermination, sickly seasons, epidemics, pestilence, and plague, advance in terrific array, and sweep off their thousands and ten thousands. Should success be still incomplete, gigantic inevitable famine stalks in the rear, and with one mighty blow, levels the population with the food of the world.

Must it not then be acknowledged by an attentive examiner of the histories of mankind, that in every age and in every state in which man has existed, or does now exist; that the increase of population is necessarily limited by the means of subsistence; that population does invariably increase when the means of subsistence increase; and, that the superior power of population is repressed, and the actual population kept equal to the means of subsistence by misery and vice.

EIGHT

Mr Wallace – Error of supposing that the difficulty arising from population is at a great distance – Mr Condorcet's sketch of the progress of the human mind – Period when the oscillation, mentioned by Mr Condorcet, ought to be applied to the human race.

To a person who draws the preceding obvious inferences, from a view of the past and present state of mankind, it cannot but be a matter of astonishment, that all the writers on the perfectibility of man and of society, who have noticed the argument of an overcharged population, treat it always very slightly, and invariably represent the difficulties arising from it, as at a great and almost immeasurable distance. Even Mr Wallace, who thought the argument itself of so much weight, as to destroy his whole system of equality, did not seem to be aware that any difficulty would occur from this cause, till the whole earth had been cultivated like a garden, and was incapable of any further increase of produce. Were this really the case, and were a beautiful system of equality in other respects practicable, I cannot think that our ardour in the pursuit of such a scheme ought to be damped by the contemplation of so remote a difficulty. An event at such a distance might fairly be left to providence: but the truth is, that if the view of the argument given in this essay be just, the difficulty so far from being remote, would be imminent, and immediate. At every period during the progress of cultivation, from the present moment, to the time when the whole earth was become like a garden, the distress for want of food would be constantly pressing on all mankind, if they were equal. Though the produce of the earth might be increasing every year, population would be increasing much faster; and the redundancy must necessarily be repressed by the periodical or constant action of misery or vice.

Mr Condorcet's *Esquisse d'un tableau historique des progrès de l'esprit humain*, was written, it is said, under the pressure of that cruel proscription which terminated in his death. If he had no hopes of its being seen during his life, and of its interesting France in his favour, it is a singular instance of the attachment of a man to principles, which every day's experience was so fatally for himself contradicting. To see the human mind in one of the most enlightened nations of the world, and after a lapse of some thousand years, debased by such a fermentation of disgusting passions, of fear, cruelty, malice, revenge, ambition, madness, and folly, as would have disgraced the most savage nation in the most barbarous age, must have been such a tremendous shock to his ideas, of the necessary and inevitable progress of the human mind, that nothing but the firmest conviction of the truth of his principles, in spite of all appearances, could have withstood.[63]

This posthumous publication, is only a sketch of a much larger work, which he proposed should be executed. It necessarily, therefore, wants that detail and application, which can alone prove the truth of any theory. A few observations will be sufficient to show how completely the theory is contradicted, when it is applied to the real, and not to an imaginary state of things.

In the last division of the work,[64] which treats of the future progress of man towards perfection, he says, that comparing, in the different civilized nations of Europe, the actual population with the extent of territory, and observing their cultivation, their industry, their divisions of labour, and their means of subsistence, we shall see that it would be impossible to preserve the same means of subsistence, and, consequently the same population, without a number of individuals, who have no other means of supplying their wants, than their industry. Having allowed the necessity of such a class of men, and adverting afterwards to the precarious revenue of those families that would depend so entirely on the life and health of their chief,* he says, very justly, 'There exists then, a necessary cause of inequality, of dependence, and even of misery, which menaces, without ceasing, the most numerous and active class of our societies.' The difficulty is just, and well stated, and I am afraid that the mode by which he proposes it should be removed, will be found inefficacious. By the application of calculations to the probabilities of life, and the interest of money, he proposes that a fund should be established, which should assure to the old an assistance, produced, in part, by their own former savings, and, in part, by the savings of individuals, who in making the same sacrifice, die before they reap the benefit of it. The same, or a similar fund, should give assistance to women and children, who lose their husbands, or fathers; and afford a capital to those who were of an age to found a new family, sufficient for the proper development of their industry. These establishments he observes, might be made, in the name, and under the protection, of the society. Going still further, he says, that by the just application of calculations, means might be found of more completely preserving a state of equality, by preventing credit from being the exclusive privilege of great fortunes, and yet giving it a basis equally solid, and by rendering the progress of industry, and the activity of commerce, less dependent on great capitalists.

Such establishments and calculations, may appear very promising upon paper, but when applied to real life, they will be found to be absolutely nugatory.[65] Mr Condorcet allows, that a class of people, which maintains itself entirely by industry, is necessary to every state. Why does he allows this? No other reason can well be assigned, than that he conceives that the labour necessary to procure subsistence for an extended population, will not be performed without the goad of necessity. If by establishments of this kind, this spur to industry be removed, if the idle and the negligent are placed upon the same

* To save time and long quotations, I shall here give the substance of some of Mr Condorcet's sentiments, and hope I shall not misrepresent them, but I refer the reader to the work itself, which will amuse, if it does not convince him.

footing with regard to their credit, and the future support of their wives and families, as the active and industrious, can we expect to see men exert that animated activity in bettering their condition, which now forms the master spring of public prosperity? If an inquisition were to be established, to examine the claims of each individual, and to determine whether he had, or had not, exerted himself to the utmost, and to grant or refuse assistance accordingly, this would be little else than a repetition upon a larger scale of the English poor laws, and would be completely destructive of the true principles of liberty and equality.

But independent of this great objection to these establishments, and supposing for a moment, that they would give no check to productive industry, by far the greatest difficulty remains yet behind.

Were every man sure of a comfortable provision for a family, almost every man would have one; and were the rising generation free from the 'killing frost'[66] of misery, population must rapidly increase. Of this, Mr Condorcet seems to be fully aware himself; and after having described further improvements, he says: 'But in this progress of industry and happiness, each generation will be called to more extended enjoyments, and in consequence, by the physical constitution of the human frame, to an increase in the number of individuals. Must not there arrive a period then, when these laws, equally necessary, shall counteract each other? When the increase of the number of men surpassing their means of subsistence, the necessary result must be, either a continual diminution of happiness and population, a movement truly retrograde, or at least, a kind of oscillation between good and evil? In societies arrived at this term, will not this oscillation be a constantly subsisting cause of periodical misery? Will it not mark the limit when all further amelioration will become impossible, and point out that term to the perfectibility of the human race, which it may reach in the course of ages, but can never pass?'

He then adds, 'There is no person who does not see how very distant such a period is from us; but shall we ever arrive at it? It is equally impossible to pronounce for or against the future realization of an event, which cannot take place, but at an era, when the human race will have attained improvements, of which we can at present scarcely form a conception.'

Mr Condorcet's picture of what may be expected to happen when the number of men shall surpass the means of their subsistence, is justly drawn. The oscillation which he describes, will certainly take place, and will, without doubt, be a constantly subsisting cause of periodical misery. The only point in which I differ from Mr Condorcet with regard to this picture, is, the period, when it may be applied to the human race. Mr Condorcet thinks, that it cannot possibly be applicable, but at an era extremely distant. If the proportion between the natural increase of population and food, which I have given, be in any degree near the truth, it will appear, on the contrary, that the period when the number of men surpass their means of subsistence, has long since arrived; and that this necessary oscillation, this constantly subsisting cause of periodical misery, has existed ever since we have had any histories of mankind, does exist at present, and will for ever continue to exist, unless some decided change take place, in the physical constitution of our nature.

Mr Condorcet, however, goes on to say, that should the period, which he conceives to be so distant, ever arrive, the human race, and the advocates for the perfectibility of man, need not be alarmed at it. He then proceeds to remove the difficulty in a manner, which I profess not to understand. Having observed, that the ridiculous prejudices of superstition, would by that time have ceased to throw over morals, a corrupt and degrading austerity, he alludes, either to a promiscuous concubinage, which would prevent breeding, or to something else as unnatural.[67] To remove the difficulty in this way, will, surely, in the opinion of most men, be, to destroy that virtue, and purity of manners, which the advocates of equality, and of the perfectibility of man, profess to be the end and object of their views.

NINE

*Mr Condorcet's conjecture concerning the organic perfect-
ibility of man, and the indefinite prolongation of human
life – Fallacy of the argument, which infers an unlimited
progress from a partial improvement, the limit of which cannot
be ascertained, illustrated in the breeding of animals, and
the cultivation of plants.*

The last question which Mr Condorcet proposes for examination, is, the organic perfectibility of man. He observes, that if
the proofs which have been already given, and which, in their
development will receive greater force in the work itself, are
sufficient to establish the indefinite perfectibility of man, upon
the supposition, of the same natural faculties, and the same
organization which he has at present; what will be the certainty, what the extent of our hope, if this organization, these
natural faculties themselves, are susceptible of amelioration?

From the improvement of medicine; from the use of more
wholesome food, and habitations; from a manner of living,
which will improve the strength of the body by exercise, without impairing it by excess; from the destruction of the two
great causes of the degradation of man, misery, and too great
riches; from the gradual removal of transmissible and contagious disorders, by the improvement of physical knowledge,
rendered more efficacious, by the progress of reason and of
social order; he infers, that though man will not absolutely
become immortal, yet that the duration between his birth, and
natural death, will increase without ceasing, will have no
assignable term, and may properly be expressed by the word
indefinite. He then defines this word to mean, either a constant
approach to an unlimited extent, without ever reaching it; or,

an increase in the immensity of ages to an extent greater than any assignable quantity.

But surely the application of this term in either of these senses, to the duration of human life, is in the highest degree unphilosophical, and totally unwarranted by any appearances in the laws of nature. Variations from different causes are essentially distinct from a regular and unretrograde increase. The average duration of human life will, to a certain degree, vary, from healthy or unhealthy climates, from wholesome or unwholesome food, from virtuous or vicious manners, and other causes; but it may be fairly doubted, whether there is really the smallest perceptible advance in the natural duration of human life, since first we have had any authentic history of man. The prejudices of all ages have indeed been directly contrary to this supposition, and though I would not lay much stress upon these prejudices, they will in some measure tend to prove, that there has been no marked advance in an opposite direction.

It may perhaps be said, that the world is yet so young, so completely in its infancy, that it ought not to be expected that any difference should appear so soon.

If this be the case, there is at once an end of all human science. The whole train of reasonings from effects to causes will be destroyed. We may shut our eyes to the book of nature, as it will no longer be of any use to read it. The wildest and most improbable conjectures may be advanced with as much certainty as the most just and sublime theories, founded on careful and reiterated experiments. We may return again to the old mode of philosophizing, and make facts bend to systems, instead of establishing systems upon facts. The grand and consistent theory of Newton, will be placed upon the same footing as the wild and eccentric hypotheses of Descartes. In short, if the laws of nature are thus fickle and inconstant; if it can be affirmed, and be believed, that they will change, when for ages and ages they have appeared immutable, the human mind will no longer have any incitements to inquiry, but must remain fixed in inactive torpor, or amuse itself only in bewildering dreams, and extravagant fancies.[68]

The constancy of the laws of nature, and of effects and causes, is the foundation of all human knowledge; though far be it from me to say, that the same power which framed and executes the laws of nature, may not change them all 'in a moment, in the twinkling of an eye.'[69] Such a change may undoubtedly happen. All that I mean to say is, that it is impossible to infer it from reasoning. If without any previous observable symptoms or indications of a change, we can infer that a change will take place, we may as well make any assertion whatever, and think it as unreasonable to be contradicted, in affirming that the moon will come in contact with the earth tomorrow, as in saying, that the sun will rise at its usual time.

With regard to the duration of human life, there does not appear to have existed, from the earliest ages of the world, to the present moment, the smallest permanent symptom, or indication, of increasing prolongation.* The observable effects of

* Many, I doubt not, will think that the attempting gravely to controvert so absurd a paradox, as the immortality of man on earth, or indeed, even the perfectibility of man and society, is a waste of time and words; and that such unfounded conjectures are best answered by neglect. I profess, however, to be of a different opinion. When paradoxes of this kind are advanced by ingenious and able men, neglect has no tendency to convince them of their mistakes. Priding themselves on what they conceive to be a mark of the reach and size of their own understandings, of the extent and comprehensiveness of their views; they will look upon this neglect merely as an indication of poverty, and narrowness, in the mental exertions of their contemporaries; and only think, that the world is not yet prepared to receive their sublime truths.

On the contrary, a candid investigation of these subjects, accompanied with a perfect readiness to adopt any theory, warranted by sound philosophy, may have a tendency to convince them, that in forming improbable and unfounded hypotheses, so far from enlarging the bounds of human science, they are contracting it; so far from promoting the improvement of the human mind, they are obstructing it: they are throwing us back again almost into the infancy of knowledge; and weakening the foundations of that mode of philosophizing, under the auspices of which, science has of late made such rapid advances. The present rage for wide and unrestrained speculation, seems to be a kind of mental intoxication, arising, perhaps, from the great and unexpected discoveries which have been made of late years, in various branches of science. To men elate, and giddy with such successes, everything appeared to be within the grasp of human powers; and, under this illusion, they confounded subjects where no real progress could be proved, with those, where the progress had been marked, certain, and acknowledged. Could they be persuaded to sober climate, habit, diet, and other causes, on length of life, have furnished the pretext for asserting its indefinite extension; and the sandy foundation on which the argument rests, is, that because the limit of human life is undefined; because you cannot mark its precise term, and say so far exactly shall it go and no further; that therefore its extent may increase for ever, and be properly termed, indefinite or unlimited. But the fallacy and absurdity of this argument will sufficiently appear from a slight examination of what Mr Condorcet calls the organic perfectibility, or degeneration, of the race of plants and animals, which he says may be regarded as one of the general laws of nature.

I am told that it is a maxim among the improvers of cattle, that you may breed to any degree of nicety you please, and they found this maxim upon another, which is, that some of the offspring will possess the desirable qualities of the parents in a greater degree. In the famous Leicestershire breed of sheep, the object is to procure them with small heads and small legs. Proceeding upon these breeding maxims, it is evident, that we might go on till the heads and legs were evanescent quantities; but this is so palpable an absurdity, that we may be quite sure that the premises are not just, and that there really is a limit, though we cannot see it, or say exactly where it is. In this case, the point of the greatest degree of improvement, or the smallest size of the head and legs, may be said to be undefined, but this is very different from unlimited, or from indefinite, in Mr Condorcet's acceptation of the term. Though I may not be able, in the present instance, to mark the limit, at which further improvement will stop, I can very easily mention a point at which it will not arrive. I should not scruple to assert, that were the breeding to continue for ever, the head and legs of these sheep would never be so small as the head and legs of a rat.

---

themselves with a little severe and chastised thinking, they would see, that the cause of truth, and of sound philosophy, cannot but suffer by substituting wild flights and unsupported assertions, for patient investigation, and well authenticated proofs.

It cannot be true, therefore, that among animals, some of the offspring will possess the desirable qualities of the parents in a greater degree; or that animals are indefinitely perfectible.

The progress of a wild plant, to a beautiful garden flower, is perhaps more marked and striking, than anything that takes place among animals, yet even here, it would be the height of absurdity to assert, that the progress was unlimited or indefinite. One of the most obvious features of the improvement is the increase of size. The flower has grown gradually larger by cultivation. If the progress were really unlimited, it might be increased *ad infinitum*; but this is so gross an absurdity, that we may be quite sure, that among plants, as well as among animals, there is a limit to improvement, though we do not exactly know where it is. It is probable that the gardeners who contend for flower prizes have often applied stronger dressing without success. At the same time, it would be highly presumptuous in any man to say, that he had seen the finest carnation or anemone that could ever be made to grow. He might however assert without the smallest chance of being contradicted by a future fact, that no carnation or anemone could ever by cultivation be increased to the size of a large cabbage; and yet there are assignable quantities much greater than a cabbage. No man can say that he has seen the largest ear of wheat, or the largest oak that could ever grow; but he might easily, and with perfect certainty, name a point of magnitude, at which they would not arrive. In all these cases therefore, a careful distinction should be made, between an unlimited progress, and a progress where the limit is merely undefined.

It will be said, perhaps, that the reason why plants and animals cannot increase indefinitely in size, is, that they would fall by their own weight. I answer, how do we know this but from experience, from experience of the degree of strength with which these bodies are formed? I know that a carnation, long before it reached the size of a cabbage, would not be supported by its stalk; but I only know this from my experience of the weakness, and want of tenacity in the materials of a carnation stalk. There are many substances in nature of the same size that would support as large a head as a cabbage.

The reasons of the mortality of plants are at present perfectly unknown to us. No man can say why such a plant is annual, another biennial, and another endures for ages. The whole affair in all these cases, in plants, animals, and in the human race, is an affair of experience; and I only conclude that man is mortal, because the invariable experience of all ages has proved the mortality of those materials of which his visible body is made. 'What can we reason but from what we know.'[70]

Sound philosophy will not authorize me to alter this opinion of the mortality of man on earth, till it can be clearly proved, that the human race has made, and is making, a decided progress towards an illimitable extent of life. And the chief reason why I adduced the two particular instances from animals and plants, was to expose, and illustrate, if I could, the fallacy of that argument, which infers an unlimited progress, merely because some partial improvement has taken place, and that the limit of this improvement cannot be precisely ascertained.

The capacity of improvement in plants and animals, to a certain degree, no person can possibly doubt. A clear and decided progress has already been made; and yet, I think it appears, that it would be highly absurd to say, that this progress has no limits. In human life, though there are great variations from different causes, it may be doubted, whether, since the world began, any organic improvement whatever in the human frame can be clearly ascertained. The foundations therefore, on which the arguments for the organic perfectibility of man rest, are unusually weak, and can only be considered as mere conjectures. It does not, however, by any means, seem impossible, that by an attention to breed, a certain degree of improvement, similar to that among animals, might take place among men. Whether intellect could be communicated may be a matter of doubt: but size, strength, beauty, complexion, and perhaps even longevity are in a degree transmissible. The error does not seem to lie, in supposing a small degree of improvement possible, but in not discriminating between a small improvement, the limit of which is undefined, and an improvement really unlimited. As the human race however could not be improved in this way, without condemning all the bad specimens to celibacy, it is not probable, that an attention to breed should ever become general; indeed, I know of no well-directed attempts of the kind, except in the ancient family of the Bickerstaffs, who are said to have been very successful in whitening the skins, and increasing the height of their race by prudent marriages, particularly by that very judicious cross with Maud, the milkmaid, by which some capital defects in the constitutions of the family were corrected.[71]

It will not be necessary, I think, in order more completely to show the improbability of any approach in man towards immortality on earth, to urge the very great additional weight that an increase in the duration of life would give to the argument of population.

Mr Condorcet's book may be considered, not only as a sketch of the opinions of a celebrated individual, but of many of the literary men in France, at the beginning of the Revolution. As such, though merely a sketch, it seems worthy of attention.

TEN

Mr Godwin's system of equality – Error of attributing all the vices of mankind to human institutions – Mr Godwin's first answer to the difficulty arising from population totally insufficient – Mr Godwin's beautiful system of equality supposed to be realized – Its utter destruction simply from the principle of population in so short a time as thirty years.

In reading Mr Godwin's ingenious and able work on political justice, it is impossible not to be struck with the spirit and energy of his style, the force and precision of some of his reasonings, the ardent tone of his thoughts, and particularly with that impressive earnestness of manner which gives an air of truth to the whole. At the same time, it must be confessed, that he has not proceeded in his inquiries with the caution that sound philosophy seems to require. His conclusions are often unwarranted by his premises. He fails sometimes in removing the objections which he himself brings forward. He relies too much on general and abstract propositions which will not admit of application. And his conjectures certainly far outstrip the modesty of nature.

The system of equality which Mr Godwin proposes, is, without doubt, by far the most beautiful and engaging of any that has yet appeared. An amelioration of society to be produced merely by reason and conviction, wears much more the promise of permanence, than any change effected and maintained by force. The unlimited exercise of private judgement, is a doctrine inexpressibly grand and captivating, and has a vast superiority over those systems where every individual is in a manner the slave of the public. The substitution of benevolence as the master-spring, and moving principle of society, instead of self-love, is a consummation devoutly to be wished. In short, it is impossible to contemplate the whole of this fair structure, without emotions of delight and admiration, accompanied with ardent longing for the period of its accomplishment. But, alas! that moment can never arrive. The whole is little better than a dream, a beautiful phantom of the imagination. These 'gorgeous palaces' of happiness and immortality, these 'solemn temples' of truth and virtue will dissolve, 'like the baseless fabric of a vision',[72] when we awaken to real life, and contemplate the true and genuine situation of man on earth.

Mr Godwin, at the conclusion of the third chapter of his eighth book, speaking of population, says, 'There is a principle in human society, by which population is perpetually kept down to the level of the means of subsistence. Thus among the wandering tribes of America and Asia, we never find through the lapse of ages that population has so increased as to render necessary the cultivation of the earth.' This principle, which Mr Godwin thus mentions as some mysterious and occult cause, and which he does not attempt to investigate, will be found to be the grinding law of necessity; misery, and the fear of misery.

The great error under which Mr Godwin labours throughout his whole work, is, the attributing almost all the vices and misery that are seen in civil society to human institutions. Political regulations, and the established administration of property, are with him the fruitful sources of all evil, the hotbeds of all the crimes that degrade mankind. Were this really a true state of the case, it would not seem a hopeless task to remove evil completely from the world; and reason seems to be the proper and adequate instrument for effecting so great a purpose. But the truth is, that though human institutions appear to be the obvious and obtrusive causes of much mischief to mankind; yet, in reality, they are light and superficial, they are mere feathers that float on the surface, in comparison with those deeper-seated causes of impurity that corrupt the springs, and render turbid the whole stream of human life.

Mr Godwin, in his chapter on the benefits attendant on a system of equality, says, 'The spirit of oppression, the spirit of servility, and the spirit of fraud, these are the immediate growth of the established administration of property. They are alike hostile to intellectual improvement. The other vices of envy, malice, and revenge, are their inseparable companions. In a state of society, where men lived in the midst of plenty, and where all shared alike the bounties of nature, these sentiments would inevitably expire. The narrow principle of selfishness would vanish. No man being obliged to guard his little store, or provide with anxiety and pain for his restless wants, each would lose his individual existence in the thought of the general good. No man would be an enemy to his neighbour, for they would have no subject of contention; and, of consequence, philanthropy would resume the empire which reason assigns her. Mind would be delivered from her perpetual anxiety about corporal support, and free to expatiate in the field of thought, which is congenial to her. Each would assist the enquiries of all.'

This would, indeed, be a happy state. But that it is merely an imaginary picture, with scarcely a feature near the truth, the reader, I am afraid, is already too well convinced.

Man cannot live in the midst of plenty. All cannot share alike the bounties of nature. Were there no established administration of property, every man would be obliged to guard with force his little store. Selfishness would be triumphant. The subjects of contention would be perpetual. Every individual mind would be under a constant anxiety about corporal support; and not a single intellect would be left free to expatiate in the field of thought.

How little Mr Godwin has turned the attention of his penetrating mind to the real state of man on earth, will sufficiently appear from the manner in which he endeavours to remove the difficulty of an overcharged population. He says, 'The obvious answer to this objection, is, that to reason thus is to foresee difficulties at a great distance. Three fourths of the habitable globe is now uncultivated. The parts already cultivated are capable of immeasurable improvement. Myriads of centuries of still increasing population may pass away, and the earth be still found sufficient for the subsistence of its inhabitants.'

I have already pointed out the error of supposing that no distress and difficulty would arise from an overcharged population before the earth absolutely refused to produce any more. But let us imagine for a moment Mr Godwin's beautiful system of equality realized in its utmost purity, and see how soon this difficulty might be expected to press under so perfect a form of society. A theory that will not admit of application cannot possibly be just.

Let us suppose all the causes of misery and vice in this island removed. War and contention cease. Unwholesome trades and manufactories do not exist. Crowds no longer collect together in great and pestilent cities for purposes of court intrigue, of commerce, and vicious gratifications. Simple, healthy, and rational amusements take place of drinking, gaming and debauchery. There are no towns sufficiently large to have any prejudicial effects on the human constitution. The greater part of the happy inhabitants of this terrestrial paradise live in hamlets and farmhouses scattered over the face of the country. Every house is clean, airy, sufficiently roomy, and in a healthy situation. All men are equal. The labours of luxury are at end. And the necessary labours of agriculture are shared amicably among all. The number of persons, and the produce of the island, we suppose to be the same as at present. The spirit of benevolence, guided by impartial justice, will divide this produce among all the members of the society according to their wants. Though it would be impossible that they should all have animal food every day, yet vegetable food, with meat occasionally, would satisfy the desires of a frugal people, and would be sufficient to preserve them in health, strength, and spirits.[73]

Mr Godwin considers marriage as a fraud and a monopoly. Let us suppose the commerce of the sexes established upon principles of the most perfect freedom. Mr Godwin does not think himself that this freedom would lead to a promiscuous intercourse; and in this I perfectly agree with him. The love of variety is a vicious, corrupt, and unnatural taste, and could not prevail in any great degree in a simple and virtuous state of society. Each man would probably select himself a partner, to whom he would adhere as long as that adherence continued to be the choice of both parties. It would be of little consequence, according to Mr Godwin, how many children a woman had, or to whom they belonged. Provisions and assistance would spontaneously flow from the quarter in which they abounded, to the quarter that was deficient.* And every man would be ready to furnish instruction to the rising generation according to his capacity.

I cannot conceive a form of society so favourable upon the whole to population. The irremediableness of marriage, as it is at present constituted, undoubtedly deters many from entering into that state. An unshackled intercourse on the contrary, would be a most powerful incitement to early attachments: and as we are supposing no anxiety about the future support of children to exist, I do not conceive that there would be one woman in a hundred, of twenty three, without a family.

With these extraordinary encouragements to population, and every cause of depopulation, as we have supposed, removed, the numbers would necessarily increase faster than in any society that has ever yet been known. I have mentioned, on the authority of a pamphlet published by a Dr Styles,[74] and referred to by Dr Price, that the inhabitants of the back settlements of America doubled their numbers in fifteen years. England is certainly a more healthy country than the back settlements of America; and as we have supposed every house in the island to be airy and wholesome, and the encouragements to have a family greater even than with the back settlers, no probable reason can be assigned, why the population should not double itself in less, if possible, than fifteen years. But to be quite sure that we do not go beyond the truth, we will only suppose the period of doubling to be twenty five years, a ratio of increase, which is well known to have taken place throughout all the northern states of America.

There can be little doubt, that the equalization of property which we have supposed, added to the circumstance of the labour of the whole community being directed chiefly to agriculture, would tend greatly to augment the produce of the

---

* W. Godwin, *Enquiry concerning political justice*, 2nd ed., 2 vols (1796), ii, p. 504.

country. But to answer the demands of a population increasing so rapidly, Mr Godwin's calculation of half an hour a day for each man, would certainly not be sufficient. It is probable that the half of every man's time must be employed for this purpose. Yet with such, or much greater exertions, a person who is acquainted with the nature of the soil in this country, and who reflects on the fertility of the lands already in cultivation, and the barrenness of those that are not cultivated, will be very much disposed to doubt, whether the whole average produce could possibly be doubled in twenty five years from the present period. The only chance of success would be the ploughing up all the grazing countries, and putting an end almost entirely to the use of animal food. Yet a part of this scheme might defeat itself. The soil of England will not produce much without dressing; and cattle seem to be necessary to make that species of manure, which best suits the land. In China, it is said, that the soil in some of the provinces is so fertile, as to produce two crops of rice in the year without dressing. None of the lands in England will answer to this description.

Difficult, however, as it might be, to double the average produce of the island in twenty five years, let us suppose it effected. At the expiration of the first period therefore, the food, though almost entirely vegetable, would be sufficient to support in health, the doubled population of 14 millions.

During the next period of doubling, where will the food be found to satisfy the importunate demands of the increasing numbers? Where is the fresh land to turn up? Where is the dressing necessary to improve that which is already in cultivation? There is no person with the smallest knowledge of land, but would say, that it was impossible that the average produce of the country could be increased during the second twenty five years by a quantity equal to what it at present yields. Yet we will suppose this increase, however improbable, to take place. The exuberant strength of the argument allows of almost any concession. Even with this concession, however, there would be 7 millions at the expiration of the second term, unprovided for. A quantity of food equal to the frugal support of 21 millions, would be to be divided among 28 millions.

Alas! what becomes of the picture where men lived in the midst of plenty; where no man was obliged to provide with anxiety and pain for his restless wants; where the narrow principle of selfishness did not exist; where mind was delivered from her perpetual anxiety about corporal support, and free to expatiate in the field of thought which is congenial to her. This beautiful fabric of imagination vanishes at the severe touch of truth. The spirit of benevolence, cherished and invigorated by plenty, is repressed by the chilling breath of want. The hateful passions that had vanished, reappear. The mighty law of self-preservation, expels all the softer and more exalted emotions of the soul. The temptations to evil are too strong for human nature to resist. The corn is plucked before it is ripe, or secreted in unfair proportions; and the whole black train of vices that belong to falsehood are immediately generated. Provisions no longer flow in for the support of the mother with a large family. The children are sickly from insufficient food. The rosy flush of health gives place to the pallid cheek and hollow eye of misery. Benevolence yet lingering in a few bosoms, makes some faint expiring struggles, till at length self-love resumes his wonted empire, and lords it triumphant over the world.

No human institutions here existed, to the perverseness of which Mr Godwin ascribes the original sin of the worst men.* No opposition had been produced by them between public and private good. No monopoly had been created of those advantages which reason directs to be left in common. No man had been goaded to the breach of order by unjust laws. Benevolence had established her reign in all hearts: and yet in so short a period as within fifty years, violence, oppression, falsehood, misery, every hateful vice, and every form of distress, which degrade and sadden the present state of society, seem to have been generated by the most imperious circumstances, by laws inherent in the nature of man, and absolutely independent of all human regulations.

If we are not yet too well convinced of the reality of this melancholy picture, let us but look for a moment into the next

* Godwin, *Political justice*, ii, p. 340.

period of twenty five years; and we shall see 28 millions of human beings without the means of support; and before the conclusion of the first century, the population would be 112 millions, and the food only sufficient for 35 millions, leaving 77 millions unprovided for. In these ages want would be indeed triumphant, and rapine and murder must reign at large: and yet all this time we are supposing the produce of the earth absolutely unlimited, and the yearly increase greater than the boldest speculator can imagine.

This is undoubtedly a very different view of the difficulty arising from population, from that which Mr Godwin gives, when he says, 'Myriads of centuries of still increasing population may pass away, and the earth be still found sufficient for the subsistence of its inhabitants.'

I am sufficiently aware that the redundant 28 millions, or 77 millions, that I have mentioned, could never have existed. It is a perfectly just observation of Mr Godwin, that, 'There is a principle in human society, by which population is perpetually kept down to the level of the means of subsistence.' The sole question is, what is this principle? Is it some obscure and occult cause? Is it some mysterious interference of heaven, which at a certain period, strikes the men with impotence, and the women with barrenness? Or is it a cause, open to our researches, within our view, a cause, which has constantly been observed to operate, though with varied force, in every state in which man has been placed? Is it not a degree of misery, the necessary and inevitable result of the laws of nature, which human institutions, so far from aggravating, have tended considerably to mitigate, though they never can remove?[75]

It may be curious to observe, in the case that we have been supposing, how some of the laws which at present govern civilized society, would be successively dictated by the most imperious necessity. As man, according to Mr Godwin, is the creature of the impressions to which he is subject, the goadings of want could not continue long, before some violations of public or private stock would necessarily take place. As these violations increased in number and extent, the more active and comprehensive intellects of the society would soon perceive, that while population was fast increasing, the yearly produce of the country would shortly begin to diminish. The urgency of the case would suggest the necessity of some immediate measures to be taken for the general safety. Some kind of convention would then be called, and the dangerous situation of the country stated in the strongest terms. It would be observed, that while they lived in the midst of plenty, it was of little consequence who laboured the least, or who possessed the least, as every man was perfectly willing and ready to supply the wants of his neighbour. But that the question was no longer, whether one man should give to another, that which he did not use himself; but whether he should give to his neighbour the food which was absolutely necessary to his own existence. It would be represented, that the number of those that were in want very greatly exceeded the number and means of those who should supply them; that these pressing wants, which from the state of the produce of the country could not all be gratified, had occasioned some flagrant violations of justice; that these violations had already checked the increase of food, and would, if they were not by some means or other prevented, throw the whole community in confusion; that imperious necessity seemed to dictate that a yearly increase of produce should, if possible, be obtained at all events; that in order to effect this first, great, and indispensable purpose, it would be advisable to make a more complete division of land, and to secure every man's stock against violation by the most powerful sanctions, even by death itself.

It might be urged perhaps by some objectors, that, as the fertility of the land increased, and various accidents occurred, the share of some men might be much more than sufficient for their support, and that when the reign of self-love was once established, they would not distribute their surplus produce without some compensation in return. It would be observed, in answer, that this was an inconvenience greatly to be lamented; but that it was an evil which bore no comparison to the black train of distresses, that would inevitably be occasioned by the insecurity of property; that the quantity of food which one man could consume, was necessarily limited by the narrow capacity of the human stomach; that it was not certainly probable that he should throw away the rest; but that even if he exchanged his surplus food for the labour of others, and made them in some degree dependent on him, this would still be better than that these others should absolutely starve.

It seems highly probable, therefore, that an administration of property, not very different from that which prevails in civilized states at present, would be established, as the best, though inadequate, remedy, for the evils which were pressing on the society.

The next subject that would come under discussion, intimately connected with the preceding, is, the commerce between the sexes.[76] It would be urged by those who had turned their attention to the true cause of the difficulties under which the community laboured, that while every man felt secure that all his children would be well provided for by general benevolence, the powers of the earth would be absolutely inadequate to produce food for the population which would inevitably ensue: that even, if the whole attention and labour of the society were directed to this sole point, and if, by the most perfect security of property, and every other encouragement that could be thought of, the greatest possible increase of produce were yearly obtained; yet still, that the increase of food would by no means keep pace with the much more rapid increase of population; that some check to population therefore was imperiously called for; that the most natural and obvious check seemed to be, to make every man provide for his own children; that this would operate in some respect, as a measure and guide, in the increase of population; as it might be expected that no man would bring beings into the world, for whom he could not find the means of support; that where this notwithstanding was the case, it seemed necessary, for the example of others, that the disgrace and inconvenience attending such a conduct, should fall upon that individual, who had thus inconsiderately plunged himself and innocent children in misery and want.

The institution of marriage, or at least, of some express or implied obligation on every man to support his own children, seems to be the natural result of these reasonings in a community under the difficulties that we have supposed.

The view of these difficulties, presents us with a very natural origin of the superior disgrace which attends a breach of chastity in the woman, than in the man. It could not be expected that women should have resources sufficient to support their own children. When therefore a woman was connected with a man, who had entered into no compact to maintain her children; and aware of the inconveniences that he might bring upon himself, had deserted her, these children must necessarily fall for support upon the society, or starve. And to prevent the frequent recurrence of such an inconvenience, as it would be highly unjust to punish so natural a fault by personal restraint or infliction, the men might agree to punish it with disgrace. The offence is besides more obvious and conspicuous in the woman, and less liable to any mistake. The father of a child may not always be known, but the same uncertainty cannot easily exist with regard to the mother. Where, the evidence of the offence was most complete, and the inconvenience to the society at the same time the greatest, there, it was agreed, that the largest share of blame should fall. The obligation on every man to maintain his children, the society would enforce, if there were occasion; and the greater degree of inconvenience or labour, to which a family would necessarily subject him, added to some portion of disgrace which every human being must incur, who leads another into unhappiness, might be considered as a sufficient punishment for the man.

That a woman should at present be almost driven from society, for an offence, which men commit nearly with impunity, seems to be undoubtedly a breach of natural justice. But the origin of the custom, as the most obvious and effectual method of preventing the frequent recurrence of a serious inconvenience to a community, appears to be natural, though not perhaps perfectly justifiable. This origin, however, is now lost in the new train of ideas which the custom has since generated. What at first might be dictated by state necessity, is now supported by female delicacy; and operates with the greatest force on that part of society, where, if the original intention of the custom were preserved, there is the least real occasion for it.

When these two fundamental laws of society, the security of property, and the institution of marriage, were once established, inequality of conditions must necessarily follow. Those who were born after the division of property, would come into a world already possessed. If their parents, from having too large a family, could not give them sufficient for their support, what are they to do in a world where everything is appropriated? We have seen the fatal effects that would result to a society, if every man had a valid claim to an equal share of the produce of the earth. The members of a family which was grown too large for the original division of land appropriated to it, could not then demand a part of the surplus produce of others, as a debt of justice. It has appeared, that from the inevitable laws of our nature, some human beings must suffer from want. These are the unhappy persons who, in the great lottery of life, have drawn a blank. The number of these claimants would soon exceed the ability of the surplus produce to supply. Moral merit is a very difficult distinguishing criterion, except in extreme cases. The owners of surplus produce would in general seek some more obvious mark of distinction. And it seems both natural and just, that except upon particular occasions, their choice should fall upon those, who were able, and professed themselves willing, to exert their strength in procuring a further surplus produce; and thus at once benefiting the community, and enabling these proprietors to afford assistance to greater numbers. All who were in want of food would be urged by imperious necessity to offer their labour in exchange for this article so absolutely essential to existence. The fund appropriated to the maintenance of labour, would be, the aggregate quantity of food possessed by the owners of land beyond their own consumption. When the demands upon this fund were great and numerous, it would naturally be divided in very small shares. Labour would be ill paid. Men would offer, to work for a bare subsistence, and the rearing of families would be checked by sickness and misery. On the contrary, when this fund was increasing fast; when it was great in proportion to the number of claimants; it would be divided in much larger shares. No man would exchange his labour without receiving an ample quantity of food in return. Labourers would live in ease and comfort; and would consequently be able to rear a numerous and vigorous offspring.

On the state of this fund, the happiness, or the degree of misery, prevailing among the lower classes of people in every known state, at present chiefly depends. And on this happiness, or degree of misery, depends the increase, stationariness, or decrease of population.

And thus it appears, that a society constituted according to the most beautiful form that imagination can conceive, with benevolence for its moving principle, instead of self-love, and with every evil disposition in all its members corrected by reason and not force, would, from the inevitable laws of nature, and not from any original depravity of man, in a very short period, degenerate into a society, constructed upon a plan not essentially different from that which prevails in every known state at present; I mean, a society divided into a class of proprietors, and a class of labourers, and with self-love for the mainspring of the great machine.

In the supposition I have made, I have undoubtedly taken the increase of population smaller, and the increase of produce greater, than they really would be. No reason can be assigned, why, under the circumstances I have supposed, population should not increase faster than in any known instance. If then we were to take the period of doubling at fifteen years, instead of twenty five years; and reflect upon the labour necessary to double the produce in so short a time, even if we allow it possible, we may venture to pronounce with certainty, that if Mr Godwin's system of society was established in its utmost perfection, instead of myriads of centuries, not thirty years could elapse, before its utter destruction from the simple principle of population.

I have taken no notice of emigration for obvious reasons. If such societies were instituted in other parts of Europe, these countries would be under the same difficulties with regard to population, and could admit no fresh members into their bosoms. If this beautiful society were confined to this island, it must have degenerated strangely from its original purity, and administer but a very small portion of the happiness it proposed; in short, its essential principle must be completely destroyed, before any of its members would voluntarily consent to leave it, and live under such governments as at present exist in Europe, or submit to the extreme hardships of first settlers in new regions. We well know, from repeated experience, how much misery and hardship men will undergo in their own country, before they can determine to desert it; and how often the most tempting proposals of embarking for new settlements have been rejected by people who appeared to be almost starving.

ELEVEN

Mr Godwin's conjecture concerning the future extinction of the passion between the sexes – Little apparent grounds for such a conjecture – Passion of love not inconsistent either with reason or virtue.

We have supposed Mr Godwin's system of society once completely established. But it is supposing an impossibility. The same cause in nature which would destroy it so rapidly, were it once established, would prevent the possibility of its establishment. And upon what grounds we can presume a change in these natural causes, I am utterly at a loss to conjecture. No move towards the extinction of the passion between the sexes has taken place in the five or six thousand years that the world has existed.[77] Men in the decline of life have, in all ages, declaimed against a passion which they have ceased to feel, but with as little reason as success. Those who from coldness of constitutional temperament have never felt what love is, will surely be allowed to be very incompetent judges, with regard to the power of this passion, to contribute to the sum of pleasurable sensations in life. Those who have spent their youth in criminal excesses, and have prepared for themselves, as the comforts of their age, corporal debility, and mental remorse, may well inveigh against such pleasures as vain and futile, and unproductive of lasting satisfaction. But the pleasures of pure love will bear the contemplation of the most improved reason, and the most exalted virtue. Perhaps there is scarcely a man who has once experienced the genuine delight of virtuous love, however great his intellectual pleasures may have been, that does not look back to the period, as the sunny spot in his whole life, where his imagination loves to bask, which he recollects and contemplates with the fondest regrets, and which he would most wish to live over again. The superiority of intellectual, to sensual pleasures, consists rather, in their filling up more time, in their having a larger range, and in their being less liable to satiety, than in their being more real and essential.

Intemperance in every enjoyment defeats its own purpose. A walk in the finest day, through the most beautiful country, if pursued too far, ends in pain and fatigue. The most wholesome and invigorating food, eaten with an unrestrained appetite, produces weakness, instead of strength. Even intellectual pleasures, though certainly less liable than others to satiety, pursued with too little intermission, debilitate the body, and impair the vigour of the mind. To argue against the reality of these pleasures from their abuse, seems to be hardly just. Morality, according to Mr Godwin, is a calculation of consequences, or, as Archdeacon Paley[78] very justly expresses it, the will of God, as collected from general expediency. According to either of these definitions, a sensual pleasure, not attended with the probability of unhappy consequences, does not offend against the laws of morality: and if it be pursued with such a degree of temperance, as to leave the most ample room for intellectual attainments, it must undoubtedly add to the sum of pleasurable sensations in life. Virtuous love, exalted by friendship, seems to be that sort of mixture of sensual and intellectual enjoyment particularly suited to the nature of man, and most powerfully calculated to awaken the sympathies of the soul, and produce the most exquisite gratifications.

Mr Godwin says, in order to show the evident inferiority of the pleasures of sense, 'Strip the commerce of the sexes of all its attendant circumstances, and it would be generally despised.'* He might as well say to a man who admired trees; strip them of their spreading branches and lovely foliage, and what beauty can you see in a bare pole? But it was the tree with the branches and foliage, and not without them, that excited admiration. One feature of an object, may be as distinct, and excite as different emotions, from the aggregate, as any two things the most

* Godwin, *Political justice*, i, p. 73.

remote, as a beautiful woman, and a map of Madagascar. It is 'the symmetry of person, the vivacity, the voluptuous softness of temper, the affectionate kindness of feelings, the imagination and the wit' of a woman that excite the passion of love, and not the mere distinction of her being a female. Urged by the passion of love, men have been driven into acts highly prejudicial to the general interests of society; but probably they would have found no difficulty in resisting the temptation, had it appeared in the form of a woman, with no other attractions whatever but her sex. To strip sensual pleasures of all their adjuncts, in order to prove their inferiority, is to deprive a magnet of some of its most essential cause of attraction, and then to say that it is weak and inefficient.

In the pursuit of every enjoyment, whether sensual or intellectual, reason, that faculty which enables us to calculate consequences, is the proper corrective and guide. It is probable therefore that improved reason will always tend to prevent the abuse of sensual pleasures, though it by no means follows that it will extinguish them.

I have endeavoured to expose the fallacy of that argument which infers an unlimited progress from a partial improvement, the limits of which cannot be exactly ascertained. It has appeared, I think, that there are many instances in which a decided progress has been observed, where yet it would be a gross absurdity to suppose that progress indefinite. But towards the extinction of the passion between the sexes, no observable progress whatever has hitherto been made. To suppose such an extinction, therefore, is merely to offer an unfounded conjecture, unsupported by any philosophical probabilities.

It is a truth, which history I am afraid makes too clear, that some men of the highest mental powers, have been addicted not only to a moderate, but even to an immoderate indulgence in the pleasures of sensual love. But allowing, as I should be inclined to do, notwithstanding numerous instances to the contrary, that great intellectual exertions tend to diminish the empire of this passion over man; it is evident that the mass of mankind must be improved more highly than the brightest ornaments of the species at present, before any difference can take place sufficient sensibly to affect population. I would by no means suppose that the mass of mankind has reached its term of improvement; but the principal argument of this essay tends to place in a strong point of view, the improbability, that the lower classes of people in any country, should ever be sufficiently free from want and labour, to attain any high degree of intellectual improvement.

TWELVE

Mr Godwin's conjecture concerning the indefinite prolongation of human life – Improper inference drawn from the effects of mental stimulants on the human frame, illustrated in various instances – Conjectures not founded on any indications in the past, not to be considered as philosophical conjectures – Mr Godwin's and Mr Condorcet's conjecture respecting the approach of man towards immortality on earth, a curious instance of the inconsistency of scepticism.

Mr Godwin's conjecture respecting the future approach of man towards immortality on earth, seems to be rather oddly placed in a chapter, which professes to remove the objection to his system of equality from the principle of population. Unless he supposes the passion between the sexes to decrease faster, than the duration of life increases, the earth would be more encumbered than ever. But leaving this difficulty to Mr Godwin, let us examine a few of the appearances from which the probable immortality of man is inferred.

To prove the power of the mind over the body, Mr Godwin observes, 'How often do we find a piece of good news dissipating a distemper? How common is the remark that those accidents which are to the indolent a source of disease, are forgotten and extirpated in the busy and active? I walk twenty miles in an indolent and half determined temper, and am extremely fatigued. I walk twenty miles full of ardour, and with a motive that engrosses my soul, and I come in as fresh and as alert as when I began my journey. Emotions excited by some unexpected word, by a letter that is delivered to us, occasions the most extraordinary revolutions in our frame, accelerates the circulation, causes the heart to palpitate, the tongue to refuse its office, and has been known to occasion death by extreme anguish or extreme joy. There is nothing indeed of which the physician is more aware than of the power of the mind in assisting or retarding convalescence.'

The instances here mentioned, are chiefly instances of the effects of mental stimulants on the bodily frame. No person has ever for a moment doubted the near, though mysterious connection, of mind and body. But it is arguing totally without knowledge of the nature of stimulants to suppose, either that they can be applied continually with equal strength, or if they could be so applied, for a time, that they would not exhaust and wear out the subject. In some of the cases here noticed, the strength of the stimulus depends upon its novelty and unexpectedness. Such a stimulus cannot, from its nature, be repeated often with the same effect, as it would by repetition lose that property which gives it its strength.

In the other cases, the argument is from a small and partial effect, to a great and general effect, which will in numberless instances be found to be a very fallacious mode of reasoning. The busy and active man may in some degree counteract, or what is perhaps nearer the truth, may disregard those slight disorders of frame, which fix the attention of a man who has nothing else to think of; but this does not tend to prove that activity of mind will enable a man to disregard a high fever, the smallpox, or the plague.

The man who walks twenty miles with a motive that engrosses his soul, does not attend to his slight fatigue of body when he comes in; but double his motive, and set him to walk another twenty miles, quadruple it, and let him start a third time, and so on; and the length of his walk will ultimately depend upon muscle and not mind. Powel, for a motive of ten guineas, would have walked further probably than Mr Godwin, for a motive of half a million.[79] A motive of uncommon power acting upon a frame of moderate strength, would, perhaps, make the man kill himself by his exertions, but it would not make him walk a hundred miles in twenty four hours. This statement of the case, shows the fallacy of supposing, that the person was really not at all tired in his first walk of twenty miles, because he did not appear to be so, or, perhaps, scarcely felt any fatigue himself. The mind cannot fix its attention strongly on more than one object at once. The twenty thousand pounds so engrossed his thoughts, that he did not attend to any slight soreness of foot, or stiffness of limb. But had he been really as fresh and as alert, as when he first set off, he would be able to go the second twenty miles with as much ease as the first, and so on, the third, etc. which leads to a palpable absurd-ity. When a horse of spirit is nearly half tired, by the stimulus of the spur, added to the proper management of the bit, he may be put so much upon his mettle, that he would appear to a stander-by, as fresh and as high-spirited, as if he had not gone a mile. Nay, probably, the horse himself, while in the heat and passion occasioned by this stimulus, would not feel any fatigue; but it would be strangely contrary to all reason and experience, to argue from such an appearance, that if the stimulus were continued, the horse would never be tired. The cry of a pack of hounds will make some horses, after a journey of forty miles on the road, appear as fresh, and as lively, as when they first set out. Were they then to be hunted, no perceptible abatement would at first be felt by their riders in their strength and spirits, but towards the end of a hard day, the previous fatigue would have its full weight and effect, and make them tire sooner. When I have taken a long walk with my gun, and met with no success, I have frequently returned home feeling a considerable degree of uncomfortableness from fatigue. Another day, per-haps, going over nearly the same extent of ground with a good deal of sport, I have come home fresh, and alert. The difference in the sensation of fatigue upon coming in, on the different days, may have been very striking, but on the following morn-ings I have found no such difference. I have not perceived that I was less stiff in my limbs, or less footsore, on the morning after the day of sport, than on the other morning.

In all these cases, stimulants upon the mind seem to act rather by taking off the attention from the bodily fatigue, than by really and truly counteracting it. If the energy of my mind had really counteracted the fatigue of my body, why should I feel tired the next morning? If the stimulus of the hounds had as completely overcome the fatigue of the journey in reality, as it did in appearance, why should the horse be tired sooner than if he had not gone the forty miles? I happen to have a very bad fit of the toothache at the time I am writing this. In the eagerness of composition, I every now and then, for a moment or two, forget it. Yet I cannot help thinking that the process which causes the pain, is still going forwards, and that the nerves, which carry the information of it to the brain, are even during these moments demanding attention, and room for their appropriate vibrations. The multiplicity of vibrations of another kind, may perhaps prevent their admission, or overcome them for a time when admitted, till a shoot of extraordinary energy puts all other vibrations to the rout, destroys the vividness of my argumentative conceptions, and rides triumphant in the brain. In this case, as in the others, the mind seems to have little or no power in counteracting, or curing the disorder, but merely possesses a power, if strongly excited, of fixing its attention on other subjects.

I do not, however, mean to say, that a sound and vigorous mind has no tendency whatever to keep the body in a similar state. So close and intimate is the union of mind and body, that it would be highly extraordinary, if they did not mutually assist each other's functions. But, perhaps, upon a comparison, the body has more effect upon the mind, than the mind upon the body. The first object of the mind is to act as purveyor to the wants of the body. When these wants are completely satisfied, an active mind is indeed apt to wander further, to range over the fields of science, or sport in the regions of imagination, to fancy that it has 'shuffled off this mortal coil',[80] and is seeking its kindred element. But all these efforts are like the vain exertions of the hare in the fable.[81] The slowly moving tortoise, the body, never fails to overtake the mind, however widely and extensively it may have ranged, and the brightest and most energetic intellects, unwillingly as they may attend to the first or second summons, must ultimately yield the empire of the brain to the calls of hunger, or sink with the exhausted body in sleep.

It seems as if one might say with certainty, that if a medicine could be found to immortalize the body, there would be no fear of its being accompanied by the immortality of the mind. But the immortality of the mind by no means seems to infer the immortality of the body. On the contrary, the greatest conceivable energy of mind would probably exhaust and destroy the strength of the body. A temperate vigour of mind appears to be favourable to health; but very great intellectual exertions tend rather, as has been often observed, to wear out the scabbard. Most of the instances which Mr Godwin has brought to prove the power of the mind over the body, and the consequent probability of the immortality of man, are of this latter description, and could such stimulants be continually applied, instead of tending to immortalize, they would tend very rapidly to destroy the human frame.

The probable increase of the voluntary power of man over his animal frame, comes next under Mr Godwin's consideration, and he concludes by saying, that the voluntary power of some men, in this respect, is found to extend to various articles in which other men are impotent. But this is reasoning against an almost universal rule from a few exceptions: and these exceptions seem to be rather tricks, than powers, that may be exerted to any good purpose. I have never heard of any man who could regulate his pulse in a fever; and doubt much, if any of the persons here alluded to, have made the smallest perceptible progress in the regular correction of the disorders of their frames, and the consequent prolongation of their lives.

Mr Godwin says, 'Nothing can be more unphilosophical, than to conclude, that, because a certain species of power is beyond the train of our present observation, that it is beyond the limits of the human mind.' I own my ideas of philosophy are in this respect widely different from Mr Godwin's. The only distinction that I see, between a philosophical conjecture, and the assertions of the prophet Mr Brothers,[82] is, that one is founded upon indications arising from the train of our present observations, and the other has no foundation at all. I expect that great discoveries are yet to take place in all the branches of human science, particularly in physics; but the moment we leave past experience as the foundation of our conjectures concerning the future; and still more, if our conjectures absolutely contradict past experience, we are thrown upon a wide field of uncertainty, and any one supposition is then just as good as another. If a person were to tell me that men would ultimately have eyes and hands behind them as well as before them, I should admit the usefulness of the addition, but should give as a reason for my disbelief of it, that I saw no indications whatever in the past, from which I could infer the smallest probability of such a change. If this be not allowed a valid objection, all conjectures are alike, and all equally philosophical. I own it appears to me, that in the train of our present observations, there are no more genuine indications that man will become immortal upon earth, than that he will have four eyes and four hands, or that trees will grow horizontally instead of perpendicularly.

It will be said, perhaps, that many discoveries have already taken place in the world that were totally unforeseen and unexpected. This I grant to be true; but if a person had predicted these discoveries, without being guided by any analogies or indications from past facts, he would deserve the name of seer or prophet, but not of philosopher. The wonder that some of our modern discoveries would excite in the savage inhabitants of Europe in the times of Theseus and Achilles, proves but little. Persons almost entirely unacquainted with the powers of a machine, cannot be expected to guess at its effects. I am far from saying, that we are at present by any means fully acquainted with the powers of the human mind; but we certainly know more of this instrument than was known four thousand years ago; and therefore, though not to be called competent judges, we are certainly much better able, than savages, to say what is, or is not, within its grasp. A watch would strike a savage with as much surprise as a perpetual motion; yet one, is to us a most familiar piece of mechanism, and the other, has constantly eluded the efforts of the most acute intellects. In many instances, we are now able to perceive the causes, which prevent an unlimited improvement in those inventions, which seemed to promise fairly for it at first. The original improvers of telescopes would probably think, that as long as the size of the specula, and the length of the tubes could be increased, the powers and advantages of the instrument would increase: but experience has since taught us, that the smallness of the field, the deficiency of light, and the circumstance of the atmosphere being magnified, prevent the beneficial results that were to be expected from telescopes of extraordinary size and power. In many parts of knowledge, man has been almost constantly making some progress; in other parts, his efforts have been invariably baffled. The savage would not probably be able to guess at the causes of this mighty difference. Our further experience has given us some little insight into these causes, and has therefore enabled us better to judge, if not, of what we are to expect in future, at least, of what we are not to expect, which, though negative, is a very useful piece of information.

As the necessity of sleep seems rather to depend upon the body than the mind, it does not appear how the improvement of the mind can tend very greatly to supersede this 'conspicuous infirmity'. A man who by great excitements on his mind, is able to pass two or three nights without sleep, proportionably exhausts the vigour of his body: and this diminution of health and strength, will soon disturb the operations of his understanding; so that by these great efforts, he appears to have made no real progress whatever, in superseding the necessity of this species of rest.

There is certainly a sufficiently marked difference in the various characters of which we have some knowledge, relative to the energies of their minds, their benevolent pursuits, etc. to enable us to judge, whether the operations of intellect have any decided effect in prolonging the duration of human life. It is certain, that no decided effect of this kind has yet been observed. Though no attention of any kind, has ever produced such an effect, as could be construed into the smallest semblance of an approach towards immortality; yet of the two, a certain attention to the body, seems to have more effect in this respect, than an attention to the mind. The man who takes his temperate meals, and his bodily exercise, with scrupulous regularity, will generally be found more healthy, than the man who, very deeply engaged in intellectual pursuits, often forgets for a time these bodily cravings. The citizen who has retired, and whose ideas, perhaps, scarcely soar above, or extend beyond his little garden, puddling all the morning about his borders of box, will, perhaps, live as long as the philosopher whose range of intellect is the most extensive, and whose views are the clearest of any of his contemporaries. It has been positively observed by those who have attended to the bills of mortality, that women live longer upon an average than men; and, though I would not by any means say that their intellectual faculties are inferior, yet, I think, it must be allowed, that from their different education, there are not so many women as men, who are excited to vigorous mental exertion.

As in these and similar instances, or to take a larger range, as in the great diversity of characters that have existed during some thousand years, no decided difference has been observed in the duration of human life from the operation of intellect, the mortality of man on earth seems to be as completely established, and exactly upon the same grounds, as any one, the most constant, of the laws of nature. An immediate act of power in the Creator of the universe might, indeed, change one or all of these laws, either suddenly or gradually; but without some indications of such a change, and such indications do not exist, it is just as unphilosophical to suppose that the life of man may be prolonged beyond any assignable limits, as to suppose that the attraction of the earth will gradually be changed into repulsion, and that stones will ultimately rise instead of fall, or that the earth will fly off at a certain period to some more genial and warmer sun.

The conclusion of this chapter presents us, undoubtedly, with a very beautiful and desirable picture, but like some of those landscapes, drawn from fancy, and not imagined with truth, it fails of that interest in the heart which nature and probability can alone give.

I cannot quit this subject without taking notice of these conjectures of Mr Godwin and Mr Condorcet, concerning the indefinite prolongation of human life, as a very curious instance of the longing of the soul after immortality. Both these gentlemen have rejected the light of revelation which absolutely promises eternal life in another state. They have also rejected the light of natural religion, which to the ablest intellects in all ages, has indicated the future existence of the soul.[83] Yet so congenial is the idea of immortality to the mind of man, that they cannot consent entirely to throw it out of their systems. After all their fastidious scepticisms concerning the only probable mode of immortality, they introduce a species of immortality of their own, not only completely contradictory to every law of philosophical probability, but in itself in the highest degree, narrow, partial, and unjust. They suppose that all the great, virtuous, and exalted minds, that have ever existed, or that may exist for some thousands, perhaps millions of years, will be sunk in annihilation; and that only a few beings, not greater in number than can exist at once upon the earth, will be ultimately crowned with immortality. Had such a tenet been advanced as a tenet of revelation, I am very sure that all the enemies of religion, and probably Mr Godwin, and Mr Condorcet among the rest, would have exhausted the whole force of their ridicule upon it, as the most puerile, the most absurd, the poorest, the most pitiful, the most iniquitously unjust, and, consequently, the most unworthy of the Deity, that the superstitious folly of man could invent.

What a strange and curious proof do these conjectures exhibit of the inconsistency of scepticism! For it should be observed, that there is a very striking and essential difference, between believing an assertion which absolutely contradicts the most uniform experience, and an assertion which contradicts nothing, but is merely beyond the power of our present observation and knowledge.* So diversified are the natural

---

* When we extend our view beyond this life, it is evident that we can have no other guides than authority, or conjecture, and perhaps, indeed, an obscure and undefined feeling. What I say here, therefore, does not appear to me in any respect to contradict what I said before, when I observed that it was unphilosophical to expect any specific event that was not indicated by some kind of analogy in the past. In ranging beyond the bourne from which no traveller returns, we must necessarily quit this rule; but with regard to events that may be expected to happen on earth, we can seldom quit it consistently with true philosophy. Analogy has, however, as I conceive, great latitude. For instance,

objects around us, so many instances of mighty power daily offer themselves to our view, that we may fairly presume, that there are many forms and operations of nature which we have not yet observed, or which, perhaps, we are not capable of observing with our present confined inlets of knowledge. The resurrection of a spiritual body from a natural body, does not appear in itself a more wonderful instance of power, than the germination of a blade of wheat from the grain, or of an oak from an acorn. Could we conceive an intelligent being, so placed, as to be conversant only with inanimate, or full grown objects, and never to have witnessed the process of vegetation or growth; and were another being to show him two little pieces of matter, a grain of wheat, and an acorn, to desire him to examine them, to analyse them if he pleased, and endeavour to find out their properties and essences; and then to tell him, that however trifling these little bits of matter might appear to him, that they possessed such curious powers of selection, combination, arrangement, and almost of creation, that upon being put into the ground, they would choose, amongst all the dirt and moisture that surrounded them, those parts which best suited their purpose, that they would collect and arrange these parts with wonderful taste, judgement, and execution, and would rise up into beautiful forms, scarcely in any respect analogous to the little bits of matter which were first placed in the earth; I feel very little doubt that the imaginary being which I have supposed, would hesitate more, would require better authority, and stronger proofs, before he believed these strange assertions, than if he had been told, that a being of mighty power, who had been the cause of all that he saw around him, and of that existence of which he himself was conscious, would, by a great act of power upon the death and corruption of human creatures, raise up the essence of thought in an incorporeal, or

---

man has discovered many of the laws of nature: analogy seems to indicate that he will discover many more; but no analogy seems to indicate that he will discover a sixth sense, or a new species of power in the human mind, entirely beyond the train of our present observations.

at least invisible form, to give it a happier existence in another state.

The only difference, with regard to our own apprehensions, that is not in favour of the latter assertion, is, that the first miracle* we have repeatedly seen, and the last miracle we have not seen. I admit the full weight of this prodigious difference; but surely no man can hesitate a moment in saying, that putting revelation out of the question, the resurrection of a spiritual body from a natural body, which may be merely one among the many operations of nature which we cannot see, is an event indefinitely more probable than the immortality of man on earth, which is not only an event, of which no symptoms or indications have yet appeared, but is a positive contradiction to one of the most constant of the laws of nature that has ever come within the observation of man.

I ought perhaps again to make an apology to my readers for dwelling so long upon a conjecture, which many I know will think too absurd and improbable, to require the least discussion. But if it be as improbable, and as contrary to the genuine spirit of philosophy as I own I think it is, why should it not be shown to be so in a candid examination? A conjecture, however improbable on the first view of it, advanced by able and ingenious men, seems at least to deserve investigation. For my own part I feel no disinclination whatever, to give that degree

---

* The powers of selection, combination, and transmutation, which every seed shows, are truly miraculous. Who can imagine that these wonderful faculties are contained in these little bits of matter? To me it appears much more philosophical to suppose that the mighty God of nature is present in full energy in all these operations. To this all powerful Being, it would be equally easy to raise an oak without an acorn as with one. The preparatory process of putting seeds into the ground, is merely ordained for the use of man, as one among the various other excitements necessary to awaken matter into mind. It is an idea that will be found, consistent equally with the natural phenomena around us, with the various events of human life, and with the successive revelations of God to man, to suppose that the world is a mighty process for the creation and formation of mind. Many vessels will necessarily come out of this great furnace in wrong shapes. These will be broken and thrown aside as useless; while those vessels whose forms are full of truth, grace, and loveliness, will be wafted into happier situations, nearer the presence of the mighty maker.

of credit to the opinion of the probable immortality of man on earth, which the appearances that can be brought in support of it deserve. Before we decide upon the utter improbability of such an event, it is but fair impartially to examine these appearances; and from such an examination I think we may conclude, that we have rather less reason for supposing that the life of man may be indefinitely prolonged, than that trees may be made to grow indefinitely high, or potatoes indefinitely large.*

---

* Though Mr Godwin advances the idea of the indefinite prolongation of human life, merely as a conjecture, yet as he has produced some appearances, which in his conception favour the supposition, he must certainly intend that these appearances should be examined; and this is all that I have meant to do.

THIRTEEN

Error of Mr Godwin in considering man too much in the light of a being merely rational – In the compound being, man, the passions will always act as disturbing forces in the decisions of the understanding – Reasonings of Mr Godwin on the subject of coercion – Some truths of a nature not to be communicated from one man to another.

In the chapter which I have been examining, Mr Godwin professes to consider the objection to his system of equality from the principle of population. It has appeared I think clearly, that he is greatly erroneous in his statement of the distance of this difficulty; and that instead of myriads of centuries, it is really not thirty years, or even thirty days, distant from us. The supposition of the approach of man to immortality on earth, is certainly not of a kind to soften the difficulty. The only argument, therefore, in the chapter, which has any tendency to remove the objection, is the conjecture concerning the extinction of the passion between the sexes; but as this is a mere conjecture, unsupported by the smallest shadow of proof, the force of the objection may be fairly said to remain unimpaired; and it is undoubtedly of sufficient weight of itself completely to overturn Mr Godwin's whole system of equality. I will, however, make one or two observations on a few of the prominent parts of Mr Godwin's reasonings, which will contribute to place in a still clearer point of view, the little hope that we can reasonably entertain of those vast improvements in the nature of man and of society, which he holds up to our admiring gaze in his political justice.

Mr Godwin considers man too much in the light of a being merely intellectual. This error, at least such I conceive it to be, pervades his whole work, and mixes itself with all his reasonings. The voluntary actions of men may originate in their opinions; but these opinions will be very differently modified in creatures compounded of a rational faculty and corporal propensities, from what they would be, in beings wholly intellectual. Mr Godwin, in proving that sound reasoning and truth, are capable of being adequately communicated, examines the proposition first practically; and then adds, 'Such is the appearance which this proposition assumes, when examined in a loose and practical view. In strict consideration it will not admit of debate. Man is a rational being, etc.* So far from calling this a strict consideration of the subject, I own I should call it the loosest, and most erroneous way possible, of considering it. It is the calculating the velocity of a falling body *in vacuo*; and persisting in it, that it would be the same through whatever resisting mediums it might fall. This was not Newton's mode of philosophizing. Very few general propositions are just in application to a particular subject. The moon is not kept in her orbit round the earth, nor the earth in her orbit round the sun, by a force that varies merely in the inverse ratio of the squares of the distances. To make the general theory just in application to the revolutions of these bodies, it was necessary to calculate accurately, the disturbing force of the sun upon the moon, and of the moon upon the earth; and till these disturbing forces were properly estimated, actual observations on the motions of these bodies, would have proved that the theory was not accurately true.[84]

I am willing to allow that every voluntary act is preceded by a decision of the mind; but it is strangely opposite to what I should conceive to be the just theory upon the subject, and a palpable contradiction to all experience, to say, that the corporal propensities of man do not act very powerfully, as disturbing forces, in these decisions. The question, therefore, does not merely depend, upon whether a man may be made to understand a distinct proposition, or be convinced by an unanswerable argument. A truth may be brought home to his conviction as a rational being, though he may determine to act

* Godwin, *Political justice*, i, p. 89.

contrary to it, as a compound being. The cravings of hunger, the love of liquor, the desire of possessing a beautiful woman, will urge men to actions, of the fatal consequences of which, to the general interests of society, they are perfectly well convinced, even at the very time they commit them. Remove their bodily cravings, and they would not hesitate a moment in determining against such actions. Ask them their opinion of the same conduct in another person, and they would immediately reprobate it. But in their own case, and under all the circumstances of their situation with these bodily cravings, the decision of the compound being is different from the conviction of the rational being.

If this be the just view of the subject, and both theory and experience unite to prove that it is, almost all Mr Godwin's reasonings on the subject of coercion in his seventh chapter, will appear to be founded on error. He spends some time in placing in a ridiculous point of view, the attempt, to convince a man's understanding, and to clear up a doubtful proposition in his mind, by blows. Undoubtedly it is both ridiculous and barbarous; and so is cock-fighting; but one has little more to do with the real object of human punishments, than the other. One frequent (indeed much too frequent) mode of punishment is death. Mr Godwin will hardly think this intended for conviction; at least it does not appear how the individual, or the society, could reap much future benefit from an understanding enlightened in this manner.

The principal objects which human punishments have in view, are undoubtedly restraint and example: restraint, or removal of an individual member, whose vicious habits are likely to be prejudicial to the society. And example, which by expressing the sense of the community with regard to a particular crime, and by associating more nearly and visibly, crime and punishment, holds out a moral motive to dissuade others from the commission of it.

Restraint, Mr Godwin thinks, may be permitted as a temporary expedient, though he reprobates solitary imprisonment, which has certainly been the most successful, and, indeed, almost the only attempt, towards the moral amelioration of offenders. He talks of the selfish passions that are fostered by solitude, and of the virtues generated in society. But surely these virtues are not generated in the society of a prison. Were the offender confined to the society of able and virtuous men, he would probably be more improved than in solitude. But is this practicable? Mr Godwin's ingenuity is more frequently employed in finding out evils, than in suggesting practical remedies.

Punishment, for example, is totally reprobated. By endeavouring to make examples too impressive and terrible, nations have, indeed, been led into the most barbarous cruelties; but the abuse of any practice is not a good argument against its use. The indefatigable pains taken in this country to find out a murder, and the certainty of its punishment, has powerfully contributed to generate that sentiment which is frequent in the mouths of the common people, that a murder will sooner or later come to light; and the habitual horror in which murder is in consequence held, will make a man, in the agony of passion, throw down his knife, for fear he should be tempted to use it in the gratification of his revenge. In Italy, where murderers by flying to a sanctuary, are allowed more frequently to escape, the crime has never been held in the same detestation, and has consequently been more frequent. No man, who is at all aware of the operation of moral motives, can doubt for a moment, that if every murder in Italy had been invariably punished, the use of the stiletto[85] in transports of passion, would have been comparatively but little known.

That human laws, either do, or can, proportion the punishment accurately to the offence, no person will have the folly to assert. From the inscrutability of motives the thing is absolutely impossible: but this imperfection, though it may be called a species of injustice, is no valid argument against human laws. It is the lot of man, that he will frequently have to choose between two evils; and it is a sufficient reason for the adoption of any institution, that it is the best mode that suggests itself of preventing greater evils. A continual endeavour should undoubtedly prevail to make these institutions as perfect as the nature of them will admit. But nothing is so easy, as to find fault with human institutions; nothing so difficult, as to suggest adequate practical improvements. It is to be lamented, that more men of talents employ their time in the former occupation, than in the latter.

The frequency of crime among men, who, as the common saying is, know better, sufficiently proves, that some truths may be brought home to the conviction of the mind without always producing the proper effect upon the conduct. There are other truths of a nature that perhaps never can be adequately communicated from one man to another. The superiority of the pleasures of intellect to those of sense, Mr Godwin considers as a fundamental truth. Taking all circumstances into consideration, I should be disposed to agree with him; but how am I to communicate this truth to a person who has scarcely ever felt intellectual pleasure? I may as well attempt to explain the nature and beauty of colours to a blind man. If I am ever so laborious, patient, and clear, and have the most repeated opportunities of expostulation, any real progress toward the accomplishment of my purpose, seems absolutely hopeless. There is no common measure between us. I cannot proceed step by step: it is a truth of a nature absolutely incapable of demonstration. All that I can say is, that the wisest and best men in all ages had agreed in giving the preference, very greatly, to the pleasures of intellect; and that my own experience completely confirmed the truth of their decisions; that I had found sensual pleasures vain, transient, and continually attended with tedium and disgust; but that intellectual pleasures appeared to me ever fresh and young, filled up all my hours satisfactorily, gave a new zest to life, and diffused a lasting serenity over my mind. If he believe me, it can only be from respect and veneration for my authority: it is credulity, and not conviction. I have not said anything, nor can anything be said of a nature to produce real conviction. The affair is not an affair of reasoning, but of experience. He would probably observe in reply, what you say may be very true with regard to yourself and many other good men, but for my own part I feel very differently upon the subject. I have very frequently taken up a book, and almost as frequently gone to sleep over it; but when I pass an evening with a gay party, or a pretty woman, I feel alive, and in spirits, and truly enjoy my existence.

Under such circumstances, reasoning and argument are not instruments from which success can be expected. At some future time perhaps, real satiety of sensual pleasures, or some accidental impressions that awakened the energies of his mind, might effect that, in a month, which the most patient and able expostulations, might be incapable of effecting in forty years.

FOURTEEN

Mr Godwin's five propositions respecting political truth, on which his whole work hinges, not established – Reasons we have for supposing from the distress occasioned by the principle of population, that the vices, and moral weakness of man can never be wholly eradicated – Perfectibility, in the sense in which Mr Godwin uses the term, not applicable to man – Nature of the real perfectibility of man illustrated.

If the reasonings of the preceding chapter are just, the corollaries respecting political truth, which Mr Godwin draws from the proposition, that the voluntary actions of men originate in their opinions, will not appear to be clearly established. These corollaries are, 'Sound reasoning and truth, when adequately communicated, must always be victorious over error; sound reasoning and truth are capable of being so communicated; truth is omnipotent; the vices and moral weakness of man are not invincible; man is perfectible, or in other words, susceptible of perpetual improvement.'

The first three propositions may be considered a complete syllogism.[86] If by adequately communicated, be meant such a conviction as to produce an adequate effect upon the conduct; the major may be allowed, and the minor denied. The consequent, or the omnipotence of truth, of course falls to the ground. If by adequately communicated be meant merely the conviction of the rational faculty; the major must be denied, the minor will be only true in cases capable of demonstration, and the consequent equally falls. The fourth proposition, Mr Godwin calls the preceding proposition, with a slight variation in the statement. If so, it must accompany the preceding proposition in its fall. But it may be worthwhile to inquire, with reference to the principal argument of this essay, into the particular reasons which we have for supposing, that the vices and moral weakness of man can never be wholly overcome in this world.

Man, according to Mr Godwin, is a creature, formed what he is, by the successive impressions which he has received, from the first moment that the germ from which he sprung was animated. Could he be placed in a situation, where he was subject to no evil impressions whatever, though it might be doubted whether in such a situation virtue could exist, vice would certainly be banished. The great bent of Mr Godwin's work on political justice, if I understand it rightly, is to show, that the greater part of the vices and weaknesses of men, proceed from the injustice of their political and social institutions: and that if these were removed, and the understandings of men more enlightened, there would be little or no temptation in the world to evil. As it has been clearly proved, however (at least as I think), that this is entirely a false conception, and that, independent of any political or social institutions whatever, the greater part of mankind, from the fixed and unalterable laws of nature, must ever be subject to the evil temptations arising from want, besides other passions; it follows from Mr Godwin's definition of man, that such impressions, and combinations of impressions, cannot be afloat in the world, without generating a variety of bad men. According to Mr Godwin's own conception of the formation of character, it is surely as improbable that under such circumstances, all men will be virtuous, as that sixes will come up a hundred times following upon the dice. The great variety of combinations upon the dice in a repeated succession of throws, appears to me not inaptly to represent the great variety of character that must necessarily exist in the world, supposing every individual to be formed what he is, by that combination of impressions which he has received since his first existence. And this comparison will, in some measure, show the absurdity of supposing, that exceptions will ever become general rules; that extraordinary and unusual combinations will be frequent; or that the individual instances of great virtue which have appeared in all ages of the world, will ever prevail universally.

I am aware that Mr Godwin might say, that the comparison is in one respect inaccurate; that in the case of the dice, the preceding causes, or rather the chances respecting the preceding causes, were always the same; and that, therefore, I could have no good reason for supposing that a greater number of sixes would come up in the next hundred times of throwing, than in the preceding same number of throws. But, that man had in some sort a power of influencing those causes that formed character, and that every good and virtuous man that was produced, by the influence which he must necessarily have, rather increased the probability that another such virtuous character would be generated; whereas the coming up of sixes upon the dice once, would certainly not increase the probability of their coming up a second time. I admit this objection to the accuracy of the comparison, but it is only partially valid. Repeated experience has assured us, that the influence of the most virtuous character will rarely prevail against very strong temptations to evil. It will undoubtedly affect some, but it will fail with a much greater number. Had Mr Godwin succeeded in his attempt to prove that these temptations to evil could by the exertions of man be removed, I would give up the comparison; or at least allow, that a man might be so far enlightened with regard to the mode of shaking his elbow, that he would be able to throw sixes every time. But as long as a great number of those impressions which form character, like the nice motions of the arm, remain absolutely independent of the will of man; though it would be the height of folly and presumption, to attempt to calculate the relative proportions of virtue and vice at the future periods of the world; it may be safely asserted, that the vices and moral weakness of mankind, taken in the mass, are invincible.

The fifth proposition, is the general deduction from the four former, and will consequently fall, as the foundations which support it have given way. In the sense in which Mr Godwin understands the term perfectible, the perfectibility of man cannot be asserted, unless the preceding propositions could have been clearly established. There is, however, one sense, which the term will bear, in which it is, perhaps, just. It may be said with truth, that man is always susceptible of improvement; or that there never has been, or will be, a period of his history, in which he can be said to have reached his possible acme of perfection. Yet it does not by any means follow from this, that our efforts to improve man will always succeed; or even, that he will ever make, in the greatest number of ages, any extraordinary strides towards perfection. The only inference that can be drawn, is, that the precise limit of his improvement cannot possibly be known. And I cannot help again reminding the reader of a distinction, which, it appears to me, ought particularly to be attended to in the present question; I mean, the essential difference there is, between an unlimited improvement, and an improvement the limit of which cannot be ascertained. The former is an improvement not applicable to man under the present laws of his nature. The latter, undoubtedly, is applicable.

The real perfectibility of man may be illustrated, as I have mentioned before, by the perfectibility of a plant. The object of the enterprising florist, is, as I conceive, to unite size, symmetry, and beauty of colour. It would surely be presumptuous in the most successful improver to affirm, that he possessed a carnation in which these qualities existed in the greatest possible state of perfection. However beautiful his flower may be, other care, other soil, or other suns, might produce one still more beautiful. Yet, although he may be aware of the absurdity of supposing that he has reached perfection; and though he may know by what means he attained that degree of beauty in the flower which he at present possesses, yet he cannot be sure that by pursuing similar means, rather increased in strength, he will obtain a more beautiful blossom. By endeavouring to improve one quality, he may impair the beauty of another. The richer mould[87] which he would employ to increase the size of his plant, would probably burst the calyx,[88] and destroy at once its symmetry. In a similar manner, the forcing manure used to bring about the French revolution, and to give a greater freedom and energy to the human mind, has burst the calyx of humanity, the restraining bond of all society; and, however large the separate petals have grown; however strongly, or even beautifully a few of them have been marked; the whole is at present a loose, deformed, disjointed mass, without union, symmetry, or harmony of colouring.

Were it of consequence to improve pinks and carnations, though we could have no hope of raising them as large as cabbages, we might undoubtedly expect, by successive efforts, to obtain more beautiful specimens than we at present possess. No person can deny the importance of improving the happiness of the human species. Every, the least advance in this respect, is highly valuable. But an experiment with the human race is not like an experiment upon inanimate objects. The bursting of a flower may be a trifle. Another will soon succeed it. But the bursting of the bonds of society is such a separation of parts as cannot take place without giving the most acute pain to thousands: and a long time may elapse, and much misery may be endured, before the wound grows up again.

As the five propositions which I have been examining may be considered as the corner stones of Mr Godwin's fanciful structure; and, indeed, as expressing the aim and bent of his whole work; however excellent much of his detached reasoning may be, he must be considered as having failed in the great object of his undertaking. Besides the difficulties arising from the compound nature of man, which he has by no means sufficiently smoothed; the principal argument against the perfectibility of man and society remains whole and unimpaired from anything that he has advanced. And as far as I can trust my own judgement, this argument appears to be conclusive, not only against the perfectibility of man, in the enlarged sense in which Mr Godwin understands the term, but against any very marked and striking change for the better, in the form and structure of general society; by which I mean, any great and decided amelioration of the condition of the lower classes of mankind, the most numerous, and, consequently, in a general view of the subject, the most important part of the human race. Were I to live a thousand years, and the laws of nature to remain the same, I should little fear, or rather little hope, a contradiction from experience, in asserting, that no possible sacrifices or exertions of the rich, in a country which had been long inhabited, could for any time place the lower classes of the community in a situation equal, with regard to circumstances, to the situation of the common people, about thirty years ago, in the northern states of America.

The lower classes of people in Europe may, at some future period, be much better instructed than they are at present; they may be taught to employ the little spare time they have in many better ways than at the alehouse; they may live under better and more equal laws than they have ever hitherto done, perhaps, in any country; and I even conceive it possible, though not probable, that they may have more leisure; but it is not in the nature of things, that they can be awarded such a quantity of money or subsistence, as will allow them all to marry early, in the full confidence that they shall be able to provide with ease for a numerous family.

FIFTEEN

*Models too perfect, may sometimes rather impede than pro-
mote improvements – Mr Godwin's essay on avarice and
profusion – Impossibility of dividing the necessary labour of a
society amicably among all – Invectives against labour may
produce present evil, with little or no chance of producing
future good – An accession to the mass of agricultural labour
must always be an advantage to the labourer.*

Mr Godwin in the preface to his *Enquirer*, drops a few expressions which seem to hint at some change in his opinions since
he wrote the *Political justice*; and as this is a work now of some
years standing, I should certainly think, that I had been arguing
against opinions, which the author had himself seen reason to
alter, but that in some of the essays of the *Enquirer*, Mr Godwin's peculiar mode of thinking, appears in as striking a light
as ever.

It has been frequently observed, that though we cannot hope
to reach perfection in anything, yet that it must always be
advantageous to us, to place before our eyes the most perfect
models. This observation has a plausible appearance, but is
very far from being generally true. I even doubt its truth in one
of the most obvious exemplifications that would occur. I doubt
whether a very young painter would receive so much benefit,
from an attempt to copy a highly finished and perfect picture,
as from copying one where the outlines were more strongly
marked, and the manner of laying on the colours was more easily discoverable. But in cases, where the perfection of the model,
is a perfection of a different and superior nature from that,
towards which we should naturally advance, we shall not only
always fail in making any progress towards it, but we shall in

all probability impede the progress, which we might have expected to make, had we not fixed our eyes upon so perfect a model. A highly intellectual being, exempt from the infirm calls of hunger or sleep, is undoubtedly a much more perfect exist-ence than man, but were man to attempt to copy such a model, he would not only fail in making any advances towards it; but by unwisely straining to imitate what was inimitable, he would probably destroy the little intellect which he was endeavouring to improve.

The form and structure of society which Mr Godwin describes, is as essentially distinct from any forms of society which have hitherto prevailed in the world, as a being that can live without food or sleep is from a man. By improving society in its present form, we are making no more advances towards such a state of things as he pictures, than we should make approaches towards a line, with regard to which we were walk-ing parallel. The question, therefore is, whether, by looking to such a form of society as our polar star, we are likely to advance or retard the improvement of the human species? Mr Godwin appears to me to have decided this question against himself in his essay on avarice and profusion in the *Enquirer*.

Dr Adam Smith has very justly observed, that nations, as well as individuals, grow rich by parsimony, and poor by pro-fusion; and that, therefore, every frugal man was a friend, and every spendthrift an enemy to his country.[89] The reason he gives is, that what is saved from revenue is always added to stock, and is therefore taken from the maintenance of labour that is generally unproductive, and employed in the mainten-ance of labour that realizes itself in valuable commodities. No observation can be more evidently just. The subject of Mr God-win's essay is a little similar in its first appearance, but in essence is as distinct as possible. He considers the mischief of profu-sion, as an acknowledged truth; and therefore makes his comparison between the avaricious man, and the man who spends his income. But the avaricious man of Mr Godwin, is totally a distinct character, at least with regard to his effect upon the prosperity of the state, from the frugal man of Dr Adam Smith. The frugal man in order to make more money, saves from his income, and adds to his capital; and this capital he either employs himself in the maintenance of productive labour, or he lends it to some other person, who will probably employ it in this way. He benefits the state, because he adds to its general capital; and because wealth employed as capital, not only sets in motion more labour, than when spent as income, but the labour is besides of a more valuable kind. But the avaricious man of Mr Godwin locks up his wealth in a chest, and sets in motion no labour of any kind, either productive or unproductive. This is so essential a difference, that Mr Godwin's decision in his essay, appears at once as evidently false, as Dr Adam Smith's position is evidently true. It could not, indeed, but occur to Mr Godwin, that some present inconvenience might arise to the poor, from thus locking up the funds destined for the maintenance of labour. The only way, therefore, he had of weakening this objection, was to compare the two characters chiefly with regard to their tendency to accelerate the approach of that happy state of cultivated equality, on which he says we ought always to fix our eyes as our polar star.

I think it has been proved in the former parts of this essay, that such a state of society is absolutely impracticable. What consequences then are we to expect from looking to such a point, as our guide and polar star, in the great sea of political discovery? Reason would teach us to expect no other, than winds perpetually adverse, constant but fruitless toil, frequent shipwreck, and certain misery. We shall not only fail in making the smallest real approach towards such a perfect form of society; but by wasting our strength of mind and body, in a direction in which it is impossible to proceed, and by the frequent distress which we must necessarily occasion by our repeated failures, we shall evidently impede that degree of improvement in society, which is really attainable.

It has appeared that a society constituted according to Mr Godwin's system, must, from the inevitable laws of our nature, degenerate into a class of proprietors, and a class of labourers; and that the substitution of benevolence, for self-love, as the moving principle of society, instead of producing the happy effects that might be expected from so fair a name, would cause the same pressure of want to be felt by the whole of society, which is now felt only by a part. It is to the established administration of property, and to the apparently narrow principle of self-love, that we are indebted for all the noblest exertions of human genius, all the finer and more delicate emotions of the soul, for everything, indeed, that distinguishes the civilized, from the savage state; and no sufficient change, has as yet taken place, in the nature of civilized man, to enable us to say, that he either is, or ever will be, in a state, when he may safely throw down the ladder by which he has risen to this eminence.

If in every society that has advanced beyond the savage state, a class of proprietors, and a class of labourers,* must necessarily exist, it is evident, that, as labour is the only property of the class of labourers, everything that tends to diminish the value of this property, must tend to diminish the possessions of this part of society. The only way that a poor man has of supporting himself in independence, is by the exertion of his bodily strength. This is the only commodity he has to give in exchange for the necessaries of life. It would hardly appear then that you benefit him, by narrowing the market for this commodity, by decreasing the demand for labour, and lessening the value of the only property that he possesses.

Mr Godwin would perhaps say, that the whole system of barter and exchange, is a vile and iniquitous traffic. If you would essentially relieve the poor man, you should take a part of his labour upon yourself, or give him your money, without exacting so severe a return for it. In answer to the first method proposed, it may be observed, that even if the rich could be

---

* It should be observed, that the principal argument of this essay, only goes to prove the necessity of a class of proprietors, and a class of labourers, but by no means infers, that the present great inequality of property, is either necessary or useful to society. On the contrary, it must certainly be considered as an evil, and every institution that promotes it, is essentially bad and impolitic. But whether a government could with advantage to society actively interfere to repress inequality of fortunes, may be a matter of doubt. Perhaps the generous system of perfect liberty, adopted by Dr Adam Smith, and the French economists, would be ill exchanged for any system of restraint.

persuaded to assist the poor in this way, the value of the assistance would be comparatively trifling. The rich, though they think themselves of great importance, bear but a small proportion in point of numbers to the poor, and would, therefore, relieve them but of a small part of their burdens by taking a share. Were all those that are employed in the labours of luxuries, added to the numbers of those employed in producing necessaries; and could these necessary labours be amicably divided among all, each man's share might indeed be comparatively light; but desirable as such an amicable division would undoubtedly be, I cannot conceive any practical principle* according to which it could take place. It has been shown, that the spirit of benevolence, guided by the strict impartial justice that Mr Godwin describes, would, if vigorously acted upon, depress in want and misery the whole human race. Let us examine what would be the consequence, if the proprietor were to retain a decent share for himself; but to give the rest away to the poor, without exacting a task from them in return. Not to mention the idleness and the vice that such a proceeding, if general, would probably create in the present state of society, and the great risk there would be, of diminishing the produce of land, as well as the labours of luxury, another objection yet remains.

It has appeared that from the principle of population, more will always be in want than can be adequately supplied. The surplus of the rich man might be sufficient for three, but four will be desirous to obtain it. He cannot make this selection of three out of the four, without conferring a great favour on those that are the objects of his choice. These persons must consider themselves as under a great obligation to him, and as dependent upon him for their support. The rich man would feel his power, and the poor man his dependence; and the evil

---

* Mr Godwin seems to have but little respect for practical principles; but I own it appears to me, that he is a much greater benefactor to mankind, who points out how an inferior good may be attained, than he who merely expatiates on the deformity of the present state of society, and the beauty of a different state, without pointing out a practical method, that might be immediately applied, of accelerating our advances from the one, to the other.

effects of these two impressions on the human heart are well known. Though I perfectly agree with Mr Godwin therefore in the evil of hard labour; yet I still think it is a less evil, and less calculated to debase the human mind, than dependence; and every history of man that we have ever read, places in a strong point of view, the danger to which that mind is exposed, which is entrusted with constant power.

In the present state of things, and particularly when labour is in request, the man who does a day's work for me, confers full as great an obligation upon me, as I do upon him. I possess what he wants; he possesses what I want. We make an amicable exchange. The poor man walks erect in conscious independence; and the mind of his employer is not vitiated by a sense of power.

Three or four hundred years ago, there was undoubtedly much less labour in England, in proportion to the population, than at present; but there was much more dependence: and we probably should not now enjoy our present degree of civil liberty, if the poor, by the introduction of manufactures, had not been enabled to give something in exchange for the provisions of the great lords, instead of being dependent upon their bounty. Even the greatest enemies of trade and manufactures, and I do not reckon myself a very determined friend to them, must allow, that when they were introduced into England, liberty came in their train.[90]

Nothing that has been said, tends in the most remote degree to undervalue the principle of benevolence. It is one of the noblest and most godlike qualities of the human heart, generated perhaps, slowly and gradually from self-love; and afterwards intended to act as a general law, whose kind office it should be, to soften the partial deformities, to correct the asperities, and to smooth the wrinkles of its parent; and this seems to be the analogy of all nature. Perhaps there is no one general law of nature that will not appear, to us at least, to produce partial evil; and we frequently observe at the same time, some bountiful provision, which acting as another general law, corrects the inequalities of the first.

The proper office of benevolence is to soften the partial evils arising from self-love, but it can never be substituted in its place. If no man were to allow himself to act, till he had completely determined, that the action he was about to perform, was more conducive than any other to the general good, the most enlightened minds would hesitate in perplexity and amazement,[91] and the unenlightened, would be continually committing the grossest mistakes.

As Mr Godwin, therefore, has not laid down any practical principle, according to which the necessary labours of agriculture might be amicably shared among the whole class of labourers; by general invectives against employing the poor, he appears to pursue an unattainable good through much present evil. For if every man who employs the poor, ought to be considered as their enemy, and as adding to the weight of their oppressions, and if the miser is, for this reason, to be preferred to the man who spends his income, it follows, that any number of men who now spend their incomes, might, to the advantage of society, be converted into misers. Suppose then, that a hundred thousand persons who now employ ten men each, were to lock up their wealth from general use, it is evident, that a million of working men of different kinds would be completely thrown out of all employment. The extensive misery that such an event would produce in the present state of society, Mr Godwin himself could hardly refuse to acknowledge; and I question whether he might not find some difficulty in proving, that a conduct of this kind tended more than the conduct of those who spend their incomes to 'place human beings in the condition in which they ought to be placed'.

But Mr Godwin says, that the miser really locks up nothing; that the point has not been rightly understood; and that the true development and definition of the nature of wealth have not been applied to illustrate it. Having defined therefore wealth, very justly, to be the commodities raised and fostered by human labour, he observes, that the miser locks up neither corn, nor oxen, nor clothes, nor houses. Undoubtedly he does not really lock up these articles, but he locks up the power of producing them, which is virtually the same. These things are certainly used and consumed by his contemporaries, as truly, and to as great an extent, as if he were a beggar; but not to as great an extent, as if he had employed his wealth, in turning up more land, in breeding more oxen, in employing more tailors, and in building more houses. But supposing, for a moment, that the conduct of the miser did not tend to check any really useful produce, how are all those, who are thrown out of employment, to obtain patents which they may show in order to be awarded a proper share of the food and raiment produced by the society? This is the unconquerable difficulty.

I am perfectly willing to concede to Mr Godwin that there is much more labour in the world than is really necessary; and that, if the lower classes of society could agree among themselves never to work more than six or seven hours in the day, the commodities essential to human happiness might still be produced in as great abundance as at present. But it is almost impossible to conceive that such an agreement could be adhered to. From the principle of population, some would necessarily be more in want than others. Those that had large families, would naturally be desirous of exchanging two hours more of their labour for an ampler quantity of subsistence. How are they to be prevented from making this exchange? It would be a violation of the first and most sacred property that a man possesses, to attempt, by positive institutions, to interfere with his command over his own labour.

Till Mr Godwin, therefore, can point out some practical plan according to which the necessary labour in a society might be equitably divided; his invectives against labour, if they were attended to, would certainly produce much present evil, without approximating us to that state of cultivated equality to which he looks forward as his polar star; and which, he seems to think, should at present be our guide in determining the nature and tendency of human actions. A mariner guided by such a polar star is in danger of shipwreck.

Perhaps there is no possible way in which wealth could, in general, be employed so beneficially to a state, and particularly to the lower orders of it, as by improving and rendering productive that land, which to a farmer would not answer the expense of cultivation. Had Mr Godwin exerted his energetic eloquence in painting the superior worth and usefulness of the character who employed the poor in this way, to him who employed them in narrow luxuries, every enlightened man must have applauded his efforts. The increasing demand for agricultural labour must always tend to better the condition of the poor; and if the accession of work be of this kind, so far is it from being true, that the poor would be obliged to work ten hours, for the same price, that they before worked eight, that the very reverse would be the fact; and a labourer might then support his wife and family as well by the labour of six hours, as he could before by the labour of eight.

The labour created by luxuries, though useful in distributing the produce of the country, without vitiating the proprietor by power, or debasing the labourer by dependence, has not, indeed, the same beneficial effects on the state of the poor. A great accession of work from manufactures, though it may raise the price of labour even more than an increasing demand for agricultural labour; yet, as in this case, the quantity of food in the country may not be proportionably increasing, the advantage to the poor will be but temporary, as the price of provisions must necessarily rise in proportion to the price of labour. Relative to this subject, I cannot avoid venturing a few remarks on a part of Dr Adam Smith's *Wealth of nations*; speaking at the same time with that diffidence, which I ought certainly to feel, in differing from a person so justly celebrated in the political world.[92]

SIXTEEN

Probable error of Dr Adam Smith in representing every increase of the revenue or stock of a society as an increase in the funds for the maintenance of labour – Instances where an increase of wealth can have no tendency to better the condition of the labouring poor – England has increased in riches without a proportional increase in the funds for the maintenance of labour – The state of the poor in China would not be improved by an increase of wealth from manufactures.

The professed object of Dr Adam Smith's inquiry, is, the nature and causes of the wealth of nations. There is another inquiry, however, perhaps still more interesting, which he occasionally mixes with it; I mean an inquiry into the causes which affect the happiness of nations, or the happiness and comfort of the lower orders of society, which is the most numerous class in every nation. I am sufficiently aware of the near connection of these two subjects, and that the causes which tend to increase the wealth of a state, tend also, generally speaking, to increase the happiness of the lower classes of the people. But perhaps Dr Adam Smith has considered these two inquiries as still more nearly connected than they really are; at least, he has not stopped to take notice of those instances, where the wealth of a society may increase (according to his definition of wealth) without having any tendency to increase the comforts of the labouring part of it. I do not mean to enter into a philosophical discussion of what constitutes the proper happiness of man; but shall merely consider two universally acknowledged ingredients, health, and the command of the necessaries and conveniences of life.

Little or no doubt can exist, that the comforts of the labouring poor depend upon the increase of the funds destined for the maintenance of labour; and will be very exactly in proportion to the rapidity of this increase. The demand for labour which such increase would occasion, by creating a competition in the market, must necessarily raise the value of labour; and, till the additional number of hands required were reared, the increased funds would be distributed to the same number of persons as before the increase, and therefore every labourer would live comparatively at his ease. But perhaps Dr Adam Smith errs in representing every increase of the revenue or stock of a society as an increase of these funds. Such surplus stock or revenues will, indeed, always be considered by the individual possessing it, as an additional fund from which he may maintain more labour: but it will not be a real and effectual fund for the maintenance of an additional number of labourers, unless the whole, or at least a great part of this increase of the stock or revenue of the society, be convertible into a proportional quantity of provisions; and it will not be so convertible, where the increase has arisen merely from the produce of labour, and not from the produce of land. A distinction will in this case occur, between the number of hands which the stock of the society could employ, and the number which its territory can maintain.

To explain myself by an instance. Dr Adam Smith defines the wealth of a nation to consist in the annual produce of its land and labour.[93] This definition evidently includes manufactured produce, as well as the produce of the land. Now supposing a nation, for a course of years, was to add what it saved from its yearly revenue, to its manufacturing capital solely, and not to its capital employed upon land, it is evident, that it might grow richer according to the above definition, without a power of supporting a greater number of labourers, and therefore, without an increase in the real funds for the maintenance of labour. There would, notwithstanding, be a demand for labour, from the power which each manufacturer would possess, or at least think he possessed, of extending his old stock in trade, or of setting up fresh works. This demand would of course raise the price of labour; but if the yearly stock of provisions in the country was not increasing, this rise would soon turn out to be merely nominal, as the price of provisions must necessarily rise with it. The demand for manufacturing labourers might, indeed, entice many from agriculture, and thus tend to diminish the annual produce of the land; but we will suppose any effect of this kind to be compensated by improvements in the instruments of agriculture, and the quantity of provisions therefore to remain the same. Improvements in manufacturing machinery would of course take place; and this circumstance, added to the greater number of hands employed in manufactures, would cause the annual produce of the labour of the country to be upon the whole greatly increased. The wealth therefore of the country would be increasing annually, according to the definition, and might not, perhaps, be increasing very slowly.

The question is, whether wealth, increasing in this way, has any tendency to better the condition of the labouring poor. It is a self-evident proposition, that any general rise in the price of labour, the stock of provisions remaining the same, can only be a nominal rise, as it must very shortly be followed by a proportional rise in provisions. The increase in the price of labour therefore, which we have supposed, would have little or no effect in giving the labouring poor a greater command over the necessaries and conveniences of life. In this respect they would be nearly in the same state as before. In one other respect they would be in a worse state. A greater proportion of them would be employed in manufacturers, and fewer, consequently, in agriculture. And this exchange of professions will be allowed, I think, by all, to be very unfavourable in respect of health, one essential ingredient of happiness, besides the greater uncertainty of manufacturing labour, arising from the capricious taste of man, the accidents of war, and other causes.

It may be said, perhaps, that such an instance as I have supposed could not occur, because the rise in the price of provisions would immediately turn some additional capital into the channel of agriculture. But this is an event which may take place very slowly, as it should be remarked, that a rise in the price of labour, had preceded the rise in provisions, and would, therefore, impede the good effects upon agriculture, which the increased value of the produce of the land might otherwise have occasioned.

It might also be said, that the additional capital of the nation would enable it to import provisions sufficient for the maintenance of those whom its stock could employ. A small country with a large navy, and great inland accommodations[94] for carriage, such as Holland, may, indeed, import and distribute an effectual quantity of provisions; but the price of provisions must be very high, to make such an importation and distribution answer in large countries, less advantageously circumstanced in this respect.

An instance, accurately such as I have supposed, may not, perhaps, ever have occurred; but I have little doubt that instances nearly approximating to it may be found without any very laborious search. Indeed I am strongly inclined to think, that England herself, since the Revolution,[95] affords a very striking elucidation of the argument in question.

The commerce of this country, internal, as well as external, has certainly been rapidly advancing during the last century. The exchangeable value, in the market of Europe, of the annual produce of its land and labour, has, without doubt, increased very considerably. But, upon examination, it will be found, that the increase has been chiefly in the produce of labour, and not in the produce of land; and therefore, though the wealth of the nation has been advancing with a quick pace, the effectual funds for the maintenance of labour have been increasing very slowly; and the result is such as might be expected. The increasing wealth of the nation has had little or no tendency to better the condition of the labouring poor. They have not, I believe, a greater command of the necessaries and conveniences of life; and a much greater proportion of them, than at the period of the Revolution, is employed in manufactures, and crowded together in close and unwholesome rooms.

Could we believe the statement of Dr Price, that the population of England has decreased since the Revolution, it would even appear, that the effectual funds for the maintenance of labour had been declining during the progress of wealth in other respects. For I conceive that it may be laid down as a general rule, that if the effectual funds for the maintenance of labour are increasing, that is, if the territory can maintain, as well as the stock employ, a greater number of labourers, this additional number will quickly spring up, even in spite of such wars as Dr Price enumerates. And, consequently, if the population of any country has been stationary, or declining, we may safely infer, that, however it may have advanced in manufacturing wealth, its effectual funds for the maintenance of labour cannot have increased.

It is difficult, however, to conceive that the population of England has been declining since the Revolution; though every testimony concurs to prove that its increase, if it has increased, has been very slow. In the controversy which the question has occasioned, Dr Price undoubtedly appears to be much more completely master of his subject, and to possess more accurate information than his opponents. Judging simply from this controversy, I think one should say, that Dr Price's point is nearer being proved than Mr Howlett's. Truth, probably, lies between the two statements, but this supposition makes the increase of population, since the Revolution, to have been very slow, in comparison with the increase of wealth.[96]

That the produce of the land has been decreasing, or even that it has been absolutely stationary during the last century, few will be disposed to believe. The enclosure of commons and waste lands, certainly tends to increase the food of the country; but it has been asserted with confidence, that the enclosure of common fields, has frequently had a contrary effect; and that large tracts of land, which formerly produced great quantities of corn, by being converted into pasture, both employ fewer hands, and feed fewer mouths, than before their enclosure. It is, indeed, an acknowledged truth, that pasture land produces a smaller quantity of human subsistence, than corn land of the same natural fertility: and could it be clearly ascertained, that from the increased demand for butcher's meat of the best quality, and its increased price in consequence, a greater quantity of good land has annually been employed in grazing, the diminution of human subsistence, which this circumstance would occasion, might have counterbalanced the advantages derived from the enclosure of waste lands, and the general improvements in husbandry.

It scarcely need be remarked, that the high price of butcher's meat at present, and its low price formerly, were not caused by the scarcity in the one case, or the plenty in the other, but by the different expense sustained at the different periods, in preparing cattle for the market. It is, however, possible, that there might have been more cattle a hundred years ago in the country, than at present; but no doubt can be entertained, that there is much more meat of a superior quality brought to market at present, than ever there was. When the price of butcher's meat was very low, cattle were reared chiefly upon waste lands; and except for some of the principal markets, were probably killed with but little other fatting. The veal that is sold so cheap in some distant countries at present, bears little other resemblance than the name, to that which is bought in London. Formerly, the price of butcher's meat would not pay for rearing, and scarcely for feeding cattle on land that would answer in tillage; but the present price will not only pay for fatting cattle on the very best land, but will even allow of the rearing many, on land that would bear good crops of corn. The same number of cattle, or even the same weight of cattle at the different periods when killed, will have consumed (if I may be allowed the expression) very different quantities of human subsistence. A fatted beast may in some respects be considered, in the language of the French economists,[97] as an unproductive labourer: he has added nothing to the value of the raw produce that he has consumed. The present system of grazing, undoubtedly tends more than the former system to diminish the quantity of human subsistence in the country, in proportion to the general fertility of the land.

I would not by any means be understood to say, that the former system either could, or ought, to have continued. The increasing price of butcher's meat, is a natural and inevitable consequence of the general progress of cultivation; but I cannot help thinking, that the present great demand for butcher's meat of the best quality, and the quantity of good land that is in consequence annually employed to produce it, together with the great number of horses at present kept for pleasure, are the chief causes, that have prevented the quantity of human food in the country, from keeping pace with the generally increased fertility of the soil; and a change of custom in these respects, would, I have little doubt, have a very sensible effect on the quantity of subsistence in the country, and consequently on its population.

The employment of much of the most fertile land in grazing, the improvements in agricultural instruments, the increase of large farms, and particularly the diminution of the number of cottages throughout the kingdom, all concur to prove, that there are not probably, so many persons employed in agricultural labour now, as at the period of the Revolution. Whatever increase of population, therefore, has taken place, must be employed almost wholly in manufactures; and it is well known, that the failure of some of these manufactures, merely from the caprice of fashion, such as, the adoption of muslins instead of silks, or of shoe-strings, and covered buttons, instead of buckles and metal buttons, combined with the restraints in the market of labour arising from corporation, and parish laws,[98] have frequently driven thousands on charity for support. The great increase of the poor's rates, is, indeed, of itself, a strong evidence, that the poor have not a greater command of the necessaries and conveniences of life; and if to the consideration, that their condition in this respect is rather worse than better, be added the circumstance, that a much greater proportion of them is employed in large manufactories, unfavourable both to health and virtue, it must be acknowledged, that the increase of wealth of late years, has had no tendency to increase the happiness of the labouring poor.

That every increase of the stock or revenue of a nation, cannot be considered as an increase of the real funds for the maintenance of labour, and, therefore, cannot have the same good effect upon the condition of the poor, will appear in a strong light, if the argument be applied to China.

Dr Adam Smith observes, that China has probably long been as rich, as the nature of her laws and institutions will admit,[99] but that with other laws and institutions, and if foreign commerce were had in honour, she might still be much richer. The question is, would such an increase of wealth, be an increase of the real funds for the maintenance of labour, and consequently, tend to place the lower classes of people in China in a state of greater plenty?

It is evident, that if trade and foreign commerce were held in great honour in China; from the plenty of labourers, and the cheapness of labour, she might work up manufactures for foreign sale to an immense amount. It is equally evident, that from the great bulk of provisions, and the amazing extent of her inland territory, she could not in return import such a quantity, as would be any sensible addition to the annual stock of subsistence in the country. Her immense amount of manufactures, therefore, she would exchange, chiefly, for luxuries collected from all parts of the world. At present, it appears, that no labour whatever is spared in the production of food. The country is rather over-peopled in proportion to what its stock can employ, and labour is, therefore, so abundant, that no pains are taken to abridge it. The consequence of this, is, probably, the greatest production of food that the soil can possibly afford: for it will be generally observed, that processes for abridging labour, though they may enable a farmer to bring a certain quantity of grain cheaper to market, tend rather to diminish, than increase the whole produce; and in agriculture, therefore, may, in some respects, be considered rather as private, than public advantages. An immense capital could not be employed in China in preparing manufactures for foreign trade, without taking off so many labourers from agriculture, as to alter this state of things, and in some degree to diminish the produce of the country. The demand for manufacturing labourers would naturally raise the price of labour; but as the quantity of subsistence would not be increased, the price of provisions would keep pace with it; or even more than keep pace with it, if the quantity of provisions were really decreasing. The country would be evidently advancing in wealth: the exchangeable value of the annual produce of its land and labour, would be annually augmented; yet the real funds for the maintenance of labour, would be stationary, or even declining; and, consequently, the increasing wealth of the nation would rather tend to depress, than to raise, the condition of the poor. With regard to the command over the necessaries and comforts of life, they would be in the same or rather worse state than before; and a great part of them would have exchanged the healthy labours of agriculture, for the unhealthy occupations of manufacturing industry.

The argument, perhaps, appears clearer when applied to China, because it is generally allowed, that the wealth of China has been long stationary. With regard to any other country it might be always a matter of dispute, at which of the two periods, compared, wealth was increasing the fastest; as it is upon the rapidity of the increase of wealth at any particular period, that Dr Adam Smith says the condition of the poor depends. It is evident, however, that two nations might increase, exactly with the same rapidity, in the exchangeable value of the annual produce of their land and labour; yet if one had applied itself chiefly to agriculture, and the other chiefly to commerce, the funds for the maintenance of labour, and consequently the effect of the increase of wealth in each nation, would be extremely different. In that which had applied itself chiefly to agriculture, the poor would live in great plenty, and population would rapidly increase. In that which had applied itself chiefly to commerce, the poor would be comparatively but little benefited, and consequently population would increase slowly.

SEVENTEEN

*Question of the proper definition of the wealth of a state –
Reason given by the French economists for considering all
manufacturers as unproductive labourers, not the true reason –
The labour of artificers, and manufacturers sufficiently
productive to individuals, though not to the state – A remarkable passage in Dr Price's two volumes of observations – Error
of Dr Price in attributing the happiness and rapid population
of America, chiefly, to its peculiar state of civilization – No
advantage can be expected from shutting our eyes to the difficulties in the way to the improvement of society.*

A question seems naturally to arise here, whether the exchangeable value of the annual produce of the land and labour, be the
proper definition of the wealth of a country; or, whether the
gross produce of the land, according to the French economists,
may not be a more accurate definition. Certain it is, that every
increase of wealth, according to the definition of the Economists, will be an increase of the funds for the maintenance of
labour, and consequently will always tend to ameliorate the
condition of the labouring poor; though an increase of wealth,
according to Dr Adam Smith's definition, will by no means
invariably have the same tendency. And yet it may not follow
from this consideration, that Dr Adam Smith's definition is not
just. It seems in many respects improper, to exclude the clothing and lodging of a whole people from any part of their
revenue. Much of it may, indeed, be of very trivial and unimportant value, in comparison with the food of the country; yet
still it may be fairly considered as a part of its revenue: and,
therefore, the only point in which I should differ from Dr Adam
Smith, is, where he seems to consider every increase of the

revenue or stock of a society, as an increase of the funds for the maintenance of labour, and consequently, as tending always to ameliorate the condition of the poor.

The fine silks and cottons, the laces, and other ornamental luxuries,[100] of a rich country, may contribute very considerably to augment the exchangeable value of its annual produce; yet they contribute but in a very small degree, to augment the mass of happiness in the society; and it appears to me, that it is with some view to the real utility of the produce, that we ought to estimate the productiveness, or unproductiveness of different sorts of labour. The French economists consider all labour employed in manufactures as unproductive. Comparing it with the labour employed upon land, I should be perfectly disposed to agree with them; but not exactly for the reasons which they give. They say, that labour employed upon land is productive, because the produce, over and above completely paying the labourer and the farmer, affords a clear rent to the landlord; and that the labour employed upon a piece of lace is unproductive, because it merely replaces the provisions that the workman had consumed, and the stock of his employer, without affording any clear rent whatever. But supposing the value of the wrought lace to be such, as that besides paying in the most complete manner the workman and his employer, it could afford a clear rent to a third person; it appears to me, that in comparison with the labour employed upon land, it would be still as unproductive as ever. Though according to the reasoning used by the French economists, the man employed in the manufacture of lace would, in this case, seem to be a productive labourer; yet according to their definition of the wealth of a state, he ought not to be considered in that light. He will have added nothing to the gross produce of the land: he has consumed a portion of this gross produce, and has left a bit of lace in return; and though he may sell this bit of lace for three times the quantity of provisions that he consumed whilst he was making it, and thus be a very productive labourer with regard to himself; yet he cannot be considered as having added by his labour to any essential part of the riches of the state. The clear rent, therefore, that a certain produce can afford, after paying the expenses of procuring it, does not appear to be the sole criterion, by which to judge of the productiveness or unproductiveness to a state, of any particular species of labour.

Suppose, that two hundred thousand men, who are now employed in producing manufactures, that only tend to gratify the vanity of a few rich people, were to be employed upon some barren and uncultivated lands, and to produce only half the quantity of food that they themselves consumed; they would be still, more productive labourers with regard to the state, than they were before; though their labour, so far from affording a rent to a third person, would but half replace the provisions used in obtaining the produce. In their former employment, they consumed a certain portion of the food of the country, and left in return, some silks and laces. In their latter employment, they consumed the same quantity of food, and left in return, provision for a hundred thousand men. There can be little doubt, which of the two legacies would be the most really beneficial to the country; and it will, I think, be allowed, that the wealth which supported the two hundred thousand men, while they were producing silks and laces, would have been more usefully employed in supporting them, while they were producing the additional quantity of food.

A capital employed upon land, may be unproductive to the individual that employs it, and yet be highly productive to the society. A capital employed in trade on the contrary, may be highly productive to the individual, and yet be almost totally unproductive to the society: and this is the reason why I should call manufacturing labour unproductive, in comparison of that which is employed in agriculture, and not for the reason given by the French economists. It is, indeed, almost impossible, to see the great fortunes that are made in trade, and the liberality with which so many merchants live, and yet agree in the statement of the Economists, that manufacturers can only grow rich by depriving themselves of the funds destined for their support. In many branches of trade the profits are so great, as would allow of a clear rent to a third person: but as there is no third person in the case, and as all the profits centre in the master manufacturer, or merchant, he seems to have a fair chance of growing rich, without much privation; and we consequently see large fortunes acquired in trade by persons who have not been remarked for their parsimony.

Daily experience proves, that the labour employed in trade and manufactures, is sufficiently productive to individuals; but it certainly is not productive in the same degree to the state. Every accession to the food of a country, tends to the immediate benefit of the whole society; but the fortunes made in trade, tend, but in a remote and uncertain manner, to the same end, and in some respects have even a contrary tendency. The home trade of consumption, is by far the most important trade of every nation. China is the richest country in the world, without any other. Putting then, for a moment, foreign trade out of the question, the man, who by an ingenious manufacture, obtains a double portion out of the old stock of provisions, will certainly not be so useful to the state, as the man who, by his labour, adds a single share to the former stock. The consumable commodities of silks, laces, trinkets, and expensive furniture, are undoubtedly a part of the revenue of the society; but they are the revenue only of the rich, and not of the society in general. An increase in this part of the revenue of a state, cannot, therefore, be considered of the same importance, as an increase of food, which forms the principal revenue of the great mass of the people.

Foreign commerce adds to the wealth of a state, according to Dr Adam Smith's definition, though not according to the definition of the Economists. Its principal use, and the reason, probably, that it has in general been held in such high estimation, is, that it adds greatly to the external power of a nation, or to its power of commanding the labour of other countries; but it will be found, upon a near examination, to contribute but little to the increase of the internal funds for the maintenance of labour, and consequently but little to the happiness of the greatest part of society. In the natural progress of a state towards riches, manufactures, and foreign commerce, would follow, in their order, the high cultivation of the soil. In Europe, this natural order of things has been inverted; and the soil has been cultivated from the redundancy of manufacturing capital, instead of manufactures rising from the redundancy of capital employed upon land. The superior encouragement that has been given to the industry of the towns, and the consequent higher price that is paid for the labour of artificers, than for the labour of those employed in husbandry, are probably the reasons why so much soil in Europe remains uncultivated. Had a different policy been pursued throughout Europe, it might undoubtedly have been much more populous than at present, and yet not be more encumbered by its population.

I cannot quit this curious subject of the difficulty arising from population, a subject, that appears to me, to deserve a minute investigation, and able discussion, much beyond my power to give it, without taking notice of an extraordinary passage in Dr Price's two volumes of *Observations*. Having given some tables on the probabilities of life, in towns and in the country, he says,* 'From this comparison, it appears, with how much truth great cities have been called the graves of mankind. It must also convince all who will consider it, that according to the observation, at the end of the fourth essay, in the former volume, it is by no means strictly proper to consider our diseases as the original intention of nature. They are, without doubt, in general our own creation. *Were there a country where the inhabitants led lives entirely natural and virtuous, few of them would die without measuring out the whole period of present existence allotted to them; pain and distemper would be unknown among them, and death would come upon them like a sleep, in consequence of no other cause than gradual and unavoidable decay.*'

I own, that I felt myself obliged to draw a very opposite conclusion from the facts advanced in Dr Price's two volumes. I had for some time been aware, that population and food, increased in different ratios; and a vague opinion had been floating in my mind, that they could only be kept equal by some species of misery or vice; but the perusal of Dr Price's two volumes of *Observations,* after that opinion had been conceived, raised it at once to conviction. With so many facts in his

* Price, *Observations,* ii, p. 243.

view, to prove the extraordinary rapidity with which population increases, when unchecked; and with such a body of evidence before him, to elucidate even the manner by which the general laws of nature repress a redundant population; it is perfectly inconceivable to me, how he could write the passage that I have quoted. He was a strenuous advocate for early marriages, as the best preservative against vicious manners. He had no fanciful conceptions about the extinction of the passion between the sexes, like Mr Godwin, nor did he ever think of eluding the difficulty in the ways hinted at by Mr Condorcet. He frequently talks of giving the prolific powers of nature room to exert themselves. Yet with these ideas, that his understanding could escape from the obvious and necessary inference, that an unchecked population would increase, beyond comparison, faster than the earth, by the best directed exertions of man, could produce food for its support, appears to me as astonishing, as if he had resisted the conclusion of one of the plainest propositions of Euclid.

Dr Price, speaking of the different stages of the civilized state, says, 'The first, or simple stages of civilization, are those which favour most the increase and the happiness of mankind.' He then instances the American colonies, as being at that time in the first, and happiest of the states, that he had described; and as affording a very striking proof of the effects of the different stages of civilization on population. But he does not seem to be aware, that the happiness of the Americans, depended much less upon their peculiar degree of civilization, than upon the peculiarity of their situation as new colonies, upon their having a great plenty of fertile uncultivated land. In parts of Norway, Denmark, or Sweden, or in this country, two or three hundred years ago, he might have found perhaps nearly the same degree of civilization; but by no means the same happiness, or the same increase of population. He quotes himself a statute of Henry VIII,[101] complaining of the decay of tillage, and the enhanced price of provisions, 'whereby a marvellous number of people were rendered incapable of maintaining themselves and families.' The superior degree of civil liberty which prevailed in America, contributed, without doubt, its share, to promote the industry, happiness, and population of these states: but even civil liberty, all powerful as it is, will not create fresh land. The Americans may be said, perhaps, to enjoy a greater degree of civil liberty, now they are an independent people, than while they were in subjection to England; but we may be perfectly sure, that population will not long continue to increase with the same rapidity as it did then.

A person who contemplated the happy state of the lower classes of people in America twenty years ago, would naturally wish to retain them for ever in that state; and might think, perhaps, that by preventing the introduction of manufactures and luxury, he might effect his purpose: but he might as reasonably expect to prevent a wife or mistress from growing old by never exposing her to the sun or air. The situation of new colonies, well governed, is a bloom of youth that no efforts can arrest. There are, indeed, many modes of treatment in the political, as well as animal body, that contribute to accelerate or retard the approaches of age: but there can be no chance of success, in any mode that could be devised, for keeping either of them in perpetual youth. By encouraging the industry of the towns more than the industry of the country, Europe may be said, perhaps, to have brought on a premature old age. A different policy in this respect, would infuse fresh life and vigour into every state. While from the law of primogeniture, and other European customs, land bears a monopoly price, a capital can never be employed in it with much advantage to the individual; and, therefore, it is not probable that the soil should be properly cultivated. And, though in every civilized state, a class of proprietors and a class of labourers must exist; yet one permanent advantage would always result from a nearer equalization of property. The greater the number of proprietors, the smaller must be the number of labourers: a greater part of society would be in the happy state of possessing property; and a smaller part in the unhappy state of possessing no other property than their labour. But the best directed exertions, though they may alleviate, can never remove the pressure of want; and it will be difficult for any person who contemplates the genuine situation of man on earth, and the general

laws of nature, to suppose it possible that any, the most enlightened efforts, could place mankind in a state where 'few would
die without measuring out the whole period of present existence allotted to them; where pain and distemper would be
unknown among them; and death would come upon them like
a sleep, in consequence of no other cause than gradual and
unavoidable decay.'

It is, undoubtedly, a most disheartening reflection, that the
great obstacle in the way to any extraordinary improvement in
society, is of a nature that we can never hope to overcome. The
perpetual tendency in the race of man to increase beyond the
means of subsistence, is one of the general laws of animated
nature, which we can have no reason to expect will change.
Yet, discouraging as the contemplation of this difficulty must
be, to those whose exertions are laudably directed to the
improvement of the human species, it is evident, that no possible good can arise from any endeavours to slur it over, or
keep it in the background. On the contrary, the most baleful
mischiefs may be expected from the unmanly conduct of not
daring to face truth, because it is unpleasing. Independently of
what relates to this great obstacle, sufficient yet remains to be
done for mankind, to animate us to the most unremitted exertion. But if we proceed without a thorough knowledge, and
accurate comprehension of the nature, extent, and magnitude,
of the difficulties we have to encounter, or if we unwisely direct
our efforts towards an object, in which we cannot hope for success; we shall not only exhaust our strength in fruitless
exertions, and remain at as great a distance as ever from the
summit of our wishes; but we shall be perpetually crushed by
the recoil of this rock of Sisyphus.[102]

The constant pressure of distress on man, from the principle of population, seems to direct our hopes to the future – State of trial inconsistent with our ideas of the foreknowledge of God – The world, probably, a mighty process for awakening matter into mind – Theory of the formation of mind – Excitements from the wants of the body – Excitements from the operation of general laws – Excitements from the difficulties of life arising from the principle of population.

The view of human life, which results from the contemplation of the constant pressure of distress on man from the difficulty of subsistence, by showing the little expectation that he can reasonably entertain of perfectibility on earth, seems strongly to point his hopes to the future. And the temptations to which he must necessarily be exposed, from the operation of those laws of nature which we have been examining, would seem to represent the world, in the light in which it has been frequently considered, as a state of trial, and school of virtue, preparatory to a superior state of happiness. But I hope I shall be pardoned, if I attempt to give a view in some degree different of the situation of man on earth, which appears to me, to be more consistent with the various phenomena of nature which we observe around us, and more consonant to our ideas of the power, goodness, and foreknowledge of the Deity.

It cannot be considered as an unimproving exercise of the human mind to endeavour to 'vindicate the ways of God to man',[104] if we proceed with a proper distrust of our own understandings, and a just sense of our insufficiency to comprehend the reason of all that we see; if we hail every ray of light with gratitude; and when no light appears, think that the darkness is from within, and not from without; and bow with humble deference to the supreme wisdom of him, whose 'thoughts are above our thoughts ... as the heavens are high above the earth.'[105]

In all our feeble attempts, however, to 'find out the Almighty to perfection',[106] it seems absolutely necessary, that we should reason from nature up to nature's God, and not presume to reason from God to nature.[107] The moment we allow ourselves to ask why some things are not otherwise, instead of endeavouring to account for them, as they are, we shall never know where to stop; we shall be led into the grossest, and most childish absurdities; all progress in the knowledge of the ways of providence must necessarily be at an end; and the study will even cease to be an improving exercise of the human mind. Infinite power is so vast and incomprehensible an idea, that the mind of man must necessarily be bewildered in the contemplation of it. With the crude and puerile conceptions which we sometimes form of this attribute of the Deity, we might imagine that God could call into being myriads, and myriads of existences; all free from pain and imperfection; all eminent in goodness and wisdom; all capable of the highest enjoyments; and unnumbered as the points throughout infinite space. But when from these vain and extravagant dreams of fancy, we turn our eyes to the book of nature, where alone we can read God as he is, we see a constant succession of sentient beings, rising apparently from so many specks of matter, going through a long and sometimes painful process in this world; but many of them attaining, ere the termination of it, such high qualities and powers, as seem to indicate their fitness for some superior state. Ought we not then to correct our crude and puerile ideas of infinite power from the contemplation of what we actually see existing? Can we judge of the Creator but from his creation? And, unless we wish to exalt the power of God at the expense of his goodness, ought we not to conclude, that even to the great Creator, almighty as he is, a certain process may be necessary, a certain time (or at least what appears to us as time) may be requisite, in order to form beings with those exalted qualities of mind which will fit them for his high purposes?

A state of trial seems to imply a previously formed existence, that does not agree with the appearance of man in infancy, and indicates something like suspicion and want of foreknowledge, inconsistent with those ideas which we wish to cherish of the supreme Being. I should be inclined, therefore, as I have hinted before in a note, to consider the world, and this life, as the mighty process of God, not for the trial, but for the creation and formation of mind; a process necessary, to awaken inert, chaotic matter, into spirit; to sublimate the dust of the earth into soul; to elicit an ethereal spark from the clod of clay. And in this view of the subject, the various impression and excitements which man receives through life, may be considered as the forming hand of his Creator, acting by general laws, and awakening his sluggish existence, by the animating touches of the Divinity, into a capacity of superior enjoyment. The original sin of man, is the torpor and corruption of the chaotic matter, in which he may be said to be born.

It could answer no good purpose to enter into the question, whether mind be a distinct substance from matter, or only a finer form of it. The question is, perhaps, after all, a question merely of words. Mind is as essentially mind, whether formed from matter, or any other substance. We know, from experience, that soul and body are most intimately united; and every appearance seems to indicate, that they grow from infancy together. It would be a supposition attended with very little probability, to believe that a complete and full-formed spirit existed in every infant; but that it was clogged and impeded in its operations, during the first twenty years of life, by the weakness, or hebetude,[108] of the organs in which it was enclosed. As we shall all be disposed to agree, that God is the creator of mind as well as of body; and as they both seem to be forming and unfolding themselves at the same time; it cannot appear inconsistent either with reason or revelation, if it appear to be consistent with the phenomena of nature, to suppose that God is constantly occupied in forming mind out of matter, and that the various impressions that man receives through life, is the process for that purpose. The employment is surely worthy of the highest attributes of the Deity.

This view of the state of man on earth will not seem to be unattended with probability, if, judging from the little experience we have of the nature of mind, it shall appear, upon investigation, that the phenomena around us, and the various events of human life, seem peculiarly calculated to promote this great end: and especially, if, upon this supposition, we can account, even to our own narrow understandings, for many of those roughnesses and inequalities in life, which querulous man too frequently makes the subject of his complaint against the God of nature.

The first great awakeners of the mind seem to be the wants of the body.* They are the first stimulants that rouse the brain of infant man into sentient activity; and such seems to be the sluggishness of original matter, that unless, by a peculiar course of excitements, other wants, equally powerful, are generated, these stimulants seem, even afterwards, to be necessary, to continue that activity which they first awakened. The savage would slumber for ever under his tree, unless he were roused from his torpor by the cravings of hunger, or the pinchings of cold; and the exertions that he makes to avoid these evils, by procuring food, and building himself a covering, are the exercises which form and keep in motion his faculties, which otherwise would sink into listless inactivity. From all that experience has taught us concerning the structure of the human mind, if those stimulants to exertion, which arise from the wants of the body, were removed from the mass of mankind, we have much more reason to think, that they would be sunk to the level of brutes, from a deficiency of excitements, than that they would be raised to the rank of philosophers by the possession of leisure. In those countries, where nature is the most redundant in spontaneous produce, the inhabitants will not be found the most remarkable for acuteness of intellect. Necessity has been with

---

* It was my intention to have entered at some length into this subject, as a kind of second part to the essay. A long interruption, from particular business, has obliged me to lay aside this intention, at least for the present. I shall now, therefore, only give a sketch of a few of the leading circumstances that appear to me to favour the general supposition that I have advanced.

great truth called the mother of invention.[109] Some of the noblest exertions of the human mind have been set in motion by the necessity of satisfying the wants of the body. Want has not infrequently given wings to the imagination of the poet; pointed the flowering periods of the historian; and added acuteness to the researches of the philosopher; and though there are undoubtedly many minds at present, so far improved by the various excitements of knowledge, or of social sympathy, that they would not relapse into listlessness, if their bodily stimulants were removed; yet, it can scarcely be doubted, that these stimulants could not be withdrawn from the mass of mankind, without producing a general and fatal torpor, destructive of all the germs of future improvement.

Locke, if I recollect, says, that the endeavour to avoid pain, rather than the pursuit of pleasure, is the great stimulus to action in life:[110] and that in looking to any particular pleasure, we shall not be roused into action in order to obtain it, till the contemplation of it has continued so long, as to amount to a sensation of pain or uneasiness under the absence of it. To avoid evil, and to pursue good, seem to be the great duty and business of man; and this world appears to be peculiarly calculated to afford opportunity of the most unremitted exertion of this kind: and it is by this exertion, by these stimulants, that mind is formed. If Locke's idea be just, and there is great reason to think that it is, evil seems to be necessary to create exertion; and exertion seems evidently necessary to create mind.

The necessity of food for the support of life, gives rise, probably, to a greater quantity of exertion, than any other want, bodily or mental. The supreme Being has ordained, that the earth shall not produce food in great quantities, till much preparatory labour and ingenuity has been exercised upon its surface. There is no conceivable connection to our comprehensions, between the seed, and the plant, or tree, that rises from it. The supreme Creator might, undoubtedly, raise up plants of all kinds, for the use of his creatures, without the assistance of those little bits of matter, which we call seed, or even without the assisting labour and attention of man. The processes of ploughing and clearing the ground, of collecting and sowing seeds, are not surely for the assistance of God in his creation; but are made previously necessary to the enjoyment of the blessings of life, in order to rouse man into action, and form his mind to reason.

To furnish the most unremitted excitements of this kind, and to urge man to further the gracious designs of providence, by the full cultivation of the earth, it has been ordained, that population should increase much faster than food. This general law (as it has appeared in the former parts of this essay) undoubtedly produces much partial evil; but a little reflection may, perhaps, satisfy us, that it produces a great overbalance of good. Strong excitements seem necessary to create exertion; and to direct this exertion, and form the reasoning faculty, it seems absolutely necessary, that the supreme Being should act always according to general laws. The constancy of the laws of nature, or the certainty, with which we may expect the same effect, from the same causes, is the foundation of the faculty of reason. If in the ordinary course of things, the finger of God were frequently visible; or to speak more correctly, if God were frequently to change his purpose (for the finger of God is, indeed, visible in every blade of grass that we see) a general and fatal torpor of the human faculties would probably ensue; even the bodily wants of mankind would cease to stimulate them to exertion, could they not reasonably expect, that if their efforts were well directed, they would be crowned with success. The constancy of the laws of nature, is the foundation of the industry and foresight of the husbandman; the indefatigable ingenuity of the artificer; the skilful researches of the physician, and anatomist; and the watchful observation, and patient investigation, of the natural philosopher. To this constancy, we owe all the greatest, and noblest efforts of intellect. To this constancy, we owe the immortal mind of a Newton.

As the reasons, therefore, for the constancy of the laws of nature, seem, even to our understandings, obvious and striking; if we return to the principle of population, and consider man as he really is, inert, sluggish, and averse from labour, unless compelled by necessity (and it is surely the height of folly to talk of man, according to our crude fancies, of what he might be), we may pronounce, with certainty, that the world would not have been peopled, but for the superiority of the power of population to the means of subsistence. Strong, and constantly operative as this stimulus is on man, to urge him to the cultivation of the earth; if we still see that cultivation proceeds very slowly, we may fairly conclude, that a less stimulus would have been insufficient. Even under the operation of this constant excitement, savages will inhabit countries of the greatest natural fertility, for a long period, before they betake themselves to pasturage or agriculture. Had population and food increased in the same ratio, it is probable that man might never have emerged from the savage state. But supposing the earth once well peopled, an Alexander, a Julius Caesar, a Tamerlane, or a bloody revolution, might irrecoverably thin the human race, and defeat the great designs of the Creator. The ravages of a contagious disorder would be felt for ages; and an earthquake might unpeople a region for ever. The principle, according to which population increases, prevents the vices of mankind, or the accidents of nature, the partial evils arising from general laws, from obstructing the high purpose of the creation. It keeps the inhabitants of the earth always fully up to the level of the means of subsistence; and is constantly acting upon man as a powerful stimulus, urging him to the further cultivation of the earth, and to enable it, consequently, to support a more extended population. But it is impossible that this law can operate, and produce the effects apparently intended by the supreme Being, without occasioning partial evil. Unless the principle of population were to be altered, according to the circumstances of each separate country (which would not only be contrary to our universal experience, with regard to the laws of nature, but would contradict even our own reason, which sees the absolute necessity of general laws, for the formation of intellect), it is evident, that the same principle, which, seconded by industry, will people a fertile region in a few years, must produce distress in countries that have been long inhabited.

It seems, however, every way probable, that even the acknowledged difficulties occasioned by the law of population, tend rather to promote, than impede the general purpose of providence. They excite universal exertion, and contribute to that infinite variety of situations, and consequently of impressions, which seems, upon the whole, favourable to the growth of mind. It is probable, that too great, or too little excitement, extreme poverty, or too great riches, may be alike unfavourable in this respect. The middle regions of society seem to be best suited to intellectual improvement; but it is contrary to the analogy of all nature, to expect that the whole of society can be a middle region. The temperate zones of the earth, seem to be the most favourable to the mental, and corporeal energies of man; but all cannot be temperate zones. A world, warmed and enlightened but by one sun, must, from the laws of matter, have some parts chilled by perpetual frosts, and others scorched by perpetual heats. Every piece of matter lying on a surface, must have an upper, and an under side: all the particles cannot be in the middle. The most valuable parts of an oak, to a timber merchant, are not either the roots, or the branches; but these are absolutely necessary to the existence of the middle part, or stem, which is the object in request. The timber merchant could not possibly expect to make an oak grow without roots or branches; but if he could find out a mode of cultivation, which would cause more of the substance to go to stem, and less to root and branch, he would be right to exert himself in bringing such a system into general use.[111]

In the same manner, though we cannot possibly expect to exclude riches, and poverty, from society; yet if we could find out a mode of government, by which, the numbers in the extreme regions would be lessened, and the numbers in the middle regions increased, it would be undoubtedly our duty to adopt it.[112] It is not, however, improbable, that as in the oak, the roots and branches could not be diminished very greatly, without weakening the vigorous circulation of the sap in the stem; so in society, the extreme parts could not be diminished beyond a certain degree, without lessening that animated exertion throughout the middle parts, which is the very cause, that they are the most favourable to the growth of intellect. If no man could hope to rise, or fear to fall, in society; if industry did not bring with it its reward, and idleness its punishment, the middle parts would not certainly be what they now are. In reasoning upon this subject, it is evident, that we ought to consider chiefly the mass of mankind, and not individual instances. There are undoubtedly many minds, and there ought to be many, according to the chances, out of so great a mass, that, having been vivified early, by a peculiar course of excitements, would not need the constant action of narrow motives, to continue them in activity. But if we were to review the various useful discoveries, the valuable writings, and other laudable exertions of mankind, I believe we should find, that more were to be attributed to the narrow motives that operate upon the many, than to the apparently more enlarged motives that operate upon the few.

Leisure is, without doubt, highly valuable to man; but taking man, as he is, the probability seems to be, that in the greater number of instances, it will produce evil rather than good. It has been not infrequently remarked, that talents are more common among younger brothers, than among elder brothers; but it can scarcely be imagined, that younger brothers are, upon an average, born with a greater original susceptibility of parts.[113] The difference, if there really is any observable difference, can only arise from their different situations. Exertion and activity, are in general absolutely necessary in the one case, and are only optional in the other.

That the difficulties of life, contribute to generate talents, every day's experience must convince us. The exertions that men find it necessary to make, in order to support themselves or families, frequently awaken faculties, that might otherwise have lain for ever dormant: and it has been commonly remarked, that new and extraordinary situations generally create minds adequate to grapple with the difficulties in which they are involved.

NINETEEN

*The sorrows of life necessary to soften and humanize the heart –
The excitements of social sympathy often produce characters of
a higher order than the mere possessors of talents – Moral evil
probably necessary to the production of moral excellence –
Excitements from intellectual wants continually kept up by the
infinite variety of nature, and the obscurity that involves metaphysical subjects – The difficulties in revelation to be accounted
for upon this principle – The degree of evidence which the scriptures contain, probably, best suited to the improvement of the
human faculties, and the moral amelioration of mankind – The
idea that mind is created by excitements, seems to account for
the existence of natural and moral evil.*

The sorrows and distresses of life form another class of excitements, which seem to be necessary, by a peculiar train of
impressions, to soften and humanize the heart, to awaken
social sympathy, to generate all the Christian virtues, and to
afford scope for the ample exertion of benevolence. The general tendency of an uniform course of prosperity is, rather to
degrade, than exalt the character. The heart that has never
known sorrow itself, will seldom be feelingly alive, to the pains
and pleasures, the wants and wishes, of its fellow beings. It will
seldom be overflowing with that warmth of brotherly love,
those kind and amiable affections, which dignify the human
character, even more than the possession of the highest talents.
Talents, indeed, though undoubtedly a very prominent and fine
feature of mind, can by no means be considered as constituting
the whole of it. There are many minds which have not been
exposed to those excitements, that usually form talents, that
have yet been vivified to a high degree, by the excitements of

social sympathy. In every rank of life, in the lowest, as frequently as in the highest, characters are to be found, overflowing with the milk of human kindness, breathing love towards God and man; and though without those peculiar powers of mind called talents, evidently holding a higher rank in the scale of beings, than many who possess them. Evangelical charity, meekness, piety, and all that class of virtues, distinguished particularly by the name of Christian virtues, do not seem necessarily to include abilities; yet a soul possessed of these amiable qualities, a soul awakened and vivified by these delightful sympathies, seems to hold a nearer commerce with the skies, than mere acuteness of intellect.

The greatest talents have been frequently misapplied, and have produced evil proportionate to the extent of their powers. Both reason and revelation seem to assure us, that such minds will be condemned to eternal death; but while on earth, these vicious instruments performed their part in the great mass of impressions, by the disgust and abhorrence which they excited. It seems highly probable, that moral evil is absolutely necessary to the production of moral excellence. A being with only good placed in view, may be justly said to be impelled by a blind necessity. The pursuit of good in this case, can be no indication of virtuous propensities. It might be said, perhaps, that infinite wisdom, cannot want such an indication as outward action, but would foreknow, with certainty, whether the being would choose good or evil. This might be a plausible argument against a state of trial; but will not hold against the supposition, that mind in this world is in a state of formation. Upon this idea, the being that has seen moral evil, and has felt disapprobation and disgust at it, is essentially different from the being that has seen only good. They are pieces of clay that have received distinct impressions; they must, therefore, necessarily be in different shapes; or, even if we allow them both to have the same lovely form of virtue, it must be acknowledged, that one has undergone the further process, necessary to give firmness and durability to its substance; while the other is still exposed to injury, and liable to be broken by every accidental impulse. An ardent love and admiration of virtue seems to imply the existence of something opposite to it; and it seems highly probable, that the same beauty of form and substance, the same perfection of character, could not be generated, without the impressions of disapprobation which arise from the spectacle of moral evil.

When the mind has been awakened into activity by the passions, and the wants of the body, intellectual wants arise; and the desire of knowledge, and the impatience under ignorance, form a new and important class of excitements. Every part of nature seems peculiarly calculated to furnish stimulants to mental exertion of this kind, and to offer inexhaustible food for the most unremitted inquiry. Our immortal bard says of Cleopatra,

'Custom cannot stale
Her infinite variety.'[114]

The expression, when applied to any one object, may be considered as a poetical amplification, but it is accurately true when applied to nature. Infinite variety, seems, indeed, eminently her characteristic feature. The shades that are here and there blended in the picture, give spirit, life, and prominence to her exuberant beauties; and those roughnesses and inequalities, those inferior parts that support the superior, though they sometimes offend the fastidious microscopic eye of short-sighted man, contribute to the symmetry, grace, and fair proportion of the whole.

The infinite variety of the forms and operations of nature, besides tending immediately to awaken and improve the mind by the variety of impressions that it creates, opens other fertile sources of improvement, by offering so wide and extensive a field for investigation and research. Uniform, undiversified perfection, could not possess the same awakening powers. When we endeavour then to contemplate the system of the universe; when we think of the stars as the suns of other systems, scattered throughout infinite space; when we reflect, that we do not probably see a millionth part of those bright orbs, that are beaming light and life to unnumbered worlds; when our minds, unable to grasp the immeasurable conception, sink, lost and confounded, in admiration at the mighty incomprehensible power of the Creator; let us not querulously complain that all climates are not equally genial; that perpetual spring does not reign throughout the year; that all God's creatures do not possess the same advantages; that clouds and tempests sometimes darken the natural world, and vice and misery, the moral world; and that all the works of the creation are not formed with equal perfection. Both reason and experience seem to indicate to us, that the infinite variety of nature (and variety cannot exist without inferior parts, or apparent blemishes) is admirably adapted to further the high purpose of the creation, and to produce the greatest possible quantity of good.

The obscurity that involves all metaphysical subjects, appears to me, in the same manner peculiarly calculated, to add to that class of excitements which arise from the thirst of knowledge. It is probable that man, while on earth, will never be able to attain complete satisfaction on these subjects; but this is by no means a reason that he should not engage in them. The darkness that surrounds these interesting topics of human curiosity, may be intended to furnish endless motives to intellectual activity and exertion. The constant effort to dispel this darkness, even if it fail of success, invigorates and improves the thinking faculty. If the subjects of human inquiry were once exhausted, mind would probably stagnate; but the infinitely diversified forms and operations of nature, together with the endless food for speculation which metaphysical subjects offer, prevent the possibility that such a period should ever arrive.

It is by no means one of the wisest sayings of Solomon, that 'there is no new thing under the sun.'[115] On the contrary, it is probable, that were the present system to continue for millions of years, continual additions would be making to the mass of human knowledge; and yet, perhaps, it may be a matter of doubt, whether, what may be called the capacity of mind, be in any marked and decided manner increasing. A Socrates, a Plato, or an Aristotle, however confessedly inferior in knowledge to the philosophers of the present day, do not appear to have been much below them in intellectual capacity. Intellect rises from a speck, continues in vigour only for a certain period, and will not, perhaps, admit, while on earth, of above a certain number of impressions. These impressions may, indeed, be infinitely modified, and from these various modifications, added probably to a difference in the susceptibility of the original germs,* arise the endless diversity of character that we see in the world; but reason and experience seem both to assure us, that the capacity of individual minds does not increase in proportion to the mass of existing knowledge. The finest minds seem to be formed rather by efforts at original thinking, by endeavours to form new combinations, and to discover new truths, than by passively receiving the impressions of other men's ideas. Could we suppose the period arrived, when there was no further hope of future discoveries; and the only employment of mind was to acquire pre-existing knowledge, without any efforts to form new and original combinations; though the mass of human knowledge were a thousand times greater than it is at present; yet it is evident that one of the noblest stimulants to mental exertion would have ceased; the finest feature of intellect would be lost; everything allied to genius would be at an end; and it appears to be impossible, that, under such circumstances, any individuals could possess the same intellectual energies, as were possessed by a Locke, a Newton, or a Shakespeare, or even by a Socrates, a Plato, an Aristotle, or a Homer.

If a revelation from heaven, of which no person could feel the smallest doubt, were to dispel the mists that now hang over metaphysical subjects; were to explain the nature and structure of mind, the affections and essences of all substances, the mode in which the supreme Being operates in the works of the creation, and the whole plan and scheme of the universe; such an accession of knowledge, so obtained, instead of giving

---

* It is probable that no two grains of wheat are exactly alike. Soil undoubtedly makes the principal difference in the blades that spring up; but probably not all. It seems natural to suppose some sort of difference in the original germs that are afterwards awakened into thought; and the extraordinary difference of susceptibility in very young children seems to confirm the supposition.

additional vigour and activity to the human mind, would, in all probability, tend to repress future exertion, and to damp the soaring wings of intellect.

For this reason I have never considered the doubts and difficulties that involve some parts of the sacred writings, as any argument against their divine original. The supreme Being might, undoubtedly, have accompanied his revelations to man by such a succession of miracles, and of such a nature, as would have produced universal overpowering conviction, and have put an end at once to all hesitation and discussion. But weak as our reason is to comprehend the plans of the great Creator, it is yet sufficiently strong, to see the most striking objections to such a revelation. From the little we know of the structure of the human understanding, we must be convinced, that an overpowering conviction of this kind, instead of tending to the improvement and moral amelioration of man, would act like the touch of a torpedo[116] on all intellectual exertion, and would almost put an end to the existence of virtue. If the scriptural denunciations of eternal punishment were brought home with the same certainty to every man's mind, as that the night will follow the day, this one vast and gloomy idea would take such full possession of the human faculties, as to leave no room for any other conceptions; the external actions of men would be all nearly alike; virtuous conduct would be no indication of virtuous disposition; vice and virtue would be blended together in one common mass; and, though the all-seeing eye of God might distinguish them, they must necessarily make the same impressions on man, who can judge only from external appearances. Under such a dispensation, it is difficult to conceive how human beings could be formed to a detestation of moral evil, and a love and admiration of God, and of moral excellence.

Our ideas of virtue and vice are not, perhaps, very accurate and well defined; but few, I think, would call an action really virtuous, which was performed simply and solely from the dread of a very great punishment, or the expectation of a very great reward. The fear of the Lord is very justly said to be the beginning of wisdom; but the end of wisdom is the love of the Lord, and the admiration of moral good. The denunciations of future punishment, contained in the scriptures, seem to be well calculated to arrest the progress of the vicious, and awaken the attention of the careless; but we see, from repeated experience, that they are not accompanied with evidence of such a nature, as to overpower the human will, and to make men lead virtuous lives with vicious dispositions, merely from a dread of hereafter. A genuine faith, by which I mean, a faith that shows itself in all the virtues of a truly Christian life, may generally be considered as an indication of an amiable and virtuous disposition, operated upon more by love than by pure unmixed fear.

When we reflect on the temptations to which man must necessarily be exposed in this world, from the structure of his frame, and the operation of the laws of nature; and the consequent moral certainty, that many vessels will come out of this mighty creative furnace in wrong shapes; it is perfectly impossible to conceive, that any of these creatures of God's hand can be condemned to eternal suffering. Could we once admit such an idea, all our natural conceptions of goodness and justice would be completely overthrown; and we could no longer look up to God as a merciful and righteous Being. But the doctrine of life and immortality which was brought to light by the gospel, the doctrine that the end of righteousness is everlasting life, but that the wages of sin are death, is in every respect just and merciful, and worthy of the great Creator. Nothing can appear more consonant to our reason, than that those beings which come out of the creative process of the world in lovely and beautiful forms, should be crowned with immortality; while those which come out misshapen, those whose minds are not suited to a purer and happier state of existence, should perish, and be condemned to mix again with their original clay. Eternal condemnation of this kind may be considered as a species of eternal punishment; and it is not wonderful that it should be represented, sometimes, under images of suffering. But life and death, salvation and destruction, are more frequently opposed to each other in the New Testament, than happiness and misery. The supreme Being would appear to us in a very different view, if we were to consider him as pursuing the creatures that had offended him with eternal hate and torture, instead of merely condemning to their original insensibility those beings, that, by the operation of general laws, had not been formed with qualities suited to a purer state of happiness.

Life is, generally speaking, a blessing independent of a future state. It is a gift which the vicious would not always be ready to throw away, even if they had no fear of death. The partial pain, therefore, that is inflicted by the supreme Creator, while he is forming numberless beings to a capacity of the highest enjoyments, is but as the dust of the balance in comparison of the happiness that is communicated; and we have every reason to think, that there is no more evil in the world, than what is absolutely necessary as one of the ingredients in the mighty process.

The striking necessity of general laws for the formation of intellect, will not in any respect be contradicted by one or two exceptions; and these evidently not intended for partial purposes, but calculated to operate upon a great part of mankind, and through many ages. Upon the idea that I have given of the formation of mind, the infringement of the general laws of nature, by a divine revelation, will appear in the light of the immediate hand of God mixing new ingredients in the mighty mass, suited to the particular state of the process, and calculated to give rise to a new and powerful train of impressions, tending to purify, exalt, and improve the human mind. The miracles that accompanied these revelations when they had once excited the attention of mankind, and rendered it a matter of most interesting discussion, whether the doctrine was from God or man, had performed their part, had answered the purpose of the Creator; and these communications of the divine will were afterwards left to make their way by their own intrinsic excellence; and by operating as moral motives, gradually to influence and improve, and not to overpower and stagnate the faculties of man.

It would be, undoubtedly, presumptuous to say, that the supreme Being could not possibly have effected his purpose in any other way than that which he has chosen; but as the revelation of the divine will, which we possess, is attended with some doubts and difficulties; and as our reason points out to us the strongest objections to a revelation, which would force immediate, implicit, universal belief; we have surely just cause to think that these doubts and difficulties are no argument against the divine origin of the scriptures; and that the species of evidence which they possess is best suited to the improvement of the human faculties, and the moral amelioration of mankind.

The idea that the impressions and excitements of this world are the instruments with which the supreme Being forms matter into mind; and that the necessity of constant exertion to avoid evil, and to pursue good, is the principal spring of these impressions and excitements, seems to smooth many of the difficulties that occur in a contemplation of human life; and appears to me, to give a satisfactory reason for the existence of natural and moral evil; and, consequently, for that part of both, and it certainly is not a very small part, which arises from the principle of population. But, though upon this supposition, it seems highly improbable, that evil should ever be removed from the world; yet it is evident, that this impression would not answer the apparent purpose of the Creator; it would not act so powerfully as an excitement to exertion, if the quantity of it did not diminish or increase, with the activity or the indolence of man. The continual variations in the weight, and in the distribution of this pressure, keep alive a constant expectation of throwing it off.

> 'Hope springs eternal in the human breast,
> Man never is, but always to be blest.'[117]

Evil exists in the world, not to create despair, but activity. We are not patiently to submit to it, but to exert ourselves to avoid it. It is not only the interest, but the duty of every individual, to use his utmost efforts to remove evil from himself, and from as large a circle as he can influence; and the more he exercises himself in this duty, the more wisely he directs his efforts, and the more successful these efforts are; the more he will probably improve and exalt his own mind, and the more completely does he appear to fulfil the will of his Creator.

THE TRAVEL DIARIES OF THOMAS ROBERT MALTHUS

The Scandinavian Journal

July 14. From Count Molk[1] after dinner I heard that when he first came to this government which was about 3 years ago, there were many discontents among the peasants, & much disposition towards the french; but that that spirit was nearly over now since they had heard that the lower classes of people in France had gained nothing by the revolution. They now rejoice at the victories of the English. There was at that time also a little difficulty about corn, & the people assembled in parties, & were not without some trouble, prevailed upon to disperse. He seems to have adopted always the most mild measures which he has constantly found to answer better than force. The people have now great confidence in him – He is Grand Bailiff of the government of Drontheim.[2]

He said that the popn had lately increased very considerably in his government, partly from their being fewer impediments to marriage from the military regulations. Cultivation also had been proceeding very rapidly – they had for some times had very fortunate years; but he was not without apprehensions that should a bad year come, the people in consequence of the increased popn would suffer most extremely. He has published a kind of proclamation to the farmers desiring that they would all keep a certain stock by them beyond their yearly consumption; & declaring that those who did not should receive no benefit from the publick stores in the event of a scarcity. It is supposed that in consequence of this proclamation most of the farmers have kept a stock by them which they were otherwise in the habit of selling to Sweden.[3]

From the remote situation of Drontheim it is extremely difficult to obtain relief in time by importation, in case of the failure of the crops; and the uncertainty of the climate renders a failure of the crops always possible, however flattering appearances may be. There are 3 nights at the end of august & beginning of september that are particularly dreaded, & I think he said were call'd the iron nights. These sometimes destroy at once the fairest promise. It is now however 15 years since there was an actual famine in the Drontheim government. The regular importation of corn into Drontheim is about 300,000 tuns. The population has greatly increased of late years; but the importation has not increased – a proof that cultivation is going rapidly forwards.

The people on the sea coast are the poorest & suffer the most. They in general marry very young & have large families which they hope to support by fishing, and in a bad year when the fisheries are unsuccessful they are reduced to extreme poverty. The people in the interior parts of the country seldom marry till they can get a place in which they can support a family, and this does not always happen while they are very young, particularly as they in general wish to be quite free with respect to the military before they settle themselves. More however have married early since it has not been necessary to obtain the permission of the officer, and Count Molk expressed some fears of the consequences. I have understood from 2 or 3 authorities that the country girls generally have sweethearts for a considerable time before they marry. A marriage seldom takes place but when a child is about to appear.

The Odels right which has been supposed with justice to impede the cultivation & population of Norway is not yet abolished – The term has been only shortened.[4]

At present if a farm has been sold, any lineal descendant of the original possessor (the eldest having always the prior right) may within ten years repurchase the farm, at the price which was paid for it. Formerly the period was 20 years. It was instituted at a time when there was emigration from Norway, & was meant to encourage those who had acquired property in other countries to return, & also to prevent an advantage being taken of the necessities of a farmer in a particular year, to buy a farm for little or nothing. The law has at present many advocates. Count Molk is not decidedly against it. I understand that 5 or 6 years ago there was an endeavour made by Government to obtain the sense of the people upon the subject of the abolition of it, & the event was that it was retained; but it was doubted whether the sense of the people was really for its being retained. As might be expected there were two parties – those who had bought estates, and the ancient possessors.

The total abolition of it is still talked of. It has occasioned more processes at law than any other subject of dispute whatever, & this is considered as one reason for its abolition. The commission of conciliation in every parish has very greatly contributed to put an end to these processes and indeed to most others, & it turns out to be a most useful institution. The lawyers have suffered by it, but they were in general considered as not a very honest race, & are not therefore much pitied.

The general law of Denmark & Norway with respect to succession is that the sons shall share equally, & have double the portion of the daughters. The reason that the farms in Norway have not been more divided is, that the population has increased very slowly till of late years; and that the eldest son has always the option of paying his brothers & sisters in money and reserving the estate, which he is generally able to do by mortgaging. Of late years however since the cultivation & population have been increasing it has been more the custom to divide the farm itself, which is the reason that we heard in our journey of many half farms & quarters of farms; but I understand now that there is no particular quantity of land which is call'd a complete farm.

The sons of housemen & small farmers generally go out to service, either in farms or with gentlemen, till they can get a houseman's place, which may enable them to marry. The Farmers sometimes, as we saw in our journey, have many unmarried servants.

The younger sons of farmers, when they have received their portions from their eldest brothers, either buy a part of a farm

with it, or lend it out to interest. The legal interest of money is
4 per cent on landed security & 5 per cent on bond.

July 15 [Monday]. A very rainy morning – passed most of it in
writing – Took a walk before dinner in the environs of the
town & saw some very fine crops of grass, & some extraordinary heavy crops of barley in full ear, laid by the wind of the
preceeding night. One field of grass was cutting. Apples ripen
at Drontheim; but not apricots, which we heard ripened pretty
well in Christiania.[5] There is not however upon the whole so
much difference in the climate as I expected, which perhaps
may arise from the greater proximity of Drontheim to the sea.

The Bay of Drontheim never freezes. The cold is not nearly so
great here as at Roraas,[6] which is further south. Last winter at
Roraas the mercury in the thermometer & Barometer froze naturally; but this intense frost lasted only 3 days, & in the northern
part of Norway it was generally considered as a mild winter, tho
they were in much apprehension on account of the small quantity of snow, that everything would be kill'd. They complain
much of the uncertainty of the weather in the summer – one day
perhaps may be excessively hot & the next quite cold – the transition is sometimes in the space of an hour. In winter the climate
is much more regular, & they have in general a clear sky.

July 16 [Tuesday]. A merchant to whom we had a letter call'd
upon us afterwards – he had been settled above 30 years at
Drontheim ... He said that since he had been here a very
marked change had taken place, & that the winters were much
less cold & the summers less warm than formerly. When he
first came the land round Drontheim was very little cultivated & almost entirely covered with woods. The road to
Christiania was quite impassable with any kind of carriage.
The cold is never so severe at Drontheim as in the interior of
the country – the lowest that he recollected the thermometer
last winter was 18, & the highest this summer 18; but sometimes they have it as high as 21. 300,000 shippunds of Copper
are exported at Drontheim from the mines of Roraas only.
Fish, wood & copper are the chief exports.

There are many grounds about the town planted to potatoes, & they have been much used by the common people within this last ten yrs. There is no wheat & not much rye sown; but barley & oats thrive very well. Rye is the chief corn imported. The most common food of the peasants is the oaten cake. Enough is in general grown in the country for its consumption, & it is seldom necessary to import much either of barley or oats.

July 17 [Wednesday]. The Count called upon us to shew us the publick institutions for the poor, & both the rooms and the people appeared to be very neat, tho there were rather too many crouded together in the same room. There is an hospital for the old & infirm; & a house of industry where any person may be employed & receive a proper price for his work. In the house of industry also, a certain number of young persons are instructed in weaving, making stockings, & are paid a dollar a week. The house of industry costs yearly about 800 or 1,000 dollars. The Count makes it a rule not to admit any person into the hospital for the old & infirm till they have done something, or at least tried to do something, in the house of industry for 2 years. All that we saw in the house of industry were employed in spinning, weaving & making stockings, & most of the old women in the hospital were spinning.

These establishments are supported chiefly by some large legacies which were left for the purpose, aided by voluntary contributions. The number of poor in Drontheim has in consequence of these establishments greatly increased. The popn of Drontheim is about 10,000 & it is said that 1,200 receive assistance. The institutions however seem to be very well inspected & great care seems to be taken not to admit any but real objects of charity into the hospital. The dress of the people in the hospital was neater than in the poor houses of England. We saw also a kind of house of correction where persons who had committed small offences were confined, & obliged to work. This house had been only established half a year – the count did not think it would answer, as they corrupted one another from being all in the same room, & he hoped to hit upon some better plan. He spoke of the prison at Philadelphia as an excellent institution.

In all parishes there are voluntary contributions for the poor – every person declares what sum he is willing to contribute yearly, and the funds are managed by persons appointed for that purpose. This seems to be a little upon the plan of the management of the poor in Scotland.

July 18 [Thursday]. I heard from Count Molke & another gentleman 2 extraordinary instances of the rapidity of vegetation in some spots, & in some years in this country. On a farm some way to the south of Drontheim a farmer had reaped two crops of barley in the same year; & a similar instance occurred last year on a farm 10 norway miles south of Drontheim. It is not uncommon for barley to be reaped 6 weeks after it was sown. Some of the vallies have a most fertile soil, & being shut out from all winds, retain the heat very much; & as the sun is so long above the horizon, & the thermometer during the short night often does not sink lower than 60, it may easily be imagined how rapid must be the vegetation when not interrupted by frosts.

AN INVESTIGATION OF
THE CAUSE OF THE
PRESENT HIGH PRICE
OF PROVISIONS

AN INVESTIGATION OF THE CAUSE OF THE PRESENT HIGH PRICE OF PROVISIONS

Among the many cause that have been assigned of the present high price of provisions, I am much inclined to suspect, that the principal one has hitherto escaped detection; at least, in the discussions on the subject, either in print or conversation, which have fallen within my knowledge, the cause, which I conceive to have operated most strongly towards increasing the price of the necessaries of life, has not yet been suggested. There are some disorders, which, though they scarcely admit of a cure, or even of any considerable mitigation, are still capable of being made greatly worse. In such misfortunes it is of great importance to know the desperate nature of the disease. The next step to the alleviation of pain, is the bearing it with composure, and not aggravating it by impatience and irritation.

It cannot admit of a doubt with persons of sense and information, that, during the last year, there was a scarcity, to a certain extent, of all sorts of grain; but it must be at the same time acknowledged, that the price was higher than the degree of that scarcity would at first sight appear to warrant.

In the summer of 1799, in the course of a northern tour, I passed through Sweden. There was at that time a general dearth of corn throughout the country, owing to a long drought the preceding year. In the province of Värmland, adjoining to Norway, it approached almost to a famine, and the lower classes of people suffered most severe distress. At the time we were passing through that part of the country, which was in July, they were reduced to two most miserable substitutes for bread; one, made of the inner bark of the fir, and the other, of the common sorrel dried, and powdered. These substances, though made into the usual shape of their rye bread, had no affinity to it whatever in taste, and but very little, I believe, in nourishment, as the effects of this miserable food were but too visible in their pallid and unhealthy countenances.

There could be little doubt, that the degree of scarcity then prevailing in that part of Sweden, was considerably greater than any we have hitherto experienced here; and yet, as far as we could learn, the price of rye, which is the grain principally used for bread, had not risen above double its usual average; whereas in this country last year, in a scarcity, that must be acknowledged to be very greatly inferior in degree, wheat rose to above three times its former price.

The continuation of extraordinary high prices, after a harvest that was at one time looked forward to as abundant, has contributed still more to astonish and perplex the public mind. Many men of sense have joined in the universal cry of the common people, that there must be roguery somewhere; and the general indignation has fallen upon monopolizers, forestallers, and regraters[1] – words, that are vented from every mouth with fearful execrations, and are applied indiscriminately to all middle men whatever, to every kind of trader that goes between the grower of the commodity and the consumer.

This popular clamour, headed by the Lord Chief Justice,[2] and enforced throughout the country by the instructions of the grand juries, must make every reflecting mind tremble for the future supply of our markets. I cannot but think therefore, that I should do an acceptable service, if I could succeed in accounting for the present high price of the necessaries of life, without criminating a class of men, who, I believe, have been accused unjustly, and who, every political economist must know, are absolutely necessary in the complicated machinery that distributes the provisions and other commodities of a large nation.

I ought first to premise, however, that I am not interested in this question, further than as a lover of truth, and a well-wisher to my country. I have no sort of connection whatever with any of these middle men or great farmers, who are now the objects of public indignation: and, as an individual with a small fixed income, I am certainly among that class of persons on whom the high price of provisions must fall the heaviest.

To proceed to the point: I am most strongly inclined to suspect, that the attempt in most parts of the kingdom to increase the parish allowances[3] in proportion to the price of corn, combined with the riches of the country, which have enabled it to proceed as far as it has done in this attempt, is, comparatively speaking, the sole cause, which has occasioned the price of provisions in this country to rise so much higher than the degree of scarcity would seem to warrant, so much higher than it would do in any other country where this cause did not operate.

It may appear, perhaps, at first, to the reader, that this cause is inadequate to the effect we experience; but, if he will kindly allow me a few minutes of patient and candid attention, I hope I shall be able to convince him, that it is not only adequate to produce the present high price of provisions of which we complain; but, admitting a real scarcity, that the attempt to carry it actually into execution, might raise the quartern loaf[4] before the expiration of a year, to as many shillings as it is now pence.

Adam Smith has most justly stated, that the actual price at which a commodity is sold, is compounded of its natural price, the price at which it can be brought to market, allowing the usual profit in times of moderate plenty, and the proportion of the supply to the demand.[5] When any commodity is scarce, its natural price is necessarily forgotten, and its actual price is regulated by the excess of the demand above the supply.

Let us suppose a commodity in great request by fifty people, but of which, from some failure in its production, there is only sufficient to supply forty. If the fortieth man from the top have two shillings which he can spend in this commodity, and the thirty nine above him, more, in various proportions, and the ten below, all less, the actual price of the article, according to the genuine principles of trade, will be two shillings. If more be asked, the whole will not be sold, because there are only forty who have as much as two shillings to spend in the article; and there is no reason for asking less, because the whole may be disposed of at that sum.

Let us suppose, now, that somebody gives the ten poor men, who were excluded, a shilling apiece. The whole fifty can now offer two shillings, the price which was before asked. According to every genuine principle of fair trading, the commodity must immediately rise. If it do not, I would ask, upon what principle are ten, out of the fifty who are all able to offer two shillings, to be rejected? For still, according to the supposition, there is only enough for forty. The two shillings of a poor man are just as good as the two shillings of a rich one; and, if we interfere to prevent the commodity from rising out of the reach of the poorest ten, whoever they may be, we must toss up, draw lots, raffle, or fight, to determine who are to be excluded. It would be beyond my present purpose, to enter into the question whether any of these modes would be more eligible, for the distribution of the commodities of a country, than the sordid distinction of money; but certainly, according to the customs of all civilized and enlightened nations, and according to every acknowledged principle of commercial dealing, the price must be allowed to rise to that point which will put it beyond the power of ten out of the fifty to purchase. This point will, perhaps, be half a crown or more, which will now become the price of the commodity. Let another shilling apiece be given to the excluded ten: all will now be able to offer half a crown. The price must in consequence immediately rise to three shillings or more, and so on *toties quoties*.[6]

In the progress of this operation the ten excluded would not be always entirely the same. The richest of the ten first excluded, would probably be raised above the poorest of the first forty. Small changes of this kind must take place. The additional allowances to the poorest, and the weight of the high prices on those above them, would tend to level the two orders; but, till a complete level had taken place, ten must be always excluded, and the price would always be fixed, as nearly as possible, at that sum which the fortieth man at the top could afford to give. This, if the donatives were continued, would raise the commodity to an extraordinary price, without the supposition of any combination and conspiracy among the vendors, or any kind of unfair dealing whatever.

The rise in the price of corn, and of other provisions, in this country, has been effected exactly in the same manner, though the operation may be a little more complicated; and I am firmly convinced, that it never could have reached its present height, but from the system of poor laws and parish allowances, which have operated precisely in the same mode as the donatives of a shilling in the instance I have just adduced.

The harvest of 1799 was bad, both in quality and quantity. Few people could deny that there appeared to be a very considerable deficiency of produce: and the price of the load[7] of wheat rose in consequence almost immediately to £20. I returned from the north in the beginning of November, and found the alarm so great and general, and the price of corn so high, that I remember thinking that it was probably fully adequate to the degree of the deficiency, and, taking into consideration the prospect of importation from the very early alarm, that it would not rise much higher during the year. In this conjecture, it appears that I was much mistaken; but I have very little doubt that in any other country equally rich, yet without the system of poor laws and parish allowances, the price would never have exceeded £25 the load of wheat; and that this sum would have been sufficiently high to have excluded such a number of people from their usual consumption, as to make the deficient crop, with the quantity imported, last throughout the year.

The system of poor laws, and parish allowances, in this country, and I will add, to their honour, the humanity and generosity of the higher and middle classes of society, naturally and necessarily altered this state of things. The poor complained to the justices[8] that their wages would not enable them to supply their families in the single article of bread. The justices very humanely, and I am far from saying improperly, listened to their complaints, inquired what was the smallest sum on which they could support their families, at the then price of wheat, and gave an order of relief on the parish accordingly. The poor were now enabled, for a short time, to purchase nearly their usual quantity of flour; but the stock in the country was not sufficient, even with the prospect of importation, to allow of the usual distribution to all its members. The crop was consuming too fast. Every market day the demand exceeded the supply; and those whose business it was to judge on these subjects, felt convinced, that in a month or two the scarcity would be greater than it was at that time. Those who were able, therefore, kept back their corn. In so doing, they undoubtedly consulted their own interest; but they, as undoubtedly, whether with the intention or not is of no consequence, consulted the true interest of the state: for, if they had not kept it back, too much would have been consumed, and there would have been a famine instead of a scarcity at the end of the year.

The corn, therefore, naturally rose. The poor were again distressed. Fresh complaints were made to the justices, and a further relief granted; but, like the water from the mouth of Tantalus,[9] the corn still slipped from the grasp of the poor; and rose again so as to disable them from purchasing a sufficiency to keep their families in health. The alarm now became still greater, and more general.* The justices in their individual capacities were not thought competent to determine on the proper modes of relief in the present crisis, a general meeting of the magistrates was called, aided by the united wisdom of other gentlemen of the county; but the result was merely the continuation and extension of the former system of relief; and, to say the truth, I hardly see what else could have been done. In some parishes this relief was given in the shape of flour; in others, which was certainly better, in money, accompanied with a recommendation not to spend the whole of it in wheaten bread, but to adopt some other kind of food. All, however, went upon the principle of inquiring what was the usual consumption of flour in the different families, and of enabling them to purchase nearly the same quantity that they did before the scarcity. With this additional command of money in the lower classes, and the consequent increased consumption, the number of purchasers at the then price would naturally exceed the supply. The corn would in consequence continue rising. The poor's rates in

---

* I am describing what took place in the neighbourhood where I then lived; and I have reason to believe that something nearly similar took place in most counties of the kingdom.

many parishes increased from 4 shillings in the pound to 14; the price of wheat necessarily kept pace with them; and before the end of the year was at near £40 a load; when probably without the operation of this cause it would not have exceeded £20 or £25.

Some of the poor would naturally make use of their additional command of money to purchase butter, cheese, bacon, pickled pork, rice, potatoes, etc. These commodities are all more limited in quantity than corn; and would, therefore, more suddenly feel the increased demand. If butter, cheese, bacon, pickled pork, and the coarser parts of meat, had continued at their usual price, they would have been purchased by so many, to come in aid of an inferior kind of bread, or to give a relish and additional nourishment to their potatoes and rice, that the supply would not have been half adequate to the quantity of these articles that was wanted. These commodities, therefore, rose as naturally and as necessarily as the corn; and, according to the genuine principles of fair trade, their price was fixed at that sum which only such a number could afford to give, as would enable the supply to answer the demand.

To fix upon this sum is the great object of every dealer and speculator in every commodity whatever, and about which he must, of course, exercise his private judgement. A reflecting mind, far from being astonished that there are now and then errors in speculation, must feel much greater astonishment that there are so few; and that the supplies of a large nation, whether plentiful or scanty, should be distributed so equally throughout the year. Most happily for society, individual interest is, in these cases, so closely and intimately interwoven with the public interest, that one cannot gain or lose without a gain or loss to the other. The man who refuses to send his corn to market when it is at £20 a load, because he thinks that in two months time it will be at £30, if he be right in his judgement, and succeed in his speculation, is a positive and decided benefactor to the state; because he keeps his supply to that period when the state is much more in want of it; and if he and some others did not keep it back in that manner, instead of its being £30 in two months, it would be £40 or £50.

If he be wrong in his speculation, he loses perhaps very considerably himself, and the state suffers a little; because, had he brought his corn to market at £20, the price would have fallen sooner, and the event showed that there was corn enough in the country to allow of it: but the slight evil that the state suffers in this case is almost wholly compensated by the glut in the market, when the corn is brought out, which makes the price fall below what it would have been otherwise.

I am far from saying that there can be no such thing as monopoly, and the other hard words that have been so much talked of. In a commodity of a confined nature, within the purchase of two or three large capitals, or of a company of merchants, we all know that it has often existed; and, in a very few instances, the article may have been in part destroyed, to enhance the price, as the Dutch Company[10] destroyed the nutmeg trees in their spice islands: but in an article which is in so many hands as corn is, in this country, monopoly, to any pernicious extent, may safely be pronounced impossible. Where are the capitals, or where is the company of merchants, rich enough to buy such a quantity of corn, as would make it answer to them to destroy, or, which is the same thing, not to sell a great part of it? As they could not, by the greatest of exertions, purchase one fourth of all the corn in the country, it is evident that, if any considerable part of their stock remained unsold, they would have enriched all the other dealers in corn at their own expense; and would not have gained half so much in proportion to their capital as the rest of the farmers and cornfactors.[11] If on the contrary all their stock sold, it would be a proof that the speculation had been just, and that the country had really benefited by it.

It seems now to be universally agreed, that the stock of old corn remaining on hand at the beginning of the harvest this year was unusually small, notwithstanding that the harvest came on nearly a month sooner than could have been expected in the beginning of June. This is a clear, decided, and unanswerable proof that there had been no speculations in corn that were prejudicial to the country. All that the large farmers and cornfactors had done, was to raise the corn to that price which excluded a sufficient number from their usual consumption, to enable the supply to last throughout the year. This price, however, has been most essentially and powerfully affected by the ability that has been given to the labouring poor, by means of parish allowances, of continuing to purchase wheat notwithstanding its extraordinary rise: and this ability must necessarily prevent the price of corn from falling very materially, till there is an actual glut in the market; for, while the whole stock will go off at £30 a load, it cannot, on any regular principle of trade, sink lower. I was in very great hopes, just before the harvest, that such a glut was about to take place; but it is now to be feared, from the nature of the present crop, that no such happy event can be hoped for during the year.

I do not know whether I have convinced my reader that the cause which I have assigned of the present extraordinary price of provisions is adequate to the effect; but I certainly feel most strongly convinced of it myself; and I cannot but believe that, if he differ from me, it can only be in degree, and from thinking that the principle of parish allowances has not yet been carried far enough to produce any material effect. With regard to the principle itself, if it were really carried into execution, it appears to me capable almost of mathematical demonstration, that, granting a real scarcity of one fourth, which could not be remedied by importation, it is adequate to the effecting any height of price that the proportion of the circulating medium to the quantity of corn daily consumed would admit.

It has often been proposed, and more than once I believe, in the House of Commons, to proportion the price of labour exactly to the price of provisions. This, though it would be always a bad plan, might pass tolerably in years of moderate plenty, or in a country that was in the habit of a considerable exportation of grain. But let us see what would be its operation in a real scarcity. We suppose, for the sake of the argument, that by law every kind of labour is to be paid accurately in proportion to the price of corn, and that the rich are to be assessed to the utmost to support those in the same manner who are thrown out of employment, and fall upon the parish. We allow the scarcity to be an irremediable deficiency of one fourth of all the provisions of the country. It is evident that, notwithstanding this deficiency, there would be no reason for economy in the labouring classes. The rise of their wages, or the parish allowances that they would receive, would enable them to purchase exactly the same quantity of corn, or other provisions, that they did before, whatever their price might be. The same quantity would of course be consumed; and, according to the regular principles of trade, as the stock continued diminishing, the price of all the necessaries of life would continue rising, in the most rapid and unexampled manner. The middle classes of society would very soon be blended with the poor; and the largest fortunes could not stand against the accumulated pressure of the extraordinary price of provisions, on the one hand, and the still more extraordinary assessments for allowances to those who had no other means of support, on the other. The cornfactors and farmers would undoubtedly be the last that suffered, but, at the expiration of the three quarters of a year, what they received with one hand, they must give away with the other; and a most complete levelling of all property would take place. All would have the same quantity of money. All the provisions of the country would be consumed: and all the people would starve together.

There is no kind of fear, that any such tragical event should ever happen in any country; but I allowed myself to make the supposition; because, it appears to me, that, in the complicated machinery of human society, the effect of any particular principle frequently escapes from the view, even of an attentive observer, if it be not magnified by pushing it to extremity.

I do not, however, by any means, intend to infer, from what I have said, that the parish allowances have been prejudicial to the state; or that, as far as the system has been hitherto pursued, or is likely to be pursued, in this country, that it is not one of the best modes of relief that the circumstances of the case will admit. The system of the poor laws, in general, I certainly do most heartily condemn, as I have expressed in another place,[12] but I am inclined to think that their operation in the present scarcity has been advantageous to the country. The principal benefit which they have produced, is exactly that which is most bitterly complained of – the high price of all the necessaries of life. The poor cry out loudly at this price; but, in so doing, they are very little aware of what they are about; for it has undoubtedly been owing to this price that a much greater number of them has not been starved.[13]

It was calculated that there were only two thirds of an average crop last year. Probably, even with the aid of all that we imported, the deficiency still remained a fifth or sixth. Supposing ten millions of people in the island; the whole of this deficiency, had things been left to their natural course, would have fallen almost exclusively on two, or perhaps three millions of the poorest inhabitants, a very considerable number of whom must in consequence have starved. The operation of the parish allowances, by raising the price of provisions so high, caused the distress to be divided among five or six millions, perhaps, instead of two or three, and to be by no means unfelt even by the remainder of the population.

The high price, therefore, which is so much complained of by the poor, has essentially mitigated their distress by bringing down to their level two or three millions more, and making them almost equal sharers in the pressure of the scarcity.

The further effects of the high price have been to enforce a strict economy in all ranks of life; to encourage an extraordinary importation, and to animate the farmer by the powerful motive of self interest to make every exertion to obtain as great a crop as possible the next year.

If economy, importation, and every possible encouragement to future production, have not the fairest chance of putting an end to the scarcity, I confess myself at a loss to say what better means can be substituted. I may undoubtedly on this subject be much mistaken; but to me, I own, they appear more calculated to answer the purpose intended, than the hanging any number of farmers and cornfactors that could be named.

No inference, therefore, is meant to be drawn against what has been done for the relief of the poor in the present scarcity, though it has without doubt greatly raised the price of provisions. All that I contend for is, that we should be aware of the effect of what we ourselves have done, and not lay the blame on the wrong persons.

If the cause, which I have detailed, be sufficient to account for the present high price of provisions, without the supposition of any unfair dealing among the farmers and cornfactors, we ought surely to bear the present pressure like men labouring under a disorder that must have its course, and not throw obstacles in the way of returning plenty, and endanger the future supplies of our markets, by encouraging the popular clamour, and keeping the farmers and corn dealers in perpetual fear for their lives and property.

To suppose that a year of scarcity can pass without distressing severely a large part of the inhabitants of a country, is to suppose a contradiction in the nature of things. I know of no other definition of a scarcity than the failure of the usual quantity of provisions; and if a great part of the people had but just enough before, they must undoubtedly have less than enough at such a period. With regard to the scarcity being artificial, it appears to me so impossible, that, till it has been proved that some man or set of men, with a capital of twenty or thirty millions sterling, has bought up half the corn in the country, I own I must still disbelieve it. On this subject, however, I know that I differ from some very respectable friends of mine, among the common people, who say that it is quite impossible that there can be a real scarcity, because you may get what quantity of corn you please, if you have but money enough; and to say the truth, many persons, who ought to be better informed, argue exactly in the same way. I have often talked with labouring men on this subject, and endeavoured to show them, that if they, or I, had a great deal of money, and other people had but little, we could undoubtedly buy what quantity of corn we liked, by taking away the shares of those who were less rich; but that if all the people had the same sum, and that there was not enough corn in the country to supply all, we could not get what we wanted for money, though we possessed millions. I never found, however, that my rhetoric produced much impression.

The cry at present is in favour of small farms, and against middle men. No two clamours can well be more inconsistent with each other, as the destruction of the middle men would, I conceive, necessarily involve with it the destruction of small farmers. The small farmer requires a quick return of his scanty capital to enable him to pay his rent and his workmen; and must therefore send his corn to market almost immediately after harvest. If he were required to perform the office of corn dealer, as well as farmer, and wait to regulate his supplies to the demands of the markets, a double capital would be absolutely necessary to him, and not having that, he would be ruined.

Many men of sense and information have attributed the dearness of provisions to the quantity of paper in circulation. There was undoubtedly great reason for apprehension, that when, by the stoppage of the Bank to pay in specie, the emission of paper ceased to have its natural check, the circulation would be overloaded with this currency; but this certainly could not have taken place to any considerable extent without a sensible depreciation of bank notes in comparison with specie. As this depreciation did not happen, the progress of the evil must have been slow and gradual, and never could have produced the sudden and extraordinary rise in the price of provisions which was so sensibly felt last year, after a season of moderate cheapness, subsequent to the stoppage of the Bank.[14]

There is one circumstance, however, that ought to be attended to. To circulate the same, or nearly the same,* quantity of commodities through a country, when they bear a much higher price, must require a greater quantity of the medium, whatever that may be. The circulation naturally takes up more. It is probable, therefore, that the Bank has found it necessary to issue a greater number of its notes on this account. Or, if it has not, this deficiency has been supplied by the country bankers, who have found that their notes now stay out longer, and in greater quantity, than they did before the scarcity, which may tempt many to overtrade their capitals.[15] If the quantity of paper, therefore, in circulation has greatly increased during the last year, I should be inclined to consider it rather as the effect than the cause of the high price of provisions. This fullness of

---

* In a scarcity the quantity of commodities in circulation is probably not so great as in years of plenty.

circulating medium, however, will be one of the obstacles in the way to returning cheapness.

The public attention is now fixed with anxiety towards the meeting of Parliament, which is to relieve us from our present difficulties; but the more considerate do not feel very sanguine on this subject, knowing how little is to be done in this species of distress by legislative interference. We interfere to fix the assize of bread.[16] Perhaps one of the best interferences of the legislature, in the present instance, would be to abolish that assize. I have certainly no tendency to believe in combinations and conspiracies; but the great interval that elapses between the fall of wheat and the fall of flour, compared with the quick succession of the rise of flour to the rise of wheat, would almost tempt one to suppose, that there might be some little manage-ment in the return of the meal weighers to the Lord Mayor.[17] If the public suffer in this instance, it is evidently owing to the assize, without which, the opportunity of any such manage-ment would not exist. And what occasion can there be for an assize in a city like London, in which there are so many bakers? If such a regulation were ever necessary, it would appear to be most so in a country village or small town, where perhaps there is but one person in the trade, and who might, therefore, for a time, have an opportunity of imposing on his customers; but this could not take place where there was such room for com-petition as in London. If there were no assize, more attention would be constantly paid to the weight and quality of the bread bought; and the bakers who sold the best in these two respects would have the most custom. The removal of this regulation would remove, in a great measure, the difficulty about brown bread, and a much grater quantity of it would probably be consumed.

The soup shops, and every attempt to make a nourishing and palatable food of what was before not in use among the common people, must evidently be of great service in the pres-ent distress.

It is a fact now generally acknowledged, and it has lately received an official sanction in a letter of the Duke of Portland to the Lord Lieutenant of the county of Oxford,[18] that of late years, even in the best seasons, we have not grown corn sufficient for our own consumption; whereas, twenty years ago, we were in the constant habit of exporting grain to a very considerable amount. Though we may suppose that the agriculture of the country has not been increasing, as it ought to have done, during this period; yet we cannot well imagine that it has gone backwards. To what then can we attribute the present inability in the country to support its inhabitants, but to the increase of population? I own that I cannot but consider the late severe pressures of distress on every deficiency in our crops, as a very strong exemplification of a principle which I endeavoured to explain in an essay published about two years ago, entitled, *An essay on the principle of population, as it affects the future improvement of society*. It was considered by many who read it, merely as a specious argument, inapplicable to the present state of society; because it contradicted some preconceived opinions on these subjects. Two years' reflection have, however, served strongly to convince me of the truth of the principle there advanced, and of its being the real cause of the continued depression and poverty of the lower classes of society, of the total inadequacy of all the present establishments in their favour to relieve them, and of the periodical returns of such seasons of distress as we have of late experienced.

The essay has now been out of print above a year; but I have deferred giving another edition of it in the hope of being able to make it more worthy of the public attention, by applying the principle directly and exclusively to the existing state of society, and endeavouring to illustrate the power and universality of its operation from the best authenticated accounts that we have of the state of other countries. Particular engagements in the former part of the time, and some most unforeseen and unfortunate interruptions latterly, have hitherto prevented me from turning my attention, with any effect, towards this subject. I still, however, have it in view. In the meantime I hope that this hasty attempt to add my mite to the public stock of information, in the present emergency, will be received with candour.

TWO SELECTIONS FROM
THE 1803 EDITION
OF THE *ESSAY*

BOOK IV, CHAPTER SIX

*Effect of the knowledge of the principal
cause of poverty on Civil Liberty*

It may appear, perhaps, that a doctrine, which attributes the
greatest part of the sufferings of the lower classes of society
exclusively to themselves, is unfavourable to the cause of liberty; as affording a tempting opportunity to governments of
oppressing their subjects at pleasure, and laying the whole
blame on the laws of nature and the imprudence of the poor.
We are not, however, to trust to first appearances; and I am
strongly disposed to believe that those who will be at the pains
to consider this subject deeply, will be convinced that nothing
would so powerfully contribute to the advancement of rational
freedom as a thorough knowledge, generally circulated, of the
principal cause of poverty; and that the ignorance of this cause,
and the natural consequences of this ignorance, form, at present, one of the chief obstacles to its progress.

The pressure of distress on the lower classes of people,
together with the habit of attributing this distress to their
rulers, appears to me to be the rock of defence, the castle, the
guardian spirit of despotism. It affords to the tyrant the fatal
and unanswerable plea of necessity. It is the reason why every
free government tends constantly to destruction; and that its
appointed guardians become daily less jealous of the encroachments of power. It is the reason why so many noble efforts in
the cause of freedom have failed, and why almost every revolution, after long and painful sacrifices, has terminated in a
military despotism. While any dissatisfied man of talents has
power to persuade the lower classes of people that all their
poverty and distress arise solely from the iniquity of the government, though perhaps the greatest part of what they suffer

is totally unconnected with this cause, it is evident that the seeds of fresh discontent and fresh revolutions are continually sowing. When an established government has been destroyed, finding that their poverty is not removed, their resentment naturally falls upon the successors to power; and when these have been immolated without producing the desired effect, other sacrifices are called for, and so on without end. Are we to be surprised that, under such circumstances, the majority of well-disposed people, finding that a government with proper restrictions is unable to support itself against the revolutionary spirit, and weary and exhausted with perpetual change, to which they can see no end, should give up the struggle in despair, and throw themselves into the arms of the first power which can afford them protection against the horrors of anarchy?

A mob, which is generally the growth of a redundant population, goaded by resentment for real sufferings, but totally ignorant of the quarter from which they originate, is of all monsters the most fatal to freedom. It fosters a prevailing tyranny, and engenders one where it was not; and though, in its dreadful fits of resentment, it appears occasionally to devour its unsightly offspring; yet no sooner is the horrid deed committed, than, however unwilling it may be to propagate such a breed, it immediately groans with the pangs of a new birth.

Of the tendency of mobs to produce tyranny, we may not be long without an example in this country. As a friend to freedom, and an enemy to large standing armies,[1] it is with extreme reluctance that I am compelled to acknowledge that, had it not been for the organized force in the country, the distresses of the people during the late scarcities, encouraged by the extreme ignorance and folly of many among the higher classes, might have driven them to commit the most dreadful outrages, and ultimately to involve the country in all the horrors of famine.[2] Should such periods often recur (a recurrence which we have too much reason to apprehend from the present state of the country) the prospect which opens to our view is melancholy in the extreme. The English constitution will be seen hastening with rapid strides to the *Euthanasia* foretold by Hume,[3] unless its progress be interrupted by some popular commotion; and this alternative presents a picture still more appalling to the imagination. If political discontents were blended with the cries of hunger, and a revolution were to take place by the instrumentality of a mob clamouring for want of food, the consequences would be unceasing change and unceasing carnage, the bloody career[4] of which nothing but the establishment of some complete despotism could arrest.

We can scarcely believe that the appointed guardians of British liberty should quietly have acquiesced in those gradual encroachments of power, which have taken place of late years, but from the apprehension of these still more dreadful evils. Great as has been the influence of corruption, I cannot yet think so meanly of the country gentlemen of England as to believe that they would thus have given up a part of their birthright of liberty, if they had not been actuated by a real and genuine fear that it was then in greater danger from the people than from the crown. They appeared to surrender themselves to government on condition of being protected from the mob; but they never would have made this melancholy and disheartening surrender, if such a mob had not existed either in reality or in imagination. That the fears on this subject were artfully exaggerated, and increased beyond the limits of just apprehension, is undeniable; but I think it is also undeniable that the frequent declamation which was heard against the unjust institutions of society, and the delusive arguments on equality which were circulated among the lower classes, gave us just reason to suppose that, if the *vox populi* had been allowed to speak, it would have appeared to be the voice of error and absurdity instead of the *vox Dei*.[5]

To say that our conduct is not to be regulated by circumstances is to betray an ignorance of the most solid and incontrovertible principles of morality. Though the admission of this principle may sometimes afford a cloak to changes of opinion that do not result from the purest motives; yet the admission of a contrary principle would be productive of infinitely worse consequences. The phrase of 'existing circumstances'[6] has, I believe, not unfrequently created a smile in the English House of Commons; but the smile should have been reserved for the application of the phrase, and not have been excited by the phrase itself. A very frequent repetition of it has indeed, of itself, rather a suspicious air; and its application should always be watched with the most jealous and anxious attention; but no man ought to be judged *in limine*[7] for saying that existing circumstances had obliged him to alter his opinions and conduct. The country gentlemen were perhaps too easily convinced that existing circumstances called upon them to give up some of the most valuable privileges of Englishmen; but, as far as they were really convinced of this obligation, they acted consistently with the clearest rule of morality.

The degree of power to be given to the civil government, and the measure of our submission to it, must be determined by general expediency; and in judging of this expediency, every circumstance is to be taken into consideration; particularly the state of public opinion, and the degree of ignorance and delusion prevailing among the common people. The patriot, who might be called upon by the love of his country to join with heart and hand in a rising of the people for some specific attainable object of reform, if he knew that they were enlightened respecting their own situation, and would stop short when they had attained their demand, would be called upon by the same motive to submit to very great oppression, rather than give the slightest countenance to a popular tumult, the members of which (at least the greater number of them) were persuaded that the destruction of the Parliament, the Lord Mayor, and the monopolizers, would make bread cheap, and that a revolution would enable them all to support their families. In this case, it is more the ignorance and delusion of the lower classes of people that occasions the oppression, than the actual disposition of the government to tyranny.

That there is, however, in all power a constant tendency to encroach is an incontrovertible truth, and cannot be too strongly inculcated. The checks which are necessary to secure the liberty of the subject will always, in some degree, embarrass and delay the operations of the executive government. The members of this government feeling these inconveniences, while they are exerting themselves, as they conceive, in the service of their country, and conscious, perhaps, of no ill intention towards the people, will naturally be disposed on every occasion to demand the suspension or abolition of these checks; but if once the convenience of ministers be put into competition with the liberties of the people, and we get into a habit of relying on fair assurances and personal character, instead of examining, with the most scrupulous and jealous care, the merits of each particular case, there is an end of British freedom. If we once admit the principle that the government must know better with regard to the quantity of power which it wants, than we can possibly do with our limited means of information, and that therefore it is our duty to surrender up our private judgments, we may just as well, at the same time, surrender up the whole of our constitution. Government is a quarter in which liberty is not, nor cannot be, very faithfully preserved. If we are wanting to ourselves, and inattentive to our great interests in this respect, it is the height of folly and unreasonableness, to expect that government will attend to them for us. Should the British constitution ultimately lapse into a despotism, as has been prophesied, I shall think that the country gentlemen of England will have really much more to answer for than the ministers.

To do the country gentlemen justice, however, I should readily acknowledge that, in the partial desertion of their posts as guardians of British freedom, which has already taken place, they have been actuated more by fear than treachery. And the principal reason of this fear was, I conceive, the ignorance and delusions of the common people, and the prospective horrors which were contemplated if, in such a state of mind, they should by any revolutionary movement obtain an ascendant.

The circulation of Paine's Rights of Man, it is supposed, has done great mischief among the lower and middling classes of people in this country.[8] This is probably true; but not because man is without rights, or that these rights ought not to be known; but because Mr Paine has fallen into some fundamental errors respecting the principles of government, and in many important points has shown himself totally unacquainted with the structure of society, and the different moral effects to be expected from the physical difference between this country and America. Mobs, of the same description as those collections of people known by this name in Europe, could not exist in America. The number of people without property is there, from the physical state of the country, comparatively small; and therefore the civil power which is to protect property cannot require the same degree of strength. Mr Paine very justly observes that whatever the apparent cause of any riots may be, the real one is always want of happiness; but when he goes on to say it shows that something is wrong in the system of government, that injures the felicity by which society is to be preserved, he falls into the common error of attributing all want of happiness to government. It is evident that this want of happiness might have existed, and from ignorance might have been the principal cause of the riots, and yet be almost wholly unconnected with any of the proceedings of government. The redundant population of an old state furnishes materials of unhappiness unknown to such a state as that of America; and if an attempt were to be made to remedy this unhappiness, by distributing the produce of the taxes to the poorer classes of society, according to the plan proposed by Mr Paine, the evil would be aggravated a hundred fold, and in a very short time no sum that the society could possibly raise would be adequate to the proposed object.

Nothing would so effectually counteract the mischiefs occasioned by Mr Paine's Rights of Man as a general knowledge of the real rights of man. What these rights are, it is not my business at present to explain; but there is one right which man has generally been thought to possess, which I am confident he neither does, nor can possess – a right to subsistence when his labour will not fairly purchase it. Our laws indeed say that he has this right, and bind the society to furnish employment and food to those who cannot get them in the regular market; but in so doing, they attempt to reverse the laws of nature; and it is in consequence to be expected, not only that they should fail in their object, but that the poor who were intended to be benefited, should suffer most cruelly from this inhuman deceit which is practised upon them.

A man who is born into a world already possessed, if he cannot get subsistence from his parents on whom he has a just demand, and if the society do not want his labour, has no claim of *right* to the smallest portion of food, and, in fact, has no business to be where he is. At nature's mighty feast there is no vacant cover for him. She tells him to be gone, and will quickly execute her own orders, if he do not work upon the compassion of some of her guests. If these guests get up and make room for him, other intruders immediately appear demanding the same favour. The report of a provision for all that come fills the hall with numerous claimants. The order and harmony of the feast is disturbed, the plenty that before reigned is changed into scarcity; and the happiness of the guests is destroyed by the spectacle of misery and dependence in every part of the hall, and by the clamorous importunity of those who are justly enraged at not finding the provision which they had been taught to expect. The guests learn too late their error, in counteracting those strict orders to all intruders, issued by the great mistress of the feast, who, wishing that all her guests should have plenty, and knowing that she could not provide for unlimited numbers, humanely refused to admit fresh comers when her table was already full.[9]

The Abbé Raynal[10] has said, that: 'Avant toutes les loix sociales l'homme avoit le droit de subsister!* He might with just as much propriety have said that, before the institution of social laws, every man had a right to live a hundred years. Undoubtedly he had then, and has still, a good right to live a hundred years, nay, a thousand *if he can*, without interfering with the right of others to live; but the affair in both cases is principally an affair of power, not of right. Social laws very greatly increase this power, by enabling a much greater number to subsist than could subsist without them, and so far very greatly enlarge *le droit de subsister*; but neither before nor after

---

* Raynal, Hist. des Indes, vol. x. s. x. p. 322. 8vo. 'Before any laws were made, man had the right to eat, to keep himself alive.'

the institution of social laws could an unlimited number subsist; and before, as well as since, he who ceased to have the power ceased to have the right.

If the great truths on these subjects were more generally circulated, and the lower classes of people could be convinced that, by the laws of nature, independently of any particular institutions, except the great one of property, which is absolutely necessary in order to attain any considerable produce, no person has any claim of right on society for subsistence, if his labour will not purchase it, the greatest part of the mischievous declamation on the unjust institutions of society would fall powerless to the ground. The poor are by no means inclined to be visionary. Their distresses are always real, though they are not attributed to the real causes. If these real causes were properly explained to them, and they were taught to know how small a part of their present distress was attributable to government, and how great a part to causes totally unconnected with it, discontent and irritation among the lower classes of people would show themselves much less frequently than at present; and when they did show themselves, would be much less to be dreaded. The efforts of turbulent and discontented men in the middle classes of society might safely be disregarded, if the poor were so far enlightened respecting the real nature of their situation, as to be aware that, by aiding them in their schemes of renovation, they would probably be promoting the ambitious views of others without in any respect benefiting themselves. And the country gentlemen and men of property in England might securely return to a wholesome jealousy of the encroachments of power; and instead of daily sacrificing the liberties of the subject on the altar of public safety, might, without any just apprehension from the people, not only tread back their late steps, but firmly insist upon those gradual reforms which the lapse of time, and the storms of circumstances, have rendered necessary, to prevent the gradual destruction of the British constitution.

All improvements in government must necessarily originate with persons of some education, and these will of course be found among the people of property. Whatever may be said of a few, it is impossible to suppose that the great mass of the people of property should be really interested in the abuses of government. They merely submit to them, from the fear that an endeavour to remove them might be productive of greater evils. Could we but take away this fear, reform and improvement would proceed with as much facility as the removal of nuisances, or the paving and lighting of the streets. In human life we are continually called upon to submit to a lesser evil in order to avoid a greater; and it is the part of a wise man to do this readily and cheerfully; but no wise man will submit to any evil if he can get rid of it without danger. Remove all apprehension from the tyranny or folly of the people, and the tyranny of government could not stand a moment. It would then appear in its proper deformity, without palliation, without pretext, without protector. Naturally feeble in itself, when it was once stripped naked, and deprived of the support of public opinion, and of the great plea of necessity, it would fall without a struggle. Its few interested defenders would hide their heads abashed, and would be ashamed any longer to advocate a cause for which no human ingenuity could invent a plausible argument.

The most successful supporters of tyranny are without doubt those general declaimers, who attribute the distresses of the poor, and almost all the evils to which society is subject, to human institutions and the iniquity of governments. The falsity of these accusations, and the dreadful consequences that would result from their being generally admitted and acted upon, make it absolutely necessary that they should at all events be resisted; not only on account of the immediate revolutionary horrors to be expected from a movement of the people acting under such impressions (a consideration which must at all times have very great weight); but also on account of the extreme probability that such a revolution would terminate in a much worse despotism than that which it had destroyed. On these grounds, a genuine friend of freedom, a zealous advocate for the real rights of man, might be found among the defenders of a considerable degree of tyranny. A cause bad in itself, might be supported by the good and the virtuous, merely because that which was opposed to it was much worse; and because it was absolutely necessary at the moment to make a choice between the two. Whatever therefore may be the intention of those indiscriminate and wholesale accusations against governments, their real effect undoubtedly is to add a weight of talents and principles to the prevailing power, which it never would have received otherwise.

It is a truth, which I trust has been sufficiently proved in the course of this work, that under a government constructed upon the best and purest principles, and executed by men of the highest talents and integrity, the most squalid poverty and wretchedness might universally prevail from the principle of population alone. And as this cause of unhappiness has hitherto been so little understood, that the efforts of society have always tended rather to aggravate than to lessen it, we have the strongest reasons for supposing that, in all the governments with which we are acquainted, a very great part of the misery to be observed among the lower classes of the people arises from this cause.

The inference therefore, which Mr Paine and others have drawn against governments from the unhappiness of the people, is palpably unfair; and before we give a sanction to such accusations, it is a debt we owe to truth and justice, to ascertain how much of this unhappiness arises from the principle of population, and how much is fairly to be attributed to government. When this distinction has been properly made, and all the vague, indefinite, and false accusations removed, government would remain, as it ought to be, clearly responsible for the rest. A tenfold weight would be immediately given to the cause of the people, and every man of principle would join in asserting and enforcing, if necessary, their rights.

I may be deceived; but I confess that if I were called upon to name the cause which, in my conception, had more than any other contributed to the very slow progress of freedom, so disheartening to every liberal mind, I should say that it was the confusion that had existed respecting the causes of the unhappiness and discontents which prevail in society; and the advantage which governments had been able to take, and indeed had been compelled to take, of this confusion, to confirm and strengthen their power. I cannot help thinking, therefore, that a knowledge generally circulated, that the principal cause of want and unhappiness is unconnected with government, and totally beyond its power to remove, and that it depends upon the conduct of the poor themselves, would, instead of giving any advantage to governments, give a great additional weight to the popular side of the question, by removing the dangers with which from ignorance it is at present accompanied; and thus tend, in a very powerful manner, to promote the cause of rational freedom.

BOOK III, CHAPTER IX

Different effects of the agricultural and commercial systems

About the middle of the last century, we were genuinely, and in the strict sense of the Economists,[1] an agricultural nation. Our commerce and manufactures were, however, then in a very respectable and thriving state; and if they had continued to bear the same relative proportion to our agriculture, they would evidently have gone on increasing considerably, with the improving cultivation of the country. There is no apparent limit to the quantity of manufactures which might in time be supported in this way. The increasing wealth of a country in such a state, seems to be out of the reach of all common accidents. There is no discoverable germ of decay in the system; and in theory, there is no reason to say, that it might not go on increasing in wealth and prosperity for thousands of years.

We have now, however, stepped out of the agricultural system, into a state, in which the commercial system clearly predominates; and there is but too much reason to fear, that even our commerce and manufactures will ultimately feel the disadvantage of the change.[2] It has been already observed, that we are exactly in that situation, in which a country feels most fully the effect of those common years of deficient crops, which, in the natural course of things, are to be expected. The competition of increasing commercial wealth, operating upon a supply of corn not increasing in the same proportion, must at all times greatly tend to raise the price of labour; but when scarce years are taken into the consideration, its effect in this way must ultimately be prodigious. We know how extremely difficult it is in England to lower the wages of labour, after they have once been raised. During the late scarcities,[3] the price of labour has been continually rising – not to fall again; the rents of land have been everywhere advancing – not to fall again; and of course, the price of produce must rise – not to fall again; as, independently of a particular competition from scarcity, or the want of competition from plenty, its price is necessarily regulated by the wages of labour, and the rent of land. We have no reason whatever for supposing that we shall be exempt in future from such scarcities as we have of late experienced. On the contrary, upon our present system, they seem to be unavoidable. And if we go on, as we have done lately, the price of labour and of provisions must soon increase in a manner out of all proportion to their price in the rest of Europe; and it is impossible that this should not ultimately check all our dealings with foreign powers, and give a fatal blow to our commerce and manufactures. The effect of capital, skill, machinery, and establishments, in their full vigour, is great; so great, indeed, that it is difficult to guess at its limit; but still it is not infinite, and without doubt has this limit. The principal states of Europe, except this fortunate island, have of late suffered so much by the actual presence of war, that their commerce and manufactures have been nearly destroyed, and we may be said in a manner to have the monopoly of the trade of Europe.[4] All monopolies yield high profits, and at present, therefore, the trade can be carried on to advantage, in spite of the high price of labour. But when the other nations of Europe shall have had time to recover themselves, and gradually to become our competitors, it would be rash to affirm, that, with the prices of provisions and of labour still going on increasing, from what they are at present, we shall be able to stand the competition. Dr Smith says, that, in his time, merchants frequently complained of the high price of British labour as the cause of their manufactures being undersold in foreign markets.* If such complaints were in any degree founded at that time, how will they be aggravated twenty years hence! And have we not some reason to fear that our present great commercial prosperity is

* Smith, *Wealth of nations*, ii, p. 413.

temporary, and belongs a little to that worst feature of the commercial system, the rising by the depression of others.

When a country, in average years, grows more corn than it consumes, and is in the habit of exporting a part of it, its price, and the price of labour as depending on it, can never rise in any very extraordinary degree above the common price in other commercial countries; and under such circumstances, England would have nothing to fear from the fullest, and most open competition. The increasing prosperity of other countries, would only open to her a more extensive market for her commodities, and give additional spirit to all her commercial transactions.

The high price of corn and of rude produce[5] in general, as far as it is occasioned by the freest competition among the nations of Europe, is a very great advantage, and is the best possible encouragement to agriculture; but when occasioned merely by the competition of monied wealth at home, its effect is totally different. In the one case, a great encouragement is given to production in general, and the more is produced, the better. In the other case, the produce is necessarily confined to the home consumption. The cultivators are justly afraid of growing too much corn, as a considerable loss will be sustained upon that part of it which is sold abroad; and a glut in the home market will universally make the price fall below the fair and proper recompense to the grower. It is impossible that a country, under such circumstances, should not be subject to great and frequent variations in the price of corn, and occasionally to severe scarcities.

If we were to endeavour to lower the price of labour by encouraging the importation of foreign corn, we should probably aggravate the evil tenfold. Experience warrants us in saying, that, from political fears, or other causes, the fall in the price of labour would be uncertain; but the ruin of our agriculture would be certain. The British grower of corn could not, in his own markets, stand the competition of the foreign grower, in average years. We should be daily thrown more and more into a dependence upon other countries for our support. Arable lands of a moderate quality would not pay the expense of cultivation. Rich soils alone would yield a rent. Round all our towns, the appearances would be the same as usual; but in the interior of the country, half of the lands would be neglected, and almost universally, where it was practicable, pasture would take place of tillage. How dreadfully precarious would our commerce and manufactures, and even our very existence be, under such circumstances! It could hardly be expected that a century should elapse without seeing our population repressed within the limits of our scanty cultivation; and suffering the same melancholy reverse, as the once flourishing population of Spain.

Nothing perhaps will show more clearly the absurdity of that artificial system, which prompts a country, with a large territory of its own, to depend upon others for its food, than the supposition of the same system being pursued by many other states. If France, Germany, and Prussia, were to become manufacturing nations, and to consider agriculture as a secondary concern, how would their wants, in the indispensable article of food, be supplied. The increasing demand for corn, would tend certainly to encourage the growth of it in Russia and America; but we know that in these countries, at present, particularly in America, the natural progress of population is not very greatly checked; and that, as their towns and manufactories increase, the demand for their own corn will of course increase with them. The Russian nobleman, whose revenue depends upon the number of his boors, will hardly be persuaded to check their increase, in order to accommodate other nations; and the independent cultivator of America will surely feed his own family and servants, and probably supply the home market, before he begins to export. But allowing that at first, and for some time, the increasing demands of these manufacturing countries might be adequately supplied; yet this could not in the nature of things last long. The manufacturers, from the decay of agriculture in their own countries, would annually want more; and Russia and America, from their rapidly increasing population, and the gradual establishment of manufactures at home, would annually be able to spare less. From these causes and the necessity of drawing a part of such vast supplies of corn from a much greater distance inland, and loaded perhaps with the expense of land carriage, the price would ultimately rise so extravagantly high, that the poor manufacturers would be totally unable to pay it, and want and famine would convince them too late of the precarious and subordinate[6] nature of their wealth. They would learn by painful experience, that, though agriculture may flourish considerably, and give plenty and happiness to great numbers, without many manufactures; yet, that manufactures cannot stir a single step, without their agricultural paymasters, either at home or abroad; and that therefore it is the height of folly and imprudence, to have these paymasters at a great distance, with different interests, and their payments precarious, instead of at home, with the same interests, and their payments always ready and certain. Nothing can be so hateful to a liberal mind, as the idea of being placed in a situation in which the growing prosperity of your neighbours will be the signal of your own approaching ruin. Yet this would be the situation of the principal countries of Europe, if they depended chiefly upon Russia and America, or any other nations for their corn. A system, which, like the present commercial system of England, throws a country into this state, without any physical necessity for it, cannot be founded on the genuine principles of the wealth of nations.

It seems almost impossible, that a country possessed of a considerable territory, should have its means of subsistence well assured, without growing at home more corn than it consumes. Nor can it be exempt from those great and sudden variations of price, which produce such severe distress throughout so large a part of the community, and are often attended with great and lasting disadvantages, unless this superfluity of produce bear some considerable proportion to the common deficiencies of unfavourable years. It has been almost universally acknowledged that there is no branch of trade, more profitable to a country, even in a commercial point of view, than the sale of rude produce. In general, its value bears a much greater proportion to the expense incurred in procuring it, than that of any other commodity whatever, and the national profit on its sale is in consequence greater. This is often noticed by Dr Smith; but in combating the arguments of the Economists, he seems for a moment to forget it, and to speak of the superior advantage of exporting manufactures.

He observes, that a trading and manufacturing country exports what can subsist and accommodate but very few, and imports the subsistence and accommodation of a great number. The other, exports the subsistence and accommodation of a great number, and imports that of a very few only. The inhabitants of the one must always enjoy a much greater quantity of subsistence, than what their own lands in the actual state of their cultivation could afford. The inhabitants of the other must always enjoy a much smaller quantity.*

In this passage he does not seem to argue with his usual accuracy. Though the manufacturing nation may export a commodity which, in its actual shape, can only subsist and accommodate a very few; yet it must be recollected, that, in order to prepare this commodity for exportation, a considerable part of the revenue of the country had been employed in subsisting and accommodating a great number of workmen. And with regard to the subsistence and accommodation which the other nation exports, whether it be of a great or a small number, it is certainly no more than sufficient to replace the subsistence that had been consumed in the manufacturing nation, together with the profits of the master manufacturer and merchant, which, probably, are not so great as the profits of the farmer and the merchant in the agricultural nation. And though it may be true, that the inhabitants of the manufacturing nation enjoy a greater quantity of subsistence than what their own lands, in the actual state of their cultivation, could afford; yet an inference in favour of the manufacturing system by no means follows, because the adoption of the one or the other system will make the greatest difference in their actual state of cultivation. If, during the course of a century, two landed nations were to pursue these two different systems, that is, if one of them were regularly to export manufactures, and

* Smith, *Wealth of nations*, iii, p. 27.

import subsistence, and the other to export subsistence, and import manufactures, there would be no comparison at the end of the period, between the state of cultivation in the two countries; and no doubt could rationally be entertained that the country which exported its raw produce, would be able to subsist and accommodate a much greater population than the other.

In the ordinary course of things, the exportation of raw produce is sufficiently profitable to the individuals concerned in it. But with regard to national profit, it possesses two peculiar and eminent advantages above any other kind of export. In the first place, raw produce, and more particularly corn, pays from its own funds the expenses of procuring it, and the whole of what is sold is a clear national profit. If I set up a new manufacture, the persons employed in it must be supported out of the funds of subsistence already existing in the country, the value of which must be deducted from the price for which the commodity is sold, before we can estimate the clear national profit; and of course, this profit can only be the profit of the master manufacturer and the exporting merchant. But if I cultivate fresh land, or employ more men in the improvement of what was before cultivated, I increase the general funds of subsistence in the country. With a part of this increase I support all the additional persons employed, and the whole of the remainder which is exported and sold, is a clear national gain, besides the advantage to the country, of supporting an additional population equal to the additional number of persons so employed, without the slightest tendency to diminish the plenty of the rest.

Secondly, it is impossible always to be secure of having enough, if we have not, in general, too much; and the habitual exportation of corn, seems to be the only practicable mode of laying by a store of sufficient magnitude to answer the emergencies, that are to be expected. The evil of scarcity is so dreadful, that any branch of commerce, the tendency of which is to prevent it, cannot but be considered, in a national point of view, as pre-eminently beneficial.

These two advantages, added to that which must necessarily accrue to manufactures from the steady and comparatively low price of provisions and of labour, are so striking, that it must be a point of the first consequence to the permanent prosperity of any country, to be able to carry on the export trade of corn, as one considerable branch of its commercial transactions.

But how to give this ability, how to turn a nation from the habit of importing corn, to the habit of exporting it, is the great difficulty. It has been generally acknowledged, and is frequently noticed by Dr Smith, that the policy of modern Europe has led it to encourage the industry of the towns more than the industry of the country, or, in other words, trade more than agriculture. In this policy, England has certainly not been behind the rest of Europe; perhaps, indeed, except in one instance,* it may be said that she has been the foremost. If things had been left to take their natural course, there is no reason to think that the commercial part of the society would have increased beyond the surplus produce of the cultivators; but the high profits of commerce from monopolies, and other peculiar encouragements, have altered this natural course of things; and the body politic[7] is in an artificial, and in some degree, diseased state, with one of its principal members out of proportion to the rest. Almost all medicine is in itself bad; and one of the great evils of illness is, the necessity of taking it. No person can well be more averse to medicine in the animal economy, or a system of expedients in political economy[8] than myself; but in the present state of the country, something of the kind may be necessary to prevent greater evils. It is a matter of very little comparative importance, whether we are fully supplied with broadcloth, linens, and muslins, or even with tea, sugar, and coffee; and no rational politician therefore, would think of proposing a bounty upon such commodities. But it is certainly a matter of the very highest importance, whether we are fully supplied with food; and if a bounty would produce such a supply, the most liberal political economist might be justified in proposing it; considering food as a commodity distinct from all others, and pre-eminently valuable.

* The bounty on the exportation of corn.

OBSERVATIONS ON THE EFFECTS OF THE CORN LAWS (1814)

OBSERVATIONS ON THE
EFFECTS OF THE CORN LAWS

A revision of the corn laws,[1] it is understood, is immediately to come under the consideration of the legislature. That the decision on such a subject, should be founded on a correct and enlightened view of the whole question, will be allowed to be of the utmost importance, both with regard to the stability of the measures to be adopted, and the effects to be expected from them.

For an attempt to contribute to the stock of information necessary to form such a decision, no apology can be necessary. It may seem indeed probable, that but little further light can be thrown on a subject, which, owing to the system adopted in this country, has been so frequently the topic of discussion; but, after the best consideration which I have been able to give it, I own, it appears to me, that some important considerations have been neglected on both sides of the question, and that the effects of the corn laws, and of a rise or fall in the price of corn, on the agriculture and general wealth of the state, have not yet been fully laid before the public.

If this be true, I cannot help attributing it in some degree to the very peculiar argument brought forward by Dr Smith,[2] in his discussion of the bounty upon the exportation of corn. Those who are conversant with the *Wealth of nations*, will be aware, that its great author has, on this occasion, left entirely in the background the broad, grand, and almost unanswerable arguments, which the general principles of political economy furnish in abundance against all systems of bounties and restrictions, and has only brought forwards, in a prominent manner, one which, it is intended, should apply to corn alone.

It is not surprising that so high an authority should have had the effect of attracting the attention of the advocates of each side of the question, in an especial manner, to this particular argument. Those who have maintained the same cause with Dr Smith, have treated it nearly in the same way; and, though they may have alluded to the other more general and legitimate arguments against bounties and restrictions, have almost universally seemed to place their chief reliance on the appropriate and particular argument relating to the nature of corn.

On the other hand, those who have taken the opposite side of the question, if they have imagined that they had combated this particular argument with success, have been too apt to consider the point as determined, without much reference to the more weighty and important arguments, which remained behind.

Among the latter description of persons I must rank myself. I have always thought, and still think, that this peculiar argument of Dr Smith, is fundamentally erroneous, and that it cannot be maintained without violating the great principles of supply and demand, and contradicting the general spirit and scope of the reasonings, which pervade the *Wealth of nations*.

But I am most ready to confess, that, on a former occasion,[3] when I considered the corn laws, my attention was too much engrossed by this one peculiar view of the subject, to give the other arguments, which belong to it, their due weight.

I am anxious to correct an error, of which I feel conscious. It is not however my intention, on the present occasion, to express an opinion on the general question. I shall only endeavour to state, with the strictest impartiality, what appear to me to be the advantages and disadvantages of each system, in the actual circumstances of our present situation, and what are the specific consequences, which may be expected to result from the adoption of either. My main object is to assist in affording the materials for a just and enlightened decision; and, whatever that decision may be, to prevent disappointment, in the event of the effects of the measure not being such as were previously contemplated. Nothing would tend so powerfully to bring the general principles of political economy into disrepute, and to prevent their spreading, as their being supported upon any occasion by reasoning, which constant and unequivocal experience should afterwards prove to be fallacious.

We must begin, therefore, by an inquiry into the truth of Dr Smith's argument, as we cannot with propriety proceed to the main question, till this preliminary point is settled.

The substance of his argument is, that corn is of so peculiar a nature, that its real price cannot be raised by an increase of its money price; and that, as it is clearly an increase of real price alone which can encourage its production, the rise of money price, occasioned by a bounty, can have no such effect.[4]

It is by no means intended to deny the powerful influence of the price of corn upon the price of labour, on an average of a considerable number of years; but that this influence is not such as to prevent the movement of capital to, or from the land, which is the precise point in question, will be made sufficiently evident by a short inquiry into the manner in which labour is paid and brought into the market, and by a consideration of the consequences to which the assumption of Dr Smith's proposition would inevitably lead.

In the first place, if we inquire into the expenditure of the labouring classes of society, we shall find, that it by no means consists wholly in food, and still less, of course, in mere bread or grain. In looking over that mine of information, for everything relating to prices and labour, Sir Frederick Morton Eden's work on the poor,[5] I find, that in a labourer's family of about an average size, the articles of house rent, fuel, soap, candles, tea, sugar, and clothing, are generally equal to the articles of bread or meal. On a very rough estimate, the whole may be divided into five parts, of which two consist of meal or bread, two of the articles above mentioned, and one of meat, milk, butter, cheese, and potatoes. These divisions are, of course, subject to considerable variations, arising from the number of the family, and the amount of the earnings. But if they merely approximate towards the truth, a rise in the price of corn must be both slow and partial in its effects upon labour. Meat, milk, butter, cheese, and potatoes are slowly affected by the price of corn; house rent, bricks, stone, timber, fuel, soap, candles, and clothing,

still more slowly; and, as far as some of them depend, in part
or in the whole, upon foreign materials (as is the case with lea-
ther, linen, cottons, soap, and candles), they may be considered
as independent of it; like the two remaining articles of tea and
sugar, which are by no means unimportant in their amount.

It is manifest therefore that the whole of the wages of labour
can never rise and fall in proportion to the variations in the
price of grain. And that the effect produced by these variations,
whatever may be its amount, must be very slow in its operation, is proved by the manner in which the supply of labour
takes place; a point, which has been by no means sufficiently
attended to.

Every change in the prices of commodities, if left to find
their natural level, is occasioned by some change, actual or
expected, in the state of the demand or supply. The reason why
the consumer pays a tax upon any manufactured commodity,
or an advance in the price of any of its component parts, is
because, if he cannot or will not pay this advance of price, the
commodity will not be supplied in the same quantity as before;
and the next year there will only be such a proportion in the
market, as is accommodated to the number of persons who will
consent to pay the tax. But, in the case of labour, the operation
of withdrawing the commodity is much slower and more painful. Although the purchasers refuse to pay the advanced price,
the same supply will necessarily remain in the market, not only
the next year, but for some years to come. Consequently, if no
increase take place in the demand, and the advanced price of
provisions be not so great, as to make it obvious that the
labourer cannot support his family, it is probable, that he will
continue to pay this advance, till a relaxation in the rate of the
increase of population causes the market to be under-supplied
with labour; and then, of course, the competition among the
purchasers will raise the price above the proportion of the
advance, in order to restore the supply. In the same manner, if
an advance in the price of labour has taken place during two or
three years of great scarcity, it is probable that, on the return of
plenty, the real recompense of labour will continue higher than
the usual average, till a too rapid increase of population causes

a competition among the labourers, and a consequent diminution of the price of labour below the usual rate.

This account of the manner in which the price of corn may
be expected to operate upon the price of labour, according to
the laws which regulate the progress of population, evidently
shows, that corn and labour rarely keep an even pace together;
but must often be separated at a sufficient distance and for a
sufficient time, to change the direction of capital.[6]

As a further confirmation of this truth, it may be useful to
consider, secondly, the consequences to which the assumption
of Dr Smith's proposition would inevitably lead.

If we suppose, that the real price of corn is unchangeable, or
not capable of experiencing a relative increase or decrease of
value, compared with labour and other commodities, it will follow, that agriculture is at once excluded from the operation of
that principle, so beautifully explained and illustrated by
Dr Smith, by which capital flows from one employment to
another, according to the various and necessarily fluctuating
wants of society. It will follow, that the growth of corn has, at
all times, and in all countries, proceeded with a uniform unvary-
ing pace, occasioned only by the equable increase of agricultural
capital, and can never have been accelerated, or retarded, by
variations of demand. It will follow, that if a country happened
to be either overstocked or understocked with corn, no motive
of interest could exist for withdrawing capital from agriculture,
in the one case, or adding to it in the other, and thus restoring
the equilibrium between its different kinds of produce. But these
consequences, which would incontestably follow from the doctrine, that the price of corn immediately and entirely regulates
the prices of labour and of all other commodities, are so directly
contrary to all experience, that the doctrine itself cannot possibly be true; and we may be assured, that, whatever influence
the price of corn may have upon other commodities, it is neither
so immediate nor so complete, as to make this kind of produce
an exception to all others.

That no such exception exists with regard to corn, is implied
in all the general reasonings of the *Wealth of nations*. Dr Smith
evidently felt this; and wherever, in consequence, he does not

shift the question from the exchangeable value of corn to its physical properties, he speaks with an unusual want of precision, and qualifies his positions by the expressions *much*, and in *any considerable degree*. But it should be recollected, that, with these qualifications, the argument is brought forward expressly for the purpose of showing, that the rise of price, acknowledged to be occasioned by a bounty, on its first establishment, is nominal and not real. Now, what is meant to be distinctly asserted here is, that a rise of price occasioned by a bounty upon the exportation or restrictions upon the importation of corn, cannot be less real than a rise of price to the same amount, occasioned by a course of bad seasons, an increase of population, the rapid progress of commercial wealth, or any other natural cause; and that, if Dr Smith's argument, with its qualifications, be valid for the purpose for which it is advanced, it applies equally to an increased price occasioned by a natural demand.

Let us suppose, for instance, an increase in the demand and the price of corn, occasioned by an unusually prosperous state of our manufactures and foreign commerce; a fact which has frequently come within our own experience. According to the principles of supply and demand, and the general principles of the *Wealth of nations*, such an increase in the price of corn would give a decided stimulus to agriculture; and a more than usual quantity of capital would be laid out upon the land, as appears obviously to have been the case in this country during the last twenty years. According to the peculiar argument of Dr Smith, however, no such stimulus could have been given to agriculture. The rise in the price of corn would have been immediately followed by a proportionate rise in the price of labour and of all other commodities; and, though the farmer and landlord might have obtained, on an average, seventy five shillings a quarter for their corn, instead of sixty, yet the farmer would not have been enabled to cultivate better, nor the landlord to live better. And thus it would appear, that agriculture is beyond the operation of that principle, which distributes the capital of a nation according to the varying profits of stock in different employments; and that no increase of price can, at any time or in any country, materially accelerate the growth of corn, or determine a greater quantity of capital to agriculture.

The experience of every person, who sees what is going forward on the land, and the feelings and conduct both of farmers and landlords, abundantly contradict this reasoning.

Dr Smith was evidently led into this train of argument, from his habit of considering labour as the standard measure of value, and corn as the measure of labour. But, that corn is a very inaccurate measure of labour, the history of our own country will amply demonstrate; where labour, compared with corn, will be found to have experienced very great and striking variations, not only from year to year, but from century to century; and for ten, twenty, and thirty years together;* and that neither labour nor any other commodity can be an accurate measure of real value in exchange, is now considered as one of the most incontrovertible doctrines of political economy; and indeed follows, as a necessary consequence, from the very definition of value in exchange. But to allow that corn regulates the prices of all commodities, is at once to erect it into a standard measure of real value in exchange; and we must either deny the truth of Dr Smith's argument, or acknowledge, that what seems to be quite impossible is found to exist; and that a given quantity of corn, notwithstanding the fluctuations to which its supply and demand must be subject, and the fluctuations to which the supply and demand of all the other commodities with which it is compared must also be subject, will, on the average of a few years, at all times and in all countries, purchase the same quantity of labour and of the necessaries and conveniences of life.

There are two obvious truths in political economy, which have not infrequently been the sources of error.

It is undoubtedly true, that corn might be just as successfully cultivated, and as much capital might be laid out upon the land, at the price of twenty shillings a quarter, as at the price of

---

* From the reign of Edward III to the reign of Henry VII, a day's earnings, in corn, rose from a peck to near half a bushel; and from Henry VII to the end of Elizabeth, it fell from near half a bushel to little more than half a peck.

one hundred shillings, *provided* that every commodity, *both at home and abroad*, were precisely proportioned to the reduced scale. In the same manner as it is strictly true, that the industry and capital of a nation would be exactly the same (with the slight exception at least of plate), if, in every exchange, both at home or abroad, one shilling only were used, where five are used now.

But to infer, from these truths, that any natural or artificial causes, which should raise or lower the values of corn or silver, might be considered as matters of indifference, would be an error of the most serious magnitude. Practically, no material change can take place in the value of either, without producing both lasting and temporary effects, which have a most powerful influence on the distribution of property, and on the demand and supply of particular commodities. The discovery of the mines of America, during the time that it raised the price of corn between three and four times, did not nearly so much as double the price of labour; and, while it permanently diminished the power of all fixed incomes, it gave a prodigious increase of power to all landlords and capitalists.[7] In a similar manner, the fall in the price of corn, from whatever cause it took place, which occurred towards the middle of the last century, accompanied as it was by a rise, rather than a fall in the price of labour, must have given a great relative check to the employment of capital upon the land, and a great relative stimulus to population; a state of things precisely calculated to produce the reaction afterwards experienced, and to convert us from an exporting to an importing nation.

It is by no means sufficient for Dr Smith's argument, that the price of corn should determine the price of labour under precisely the same circumstances of supply and demand. To make it applicable to his purpose, he must show, in addition, that a natural or artificial rise in the price of corn, or in the value of silver, will make no alteration in the state of property, and in the supply and demand of corn and labour; a position which experience uniformly contradicts.

Nothing then can be more evident both from theory and experience, than that the price of corn does not immediately

and generally regulate the prices of labour and all other commodities; and that the real price of corn is capable of varying
for periods of sufficient length to give a decided stimulus or
discouragement to agriculture. It is, of course, only to a temporary encouragement or discouragement, that any commodity,
where the competition is free, can be subjected. We may
increase the capital employed either upon the land or in the
cotton manufacture, but it is impossible permanently to raise
the profits of farmers or particular manufacturers above the
level of other profits; and, after the influx of a certain quantity
of capital, they will necessarily be equalized. Corn, in this
respect, is subjected to the same laws as other commodities,
and the difference between them is by no means so great as
stated by Dr Smith.

In discussing therefore the present question, we must lay
aside the peculiar argument relating to the nature of corn; and
allowing that it is possible to encourage cultivation by corn
laws, we must direct our chief attention to the question of the
policy or impolicy of such a system.

While our great commercial prosperity continues, it is
scarcely possible that we should become again an exporting
nation with regard to corn. The bounty has long been a dead
letter; and will probably remain so. We may at present then
confine our inquiry to the restrictions upon the importation of
foreign corn with a view to an independent supply.

The determination of the question, respecting the policy or
impolicy of continuing the corn laws, seems to depend upon
the three following points.

First, whether, upon the supposition of the most perfect
freedom of importation and exportation, it is probable that
Great Britain and Ireland would grow an independent supply
of corn.

Secondly, whether an independent supply, if it do not come
naturally, is an object really desirable, and one which justifies
the interference of the legislature.

And, thirdly, if an independent supply be considered as such
an object, how far, and by what sacrifices, are restrictions upon
importation adapted to attain the end in view.

Of the first point, it may be observed, that it cannot, in the nature of things, be determined by general principles, but must depend upon the size, soil, facilities of culture, and demand for corn in the country in question. We know that it answers to almost all small well-peopled states, to import their corn; and there is every reason to suppose, that even a large landed nation, abounding in a manufacturing population, and having cultivated all its good soil, might find it cheaper to purchase a considerable part of its corn in other countries, where the supply, compared with the demand, was more abundant. If the intercourse between the different parts of Europe were perfectly easy and perfectly free, it would be by no means natural that one country should be employing a great capital in the cultivation of poor lands, while at no great distance, lands comparatively rich were lying very ill cultivated, from the want of an effectual demand.[8] The progress of agricultural improvement ought naturally to proceed more equably. It is true indeed that the accumulation of capital, skill, and population in particular districts, might give some facilities of culture not possessed by poorer nations; but such facilities could not be expected to make up for great differences in the quality of the soil and the expenses of cultivation. And it is impossible to conceive that under very great inequalities in the demand for corn in different countries, occasioned by a very great difference in the accumulation of mercantile and manufacturing capital and in the number of large towns, an equalization of price could take place, without the transfer of a part of the general supply of Europe, from places where the demand was comparatively deficient, to those where it was comparatively excessive.

According to Oddy's *European commerce*, the Poles can afford to bring their corn to Danzig at thirty two shillings a quarter.[9] The Baltic merchants are said to be of opinion that the price is not very different at present; and there can be little doubt, that if the corn growers in the neighbourhood of the Baltic could look forward to a permanently open market in the British ports, they would raise corn expressly for the purpose. The same observation is applicable to America; and under such circumstances it would answer to both countries, for many years to come, to afford us supplies of corn, in much larger quantities than we have ever yet received from them.

During the five years from 1804 to 1808, both inclusive, the bullion price of corn was about seventy five shillings per quarter; yet, at this price, it answered to us better to import some portion of our supplies than to bring our land into such a state of cultivation as to grow our own consumption. We have already shown how slowly and partially the price of corn affects the price of labour and some of the other expenses of cultivation. Is it credible then that if by the freedom of importation the prices of corn were equalized, and reduced to about forty five or fifty shillings a quarter, it could answer to us to go on improving our agriculture with our increasing population, or even to maintain our produce in its actual state?

It is a great mistake to suppose that the effects of a fall in the price of corn on cultivation may be fully compensated by a diminution of rents. Rich land which yields a large net rent, may indeed be kept up in its actual state, notwithstanding a fall in the price of its produce: as a diminution of rent may be made entirely to compensate this fall and all the additional expenses that belong to a rich and highly taxed country. But in poor land, the fund of rent will often be found quite insufficient for this purpose. There is a good deal of land in this country of such a quality that the expenses of its cultivation, together with the outgoings of poor rates, tithes and taxes, will not allow the farmer to pay more than a fifth or sixth of the value of the whole produce in the shape of rent. If we were to suppose the prices of grain to fall from seventy five shillings to fifty shillings the quarter, the whole of such a rent would be absorbed, even if the price of the whole produce of the farm did not fall in proportion to the price of grain, and making some allowance for a fall in the price of labour. The regular cultivation of such land for grain would of course be given up, and any sort of pasture, however scanty, would be more beneficial both to the landlord and farmer.

But a diminution in the real price of corn is still more efficient, in preventing the future improvement of land, than in throwing land, which has been already improved, out of cultivation. In all progressive countries, the average price of corn is never higher than what is necessary to continue the average increase of produce. And though, in much the greater part of the improved lands of most countries, there is what the French economists call a disposable produce, that is, a portion which might be taken away without interfering with future production, yet, in reference to the whole of the actual produce and the rate at which it is increasing, there is no part of the price so disposable. In the employment of fresh capital upon the land to provide for the wants of an increasing population, whether this fresh capital be employed in bringing more land under the plough or in improving land already in cultivation, the main question always depends upon the expected returns of this capital; and no part of the gross profits can be diminished without diminishing the motive to this mode of employing it. Every diminution of price not fully and immediately balanced by a proportionate fall in all the necessary expenses of a farm, every tax on the land, every tax on farming stock, every tax on the necessaries of farmers, will tell in the computation; and if, after all these outgoings are allowed for, the price of the produce will not leave a fair remuneration for the capital employed, according to the general rate of profits and a rent at least equal to the rent of the land in its former state, no sufficient motive can exist to undertake the projected improvement.

It was a fatal mistake in the system of the Economists to consider merely production and reproduction, and not the provision for an increasing population, to which their territorial tax would have raised the most formidable obstacles.

On the whole then considering the present accumulation of manufacturing population in this country, compared with any other in Europe, the expenses attending enclosures, the price of labour and the weight of taxes, few things seem less probable, than that Great Britain should naturally grow an independent supply of corn; and nothing can be more certain, than that if the prices of wheat in Great Britain were reduced by free importation nearly to a level with those of America and the continent, and if our manufacturing prosperity were to continue increasing, it would incontestably answer to us to support a part of our present population on foreign corn, and nearly the whole probably of the increasing population, which we may naturally expect to take place in the course of the next twenty or twenty five years.

The next question for consideration is, whether an independent supply, if it do not come naturally, is an object really desirable and one which justifies the interference of the legislature.

The general principles of political economy teach us to buy all our commodities where we can have them the cheapest; and perhaps there is no general rule in the whole compass of the science to which fewer justifiable exceptions can be found in practice. In the simple view of present wealth, population, and power, three of the most natural and just objects of national ambition, I can hardly imagine an exception; as it is only by a strict adherence to this rule that the capital of a country can ever be made to yield its greatest amount of produce.

It is justly stated by Dr Smith that by means of trade and manufactures a country may enjoy a much greater quantity of subsistence, and consequently may have a much greater population, than what its own lands could afford. If Holland, Venice, and Hamburg had declined a dependence upon foreign countries for their support, they would always have remained perfectly inconsiderable states, and never could have risen to that pitch of wealth, power, and population, which distinguished the meridian of their career.

Although the price of corn affects but slowly the price of labour, and never regulates it wholly, yet it has unquestionably a powerful influence upon it. A most perfect freedom of intercourse between different nations in the article of corn, greatly contributes to an equalization of prices and a level in the value of the precious metals. And it must be allowed that a country which possesses any peculiar facilities for successful exertion in manufacturing industry, can never make a full and complete use of its advantages; unless the price of its labour and other commodities be reduced to that level compared with other countries, which results from the most perfect freedom of the corn trade.

It has been sometimes urged as an argument in favour of the corn laws, that the great sums which the country has had to pay for foreign corn during the last twenty years must have been injurious to her resources, and might have been saved by the improvement of our agriculture at home. It might with just as much propriety be urged that we lose every year by our forty millions worth of imports, and that we should gain by diminishing these extravagant purchases. Such a doctrine cannot be maintained without giving up the first and most fundamental principles of all commercial intercourse. No purchase is ever made, either at home or abroad, unless that which is received is, in the estimate of the purchaser, of more value than that which is given; and we may rest quite assured, that we shall never buy corn or any other commodities abroad, if we cannot by so doing supply our wants in a more advantageous manner, and by a smaller quantity of capital, than if we had attempted to raise these commodities at home.

It may indeed occasionally happen that in an unfavourable season, our exchanges with foreign countries may be affected by the necessity of making unusually large purchases of corn; but this is in itself an evil of the slightest consequence, which is soon rectified, and in ordinary times is not more likely to happen, if our average imports were two millions of quarters, than if, on an average, we grew our own consumption.

The *unusual* demand is in this case the sole cause of the evil, and not the average amount imported. The habit on the part of foreigners of supplying this amount, would on the contrary rather facilitate than impede further supplies; and as all trade is ultimately a trade of barter, and the power of purchasing cannot be permanently extended without an extension of the power of selling, the foreign countries which supplied us with corn would evidently have their power of purchasing our commodities increased, and would thus contribute more effectually to our commercial and manufacturing prosperity.

It has further been intimated by the friends of the corn laws, that by growing our own consumption we shall keep the price of corn within moderate bounds and to a certain degree steady. But this also is an argument which is obviously not tenable; as in our actual situation, it is only by keeping the price of corn up, very considerably above the average of the rest of Europe, that we can possibly be made to grow our own consumption.

A bounty upon exportation in one country, may be considered, in some degree, as a bounty upon production in Europe; and if the growing price of corn in the country where the bounty is granted be not higher than in others, such a premium might obviously after a time have some tendency to create a temporary abundance of corn and a consequent fall in its price. But restrictions upon importation cannot have the slightest tendency of this kind. Their whole effect is to stint the supply of the general market, and to raise, not to lower, the price of corn.

Nor is it in their nature permanently to secure what is of more consequence, steadiness of prices. During the period indeed, in which the country is obliged regularly to import some foreign grain, a high duty upon it is effectual in steadily keeping up the price of home corn, and giving a very decided stimulus to agriculture. But as soon as the average supply becomes equal to the average consumption, this steadiness ceases. A plentiful year will occasion a sudden fall; and from the average price of the home produce being so much higher than in the other markers of Europe, such a fall can be but little relieved by exportation. It must be allowed, that a free trade in corn would in all ordinary cases not only secure a cheaper, but a more steady, supply of grain.

To counterbalance these striking advantages of a free trade in corn, what are the evils which are apprehended from it?

It is alleged, first, that security is of still more importance than wealth, and that a great country likely to excite the jealousy of others, if it become dependent for the support of any considerable portion of its people upon foreign corn, exposes itself to the risk of having its most essential supplies suddenly fail at the time of its greatest need. That such a risk is not very great will be readily allowed. It would be as much against the interest of those nations which raised the superabundant supply as against the one which wanted it, that the intercourse should at any time be interrupted; and a rich country, which could afford to pay high for its corn, would not be likely to starve, while there was any to be purchased in the market of the commercial world.

At the same time it should be observed that we have latterly seen the most striking instances in all quarters, of governments acting from passion rather than interest.[10] And though the recurrence of such a state of things is hardly to be expected, yet it must be allowed that if anything resembling it should take place in future, when, instead of very nearly growing our own consumption, we were indebted to foreign countries for the support of two millions of our people, the distresses which our manufacturers suffered in 1812 would be nothing compared with the wide-wasting calamity which would be then experienced.[11]

According to the returns made to Parliament in the course of the last session, the quantity of grain and flour exported in 1811 rather exceeded, than fell short of, what was imported; and in 1812, although the average price of wheat was one hundred and twenty five shillings the quarter, the balance of the importations of grain and flour was only about one hundred thousand quarters. From 1805, partly from the operation of the corn laws passed in 1804,[12] but much more from the difficulty and expense of importing corn in the actual state of Europe and America, the price of grain had risen so high and had given such a stimulus to our agriculture, that with the powerful assistance of Ireland, we had been rapidly approaching to the growth of an independent supply. Though the danger therefore may not be great of depending for a considerable portion of our subsistence upon foreign countries, yet it must be acknowledged that nothing like an experiment has yet been made of the distresses that might be produced, during a widely extended war, by the united operation, of a great difficulty in finding a market for our manufactures, accompanied by the absolute necessity of supplying ourselves with a very large quantity of corn.

Secondly, it may be said, that an *excessive* proportion of manufacturing population does not seem favourable to national quiet and happiness. Independently of any difficulties respecting the import of corn, variations in the channels of manufacturing industry and in the facilities of obtaining a vent for its produce are perpetually recurring. Not only during the last four or five years, but during the whole course of the war, have the wages of manufacturing labour been subject to great fluctuations. Sometimes they have been excessively high, and at other times proportionably low; and even during a peace they must always remain subject to the fluctuations which arise from the caprices of taste and fashion, and the competition of other countries. These fluctuations naturally tend to generate discontent and tumult and the evils which accompany them; and if to this we add, that the situation and employment of a manufacturer and his family are even in their best state unfavourable to health and virtue, it cannot appear desirable that a very large proportion of the whole society should consist of manufacturing labourers. Wealth, population and power are, after all, only valuable, as they tend to improve, increase, and secure the mass of human virtue and happiness.[13]

Yet though the condition of the individual employed in common manufacturing labour is not by any means desirable, most of the effects of manufactures and commerce on the general state of society are in the highest degree beneficial. They infuse fresh life and activity into all classes of the state, afford opportunities for the inferior orders to rise by personal merit and exertion, and stimulate the higher orders to depend for distinction upon other grounds than mere rank and riches. They excite invention, encourage science and the useful arts, spread intelligence and spirit, inspire a taste for conveniences and comforts among the labouring classes; and, above all, give a new and happier structure to society, by increasing the proportion of the middle classes, that body on which the liberty, public spirit, and good government of every country must mainly depend.

If we compare such a state of society with a state merely agricultural, the general superiority of the former is incontestable; but it does not follow that the manufacturing system may not be carried to excess, and that beyond a certain point the evils which accompany it may not increase further than its advantages. The question, as applicable to this country, is not whether a manufacturing state is to be preferred to one merely agricultural but whether a country the most manufacturing of any ever recorded in history, with an agriculture however as yet nearly keeping pace with it, would be improved in its happiness, by a great relative increase to its manufacturing population and relative check to its agriculture population.

Many of the questions both in morals and politics seem to be of the nature of the problems *de maximis* and *minimis* in fluxions;[14] in which there is always a point where a certain effect is the greatest, while on either side of this point it gradually diminishes.

With a view to the permanent happiness and security from great reverses of the lower classes of people in this country, I should have little hesitation in thinking it desirable that its agriculture should keep pace with its manufactures, even at the expense of retarding in some degree the growth of manufactures; but it is a different question, whether it is wise to break through a general rule, and interrupt the natural course of things, in order to produce and maintain such an equalization.

Thirdly, it may be urged, that though a comparatively low value of the precious metals, or a high nominal price of corn and labour, tends rather to check commerce and manufactures, yet its effects are permanently beneficial to those who live by the wages of labour.

If the labourers in two countries were to earn the same quantity of corn, yet in one of them the nominal price of this corn were twenty five per cent higher than in the other, the condition of the labourers where the price of corn was the highest, would be decidedly the best. In the purchase of all commodities purely foreign; in the purchase of those commodities, the raw materials of which are wholly or in part foreign, and therefore influenced in a great degree by foreign prices, and in the purchase of all home commodities which are taxed, and not taxed *ad valorem*, they would have an unquestionable advantage: and these articles altogether are not inconsiderable even in the expenditure of a cottager.

As one of the evils therefore attending the throwing open our ports, it may be stated, that if the stimulus to population, from the cheapness of grain, should in the course of twenty or twenty five years reduce the earnings of the labourer to the same quantity of corn as at present, at the same price as in the rest of Europe, the condition of the lower classes of people in this country would be deteriorated. And if they should not be so reduced, it is quite clear that the encouragement to the growth of corn will not be fully restored, even after the lapse of so long a period.

Fourthly, it may be observed, that though it might by no means be advisable to *commence* an artificial system of regulations in the trade of corn; yet if, by such a system already established and other concurring causes, the prices of corn and of many commodities had been raised above the level of the rest of Europe, it becomes a different question, whether it would be advisable to risk the effects of so great and sudden a fall in the price of corn, as would be the consequence of at once throwing open our ports. One of the cases in which, according to Dr Smith, 'it may be a matter of deliberation how far it is proper to restore the free importation of foreign goods after it has been for some time interrupted, is, when particular manufactures, by means of high duties and prohibitions upon all foreign goods which can come into competition with them, have been so far extended as to employ a great multitude of hands.'*

That the production of corn is not exempted from the operation of this rule has already been shown; and there can be no doubt that the interests of a large body of landholders and farmers, the former to a certain extent permanently, and the latter temporarily, would be deeply affected by such a change of policy. These persons too may further urge, with much appearance of justice, that in being made to suffer this injury, they would not be treated fairly and impartially. By protecting duties of various kinds, an unnatural quantity of capital is

* Adam Smith, *An inquiry into the nature and causes of the wealth of nations*, 6th ed., 3 vols (1791), ii, p. 202.

directed towards manufactures and commerce and taken from the land; and while, on account of these duties, they are obliged to purchase both home-made and foreign goods at a kind of monopoly price, they would be obliged to sell their own at the price of the most enlarged competition. It may fairly indeed be said, that to restore the freedom of the corn trade, while protecting duties on various other commodities are allowed to remain, is not really to restore things to their natural level, but to depress the cultivation of the land below other kinds of industry. And though, even in this case, it might still be a national advantage to purchase corn where it could be had the cheapest; yet it must be allowed that the owners of property in land would not be treated with impartial justice.

If under all the circumstances of the case, it should appear impolitic to check our agriculture; and so desirable to secure an independent supply of corn, as to justify the continued interference of the legislature for this purpose, the next question for our consideration is;

Fifthly, how far and by what sacrifices, restrictions upon the importation of foreign corn are calculated to attain the end in view.

With regard to the mere practicability of effecting an independent supply, it must certainly be allowed that foreign corn may be so prohibited as completely to secure this object. A country with a large territory, which determines never to import corn, except when the price indicates a scarcity, will unquestionably in average years supply its own wants. But a law passed with this view might be so framed as to effect its object rather by a diminution of the people than an increase of the corn: and even if constructed in the most judicious manner, it can never be made entirely free from objections of this kind.

The evils which must always belong to restrictions upon the importation of foreign corn, are the following:

1. A certain waste of the national resources, by the employment of a greater quantity of capital than is necessary for procuring the quantity of corn required.

2. A relative disadvantage in all foreign commercial transactions, occasioned by the high comparative prices of corn and

labour, and the low value of silver, as far as they affect export-able commodities.

3. Some check to population, occasioned by a check to that abundance of corn, and demand for manufacturing labours, which would be the result of a perfect freedom of importation.

4. The necessity of constant revision and interference, which belongs to almost every artificial system.

It is true, that during the last twenty years we have witnessed a very great increase of population and of our exported com-modities, under a high price of corn and labour; but this must have happened in spite of these high prices, not in consequence of them; and is to be attributed chiefly to the unusual success of our inventions for saving labour and the unusual monopoly of the commerce of Europe which has been thrown into our hands by the war.[15] When these inventions spread and Europe recov-ers in some degree her industry and capital, we may not find it so easy to support the competition. The more strongly the nat-ural state of the country directs it to the purchase of foreign corn, the higher must be the protecting duty or the price of importation, in order to secure an independent supply; and the greater consequently will be the relative disadvantage which we shall suffer in our commerce with other countries. This drawback may, it is certain, ultimately be so great as to coun-terbalance the effects of our extraordinary skill, capital and machinery.

The whole, therefore, is evidently a question of contending advantages and disadvantages; and, as interests of the highest importance are concerned, the most mature deliberation is required in its decision.

In whichever way it is settled, some sacrifices must be sub-mitted to. Those who contend for the unrestrained admission of foreign corn, must not imagine that the cheapness it will occa-sion will be an unmixed good; and that it will give an additional stimulus to the commerce and population of the country, while it leaves the present state of agriculture and its future increase undisturbed. They must be prepared to see a sudden stop put to the progress of our cultivation, and even some diminution of its actual state; and they must be ready to encounter the as yet untried risk, of making a considerable proportion of our population dependent upon foreign supplies of grain, and of exposing them to those vicissitudes and changes in the channels of commerce to which manufacturing states are of necessity subject.

On the other hand, those who contend for a continuance and increase of restrictions upon importation, must not imagine that the present state of agriculture and its present rate of eminence can be maintained without injuring other branches of the national industry. It is certain that they will not only be injured, but that they will be injured rather more than agriculture is benefited; and that a determination at all events to keep up the prices of our corn might involve us in a system of regulations, which, in the new state of Europe which is expected, might not only retard in some degree, as hitherto, the progress of our foreign commerce, but ultimately begin to diminish it; in which case our agriculture itself would soon suffer, in spite of all our efforts to prevent it.

If, on weighing fairly the good to be obtained and the sacrifices to be made for it, the legislature should determine to adhere to its present policy of restrictions, it should be observed, in reference to the mode of doing it, that the time chosen is by no means favourable for the adoption of such a system of regulations as will not need future alterations. The state of the currency must throw the most formidable obstacles in the way of all arrangements respecting the prices of importation.

If we return to cash payments,[16] while bullion continues of its present value compared with corn, labour, and most other commodities; little alteration will be required in the existing corn laws. The bullion price of corn is now very considerably under sixty three shillings, the price at which the high duty ceases according to the Act of 1804.

If our currency continues at its present nominal value, it will be necessary to make very considerable alterations in the laws, or they will be a mere dead letter and become entirely inefficient in restraining the importation of foreign corn.

If, on the other hand, we should return to our old standard, and at the same time the value of bullion should fall from the restoration of general confidence, and the ceasing of an extraordinary demand for bullion; an intermediate sort of alteration will be necessary, greater than in the case first mentioned, and less than in the second.

In this state of necessary uncertainty with regard to our currency, it would be extremely impolitic to come to any *final regulation*, founded on an average which would be essentially influenced by the nominal prices of the last five years.

To these considerations it may be added, that there are many reasons to expect a more than usual abundance of corn in Europe during the repose to which we may now look forward.[17] Such an abundance* took place after the termination of the war of Louis XIV, and seems still more probable now, if the late devastation of the human race and interruption to industry should be succeeded by a peace of fifteen or twenty years.

The prospect of an abundance of this kind, may to some perhaps appear to justify still greater efforts to prevent the introduction of foreign corn; and to secure our agriculture from too sudden a shock, it may be necessary to give it some protection. But if, under such circumstances with regard to the price of corn in Europe, we were to endeavour to retain the prices of the last five years, it is scarcely possible to suppose that our foreign commerce would not in a short time begin to languish. The difference between ninety shillings a quarter and thirty two shillings a quarter, which is said to be the price of the best wheat in France, is almost too great for our capital and machinery to contend with. The wages of labour in this country, though they have not risen in proportion to the price of corn, have been beyond all doubt considerably influenced by it.

If the whole of the difference in the expense of raising corn in this country and in the corn countries of Europe was occasioned by taxation, and the precise amount of that taxation as affecting corn, could be clearly ascertained; the simple and obvious way of restoring things to their natural level and

---

* The cheapness of corn, during the first half of the last century, was rather oddly mistaken by Dr Smith for a rise in the value of silver. That it was owing to peculiar abundance was obvious, from all other commodities rising instead of falling.

enabling us to grow corn, as in a state of perfect freedom, would be to lay precisely the same amount of tax on imported corn and grant the same amount in a bounty upon exportation. Dr Smith observes, that when the necessities of a state have obliged it to lay a tax upon a home commodity, a duty of equal amount upon the same kind of commodity when imported from abroad, only tends to restore the level of industry which had necessarily been disturbed by the tax.

But the fact is that the whole difference of price does not by any means arise solely from taxation. A part of it, and I should think, no inconsiderable part, is occasioned by the necessity of yearly cultivating and improving more poor land, to provide for the demands of an increasing population; which land must of course require more labour and dressing, and expense of all kinds in its cultivation. The growing price of corn therefore, independently of all taxation, is probably higher than in the rest of Europe; and this circumstance not only increases the sacrifice that must be made for an independent supply, but enhances the difficulty of framing a legislative provision to secure it.

When the former very high duties upon the importation of foreign grain were imposed, accompanied by the grant of a bounty, the growing price of corn in this country was not higher than in the rest of Europe; and the stimulus given to agriculture by these laws aided by other favourable circumstances occasioned so redundant a growth, that the average price of corn was not affected by the prices of importation. Almost the only sacrifice made in this case was the small rise of price occasioned by the bounty on its first establishment, which, after it had operated as a stimulus to cultivation, terminated in a period of increased cheapness.

If we were to attempt to pursue the same system in a very different state of the country, by raising the importation prices and the bounty in proportion to the fall in the value of money, the effects of the measure might bear very little resemblance to those which took place before. Since 1740 Great Britain has added nearly four millions and a half to her population, and with the addition of Ireland probably eight millions, a greater proportion I believe than in any other country in Europe,[18] and from the structure of our society and the great increase of the middle classes, the demands for the products of pasture have probably been augmented in a still greater proportion.[19] Under these circumstances it is scarcely conceivable that any effects could make us again export corn to the same comparative extent as in the middle of the last century. An increase of the bounty in proportion to the fall in the value of money, would certainly not be sufficient; and probably nothing could accomplish it but such an excessive premium upon exportation, as would at once stop the progress of the population and foreign commerce of the country, in order to let the produce of corn get before it.

In the present state of things then we must necessarily give up the idea of creating a large average surplus. And yet very high duties upon importation, operating alone, are peculiarly liable to occasion great fluctuations of price. It has been already stated, that after they have succeeded in producing an independent supply by steady high prices, an abundant crop which cannot be relieved by exportation, must occasion a very sudden fall.* Should this continue a second or third year, it would unquestionably discourage cultivation, and the country would again become partially dependent. The necessity of importing foreign corn would of course again raise the price of importation, and the same causes might make a similar fall and a subsequent rise recur; and thus prices would tend to vibrate between the high prices occasioned by the high duties on importation and the low prices occasioned by a glut which could not be relieved by exportation.

It is under these difficulties that the parliament is called upon to legislate. On account of the deliberation which the subject naturally requires, but more particularly on account of the present uncertain state of the currency, it would be desirable to delay any final regulation. Should it however be determined to proceed *immediately* to a revision of the present laws, in order

---

* The sudden fall of the price of corn this year seems to be a case precisely in point. It should be recollected however that quantity always in some degree balances cheapness.

to render them more efficacious, there would be some obvious advantages, both as a temporary and permanent measure, in giving to the restrictions the form of a constant duty upon foreign corn, not to act as a prohibition, but as a protecting, and at the same time, profitable tax. And with a view to prevent the great fall that might be occasioned by a glut, under the circumstances before adverted to, but not to create an average surplus, the old bounty might be continued, and allowed to operate in the same way as the duty at all times, except in extreme cases.

These regulations would be extremely simple and obvious in their operations, would give greater certainty to the foreign grower, afford a profitable tax to the government, and would be less affected even by the expected improvement of the currency, than high importation prices founded upon any past average.*

---

* Since sending the above to the press I have heard of the new resolutions that are to be proposed. The machinery seems to be a little complicated; but if it will work easily and well, they are greatly preferable to those which were suggested last year.

To the free exportation asked, no rational objection can of course be made, though its efficiency in the present state of things may be doubted. With regard to the duties, if any be imposed, there must always be a question of degree. The principal objection which I see to the present scale, is that with an average price of corn in the actual state of the currency, there will be a pretty strong competition of foreign grain; whereas with an average price on the restoration of the currency, foreign competition will be absolutely and entirely excluded.

SELECTIONS FROM PRINCIPLES OF POLITICAL ECONOMY (1820)

PRINCIPLES OF
POLITICAL ECONOMY

INTRODUCTION

It has been said, and perhaps with truth, that the conclusions of Political Economy partake more of the certainty of the stricter sciences than those of most of the other branches of human knowledge. Yet we should fall into a serious error if we were to suppose that any propositions, the practical results of which depend upon the agency of so variable a being as man, and the qualities of so variable a compound as the soil, can ever admit of the same kinds of proof, or lead to the same certain conclusions, as those which relate to figure and number. There are indeed in political economy great general principles, to which exceptions are of the most rare occurrence, and prominent land-marks which may almost always be depended upon as safe guides; but even these, when examined, will be found to resemble in most particulars the great general rules in morals and politics founded upon the known passions and propensities of human nature: and whether we advert to the qualities of man, or of the earth he is destined to cultivate, we shall be compelled to acknowledge, that the science of political economy bears a nearer resemblance to the science of morals and politics than to that of mathematics.

This conclusion, which could hardly fail to be formed merely from a view of the subjects about which political economy is conversant, is further strengthened by the differences of opinion which have prevailed among those who have directed a large share of talent and attention to this study.

During the prevalence of the mercantile system,[1] the interest which the subject excited was confined almost exclusively to those who were engaged in the details of commerce, or expected immediate benefit from its results. The differences which prevailed among merchants and statesmen, which were differences rather in practice than principle, were not calculated to attract much attention. But no sooner was the subject raised into a science by the works of the Economists[2] and of Adam Smith, than a memorable schism divided, for a considerable time, the students of this new branch of knowledge, on the fundamental questions – What is wealth? and from what source or sources is it derived?

Happily for the interests of the science and its usefulness to society, the Economists and Adam Smith entirely agreed on some of those great general principles which lead to the most important practical conclusions; such as the freedom of trade, and the leaving every person, while he adheres to the rules of justice, to pursue his own interest his own way, together with some others: and unquestionably their agreement on these principles affords the strongest presumption of their truth. Yet the differences of the Economists and Adam Smith were not mere differences in theory; they were not different interpretations of the same phenomena, which would have no influence on practice; but they involved such views of the nature and origin of wealth, as, if adopted, would lead, in almost every country, to great practical changes, particularly on the very important subject of taxation.

Since the era of these distinguished writers, the subject has gradually attracted the attention of a greater number of persons, particularly during the last twenty or thirty years.[3] All the main propositions of the science have been examined, and the events which have since occurred, tending either to illustrate or confute them, have been repeatedly discussed. The result of this examination and discussion seems to be, that on some very important points there are still great differences of opinion. Among these, perhaps, may be reckoned – The definitions of wealth and of productive labour – The nature and measures of value – The nature and extent of the principles of demand and supply – The origin and progress of rent – The causes which determine the wages of labour and the profits of stock – The causes which practically retard and limit the progress of wealth – The level of the precious metals in different countries – The principles of taxation, &c. On all these points, and many others among the numerous subjects which belong to political economy, differences have prevailed among persons whose opinions are entitled to attention. Some of these questions are to a certain degree theoretical; and the solution of them, though obviously necessary to the improvement of the science, might not essentially affect its practical rules; but others are of such a nature, that the determination of them one way or the other will necessarily influence the conduct both of individuals and of governments; and their correct determination therefore must be a matter of the highest practical importance.

In a science such as that of political economy, it is not to be expected that an *universal* assent should be obtained to all its important propositions; but, in order to give them their proper weight and justify their being acted upon, it is extremely desirable, indeed almost necessary, that a considerable *majority* of those who, from their attention to the subject, are considered by the public as likely to be the most competent judges, should agree in the truth of them.

Among those writers who have treated the subject scientifically, there is not perhaps, at the present moment, so general an agreement as would be desirable to give effect to their conclusions; and the writers who peculiarly call themselves practical, either draw no general inferences, or are so much influenced by narrow, partial, and sometimes interested views, that no reliance can be placed on them for the establishment of general rules.[4] The last twenty or thirty years have besides been marked by a train of events of a most extraordinary kind; and there has hardly yet been time so to arrange and examine them as to see to what extent they confirm or invalidate the received principles of the science to which they relate.

The present period, therefore, seems to be unpropitious to the publication of a new systematic treatise on political economy. The treatise which we already possess is still of the very highest value; and till a more general agreement shall be found to take place, both with respect to the controverted points of Adam Smith's work, and the nature and extent of the additions to it, which the more advanced stage of the science has rendered necessary, it is obviously more advisable that the different subjects which admit of doubt should be treated separately. When these discussions have been for some time before the public, and a sufficient opportunity has been given, by the collision of different opinions and an appeal to experience, to separate what is true from what is false, the different parts may then be combined into a consistent whole, and may be expected to carry with it such weight and authority as to produce the most useful practical results.

The principal cause of error, and of the differences which prevail at present among the scientific writers on political economy, appears to me to be a precipitate attempt to simplify and generalize; and while their more practical opponents draw too hasty inferences from a frequent appeal to partial facts, these writers run into a contrary extreme, and do not sufficiently try their theories by a reference to that enlarged and comprehensive experience which, on so complicated a subject, can alone establish their truth and utility.[5]

To minds of a certain cast there is nothing so captivating as simplification and generalization. It is indeed the desirable and legitimate object of genuine philosophy, whenever it can be effected consistently with truth; and for this very reason, the natural tendency towards it has, in almost every science with which we are acquainted, led to crude and premature theories.

In political economy the desire to simplify has occasioned an unwillingness to acknowledge the operation of more causes than one in the production of particular effects; and if one cause would account for a considerable portion of a certain class of phenomena, the whole has been ascribed to it without sufficient attention to the facts, which would not admit of being so solved.

It is certain that we cannot too highly respect and venerate that admirable rule of Newton, not to admit more causes than are necessary to the solution of the phenomena we are considering, but the rule itself implies, that those which really are necessary must be admitted. Before the shrine of truth, as discovered by facts and experience, the fairest theories and the most beautiful classifications must fall.[6] The chemist of thirty years ago may be allowed to regret, that new discoveries in the science should disturb and confound his previous systems and arrangements; but he is not entitled to the name of philosopher, if he does not give them up without a struggle, as soon as the experiments which refute them are fully established.[7]

The same tendency to simplify and generalize, produces a still greater disinclination to allow of modifications, limitations, and exceptions to any rule or proposition, than to admit the operation of more causes than one. Nothing indeed is so unsatisfactory, and gives so unscientific and unmasterly an air to a proposition as to be obliged to make admissions of this kind; yet there is no truth of which I feel a stronger conviction than that there are many important propositions in political economy which absolutely require limitations and exceptions; and it may be confidently stated that the frequent combination of complicated causes, the action and reaction of cause and effect on each other, and the necessity of limitations and exceptions in a considerable number of important propositions, form the main difficulties of the science, and occasion those frequent mistakes which it must be allowed are made in the prediction of results.

To explain myself by an instance. Adam Smith has stated, that capitals are increased by parsimony, that every frugal man is a public benefactor,* and that the increase of wealth depends upon the balance of produce above consumption.† That these propositions are true to a great extent is perfectly unquestionable. No considerable and continued increase of wealth could possibly take place without that degree of frugality which occasions, annually, the conversion of some revenue into capital, and creates a balance of produce above consumption; but it is

---

* *Wealth of Nations*, Book II. c. iii. pp. 15–18. 6th edit.
† Book IV. c. iii. p. 250.

quite obvious that they are not true to an indefinite extent, and that the principle of saving, pushed to excess, would destroy the motive to production. If every person were satisfied with the simplest food, the poorest clothing, and the meanest houses, it is certain that no other sort of food, clothing, and lodging would be in existence; and as there would be no adequate motive to the proprietors of land to cultivate well, not only the wealth derived from conveniences and luxuries would be quite at an end, but if the same divisions of land continued, the production of food would be prematurely checked, and population would come to a stand long before the soil had been well cultivated. If consumption exceed production, the capital of the country must be diminished, and its wealth must be gradually destroyed from its want of power to produce; if production be in a great excess above consumption, the motive to accumulate and produce must cease from the want of will to consume. The two extremes are obvious; and it follows that there must be some intermediate point, though the resources of political economy may not be able to ascertain it, where, taking into consideration both the power to produce and the will to consume, the encouragement to the increase of wealth is the greatest.

The division of landed property presents another obvious instance of the same kind. No person has ever for a moment doubted that the division of such immense tracts of land as were formerly in possession of the great feudal proprietors must be favourable to industry and production. It is equally difficult to doubt that a division of landed property may be carried to such an extent as to destroy all the benefits to be derived from the accumulation of capital and the division of labour, and to occasion the most extended poverty. There is here then a point as well as in the other instance, though we may not know how to place it, where the division of property is best suited to the actual circumstances of the society, and calculated to give the best stimulus to production and to the increase of wealth and population. It follows clearly that no general rule can be laid down respecting the advantage to be derived from saving, or the division of property, without limitations and exceptions; and it is particularly worthy of attention that in cases of this kind, where the extremes are obvious and striking, but the most advantageous mean cannot be marked, that in the progress of society effects may be produced by an unnoticed approximation to this middle point, which are attributed to other causes, and lead to false conclusions.

The tendency to premature generalization occasions also, in some of the principal writers on political economy, an unwillingness to bring their theories to the test of experience. I should be the last person to lay an undue stress upon isolated facts, or to think that a consistent theory, which would account for the great mass of phenomena observable, was immediately invalidated by a few discordant appearances, the reality and the bearings of which, there might not have been an opportunity of fully examining. But certainly no theory can have any pretension to be accepted as correct, which is inconsistent with general experience. Such inconsistency appears to me at once a full and sufficient reason for its rejection. Under such circumstances it must be either radically false, or essentially incomplete; and in either case, it can neither be adopted as a satisfactory solution of existing phenomena, nor acted upon with any degree of safety for the future.

The first business of philosophy is to account for things as they are; and till our theories will do this, they ought not to be the ground of any practical conclusion. I should never have had that steady and unshaken confidence in the theory of population which I have invariably felt, if it had not appeared to me to be confirmed, in the most remarkable manner, by the state of society as it actually exists in every country with which we are acquainted. To this test I appealed in laying it down; and a frequent appeal to this sort of experience is pre-eminently necessary in most of the subjects of political economy, where various and complicated causes are often in operation, the presence of which can only be ascertained in this way. A theory may appear to be correct, and may really be correct under given premises; it may further *appear* that these premises are the same as those under which the theory is about to be applied; but a difference, which might before have been unobserved, may shew itself in the difference of the results from those which were expected; and the theory may justly be considered as failing, whether this failure arises from an original error in its formation, or from its general inapplicability, or specific misapplication, to actual circumstances.

Where unforeseen causes may possibly be in operation, and the causes that are foreseen are liable to great variations in their strength and efficacy, an accurate yet comprehensive attention to facts is necessary, both to prevent the multiplication of erroneous theories, and to confirm and sanction those that are just.

The science of political economy is essentially practical, and applicable to the common business of human life. There are few branches of human knowledge where false views may do more harm, or just views more good. I cannot agree, therefore, with a writer in one of our most popular critical journals, who considers the subjects of population, bullion, and corn laws in the same light as the scholastic questions of the middle ages, and puts marks of admiration to them expressive of his utter astonishment that such perishable stuff should engage any portion of the public attention.*[8]

In the very practical science of political economy perhaps it might be difficult to mention three subjects more practical than those unfortunately selected for a comparison with scholastic questions. But in fact, most of the subjects which belong to it are peculiarly applicable to the common concerns of mankind. What shall we say of all the questions relating to taxation, various and extensive as they are? It will hardly be denied that they come home to the business and bosoms of mankind. What shall we say of the laws which regulate exchangeable value, or every act of purchase and exchange which takes place in our markets? What of the laws which regulate the profits of stock, the interest of money, the rent of land, the value of the precious metals in different countries, the rates of exchange, &c. &c.?

* *Quarterly Review*, No. xxix. Art. viii.

The study of the laws of nature is, in all its branches, interesting. Even those physical laws by which the more distant parts of the universe are governed, and over which, of course, it is impossible for man to have the slightest influence, are yet noble and rational objects of curiosity; but the laws which regulate the movements of human society have an infinitely stronger claim to our attention, both because they relate to objects about which we are daily and hourly conversant, and because their effects are continually modified by human interference.

There are some eminent persons so strongly attached to the received general rules of political economy, that, though they are aware that in practice some exceptions to them may occasionally occur; yet they do not think it wise and politic to notice them, for fear of directing the public attention too much and too frequently to exceptions, and thus weakening the force and utility of the general rules.

It is, for instance, one of the most general rules in political economy, that governments should not interfere in the direction of capital and industry, but leave every person, so long as he obeys the laws of justice, to pursue his own interest in his own way, as the best security for the constant and equable supply of the national wants. Though to this rule they allow that exceptions may possibly occur; yet thinking that the danger from the officious meddling of governments is so much greater than any which could arise from the neglect of such exceptions, they would be inclined to make the rule universal.

In this, however, I cannot agree. Though I should most readily allow that altogether more evil is likely to arise from governing too much, than from a tendency to the other extreme; yet, still, if the consequences of not attending to these exceptions were of sufficient magnitude and frequency to be conspicuous to the public, I should be decidedly of opinion, that the cause of general principles was much more likely to lose than to gain by concealment. Nothing can tend so strongly to bring theories and general principles into discredit as the occurrence of consequences, from particular measures, which have not been foreseen. Though in reality such an event forms no just objection to theory, in the general and proper sense of the term; yet it forms a most valid objection to the specific theory in question, as proving it in some way or other wrong; and with the mass of mankind this will pass for an impeachment of general principles, and of the knowledge or good faith of those who are in the habit of inculcating them. It appears to me, I confess, that the most perfect sincerity, together with the greatest degree of accuracy attainable, founded upon the most comprehensive view of all the circumstances of the case, are necessary to give that credit and circulation to general principles which is so desirable. And no views of temporary advantage, nor, what is more likely to operate, the fear of destroying the simplicity of a general rule, should ever tempt us to deviate from the strict line of truth, or to conceal or overlook any circumstances that may interfere with the universality of the principle.

There is another class of persons who set a very high value upon the received general rules of political economy, as of the most extensive practical use. They have seen the errors of the mercantile system refuted and replaced by a more philosophical and correct view of the subject; and having made themselves masters of the question so far, they seem to be satisfied with what they have got, and do not look with a favorable eye on new and further inquiries, particularly if they do not see at once clearly and distinctly to what beneficial effects they lead.

This indisposition to innovation, even in science, may possibly have its use, by tending to check crude and premature theories; but it is obvious that, if carried too far, it strikes at the root of all improvement. It is impossible to observe the great events of the last twenty-five years in their relation to subjects belonging to political economy, and sit down satisfied with what has been already done in the science. But if the science be manifestly incomplete, and yet of the highest importance, it would surely be most unwise to restrain inquiry, conducted upon just principles, even where the immediate practical utility of it was not visible. In mathematics, chemistry, and every branch of natural philosophy, how many are the inquiries necessary to their improvement and completion, which, taken separately, do not appear to lead to any specifically advantageous purpose! How many useful inventions, and how much valuable and improving knowledge would have been lost, if a rational curiosity and a mere love of information had not generally been allowed to be a sufficient motive for the search after truth!

I should not, therefore, consider it as by any means conclusive against further inquiries in political economy, if they would not always bear the rigid application of the test of *cui bono?*[9] But such, in fact, is the nature of the science, so intimately is it connected with the business of mankind, that I really believe more of its propositions will bear this test than those of any other department of human knowledge.

To trace distinctly the operations of that circle of causes and effects in political economy which are acting and re-acting on each other, so as to foresee their results, and lay down general rules accordingly, is, in many cases, a task of very great difficulty. But there is scarcely a single inquiry belonging to these subjects, however abstruse and remote it may at first sight appear, which in some point or other does not bear directly upon practice. It is unquestionably desirable, therefore, both with a view to the improvement and completion of the science, and the practical advantages which may be expected from it, that such inquiries should be pursued; and no common difficulty or obscurity should be allowed to deter those who have leisure and ability for such researches.

In many cases, indeed, it may not be possible to predict results with certainty, on account of the complication of the causes in action, the different degrees of strength and efficacy with which they may operate, and the number of unforeseen circumstances which are likely to interfere; but it is surely knowledge of the highest importance to be able to draw a line, with tolerable precision, between those cases where the expected results are certain, and those where they are doubtful; and further to be able satisfactorily to explain, in the latter case, the reasons of such uncertainty.

To know what can be done, and how to do it, is, beyond a doubt, the most valuable species of information. The next to it is, to know what cannot be done, and why we cannot do it.

The first enables us to attain a positive good, to increase our powers, and augment our happiness: the second saves us from the evil of fruitless attempts, and the loss and misery occasioned by perpetual failure.

But these inquiries demand more time and application than the practical statesman, whom of all others they most nearly concern, can give to them. In the public measures of every state all are, no doubt, interested; but a peculiar responsibility, as well as interest, must be felt by those who are the principal advisers of them, and have the greatest influence in their enactment; and if they have not leisure for such researches themselves, they should not be unwilling, under the guidance of a sound discretion, to make use of the advantages which may be afforded by the leisure of others. They will not indeed be justified in taking any decided steps, if they do not themselves see, or at least think they see, the way they are going; but they may be fairly expected to make use of all the lights which are best calculated to illumine their way, and enable them to reach the object which they have in view.

It may perhaps be thought that, if the great principle so ably maintained by Adam Smith be true, namely, that the best way of advancing a people towards wealth and prosperity is *not* to interfere with them, the business of government, in matters relating to political economy, must be most simple and easy.

But it is to be recollected, in the first place, that there is a class of duties connected with these subjects, which, it is universally acknowledged, belongs to the Sovereign; and though the line appears to be drawn with tolerable precision, when it is considered generally; yet when we come to particulars, doubts may arise, and certainly in many instances have arisen, as to the subjects to be included in this classification. To what extent education and the support of the poor should be public concerns? What share the Government should take in the construction and maintenance of roads, canals, public docks? What course it should adopt with regard to colonization and emigration, and in the support of forts and establishments in foreign countries? On all these questions, and many others, there may be differences of opinion; and on all these questions the sovereign and his ministers are called upon to decide.

Secondly, every actual government has to administer a body of laws relating to agriculture, manufactures, and commerce, which was formed at a period comparatively unenlightened, and many of which, therefore, it must be desirable to repeal: but to see fully the amount of partial evil arising from present change, and the extent of general good to be effected by it, so as to warrant active interference, requires no inconsiderable share of knowledge and judgment; while to remain inactive under such circumstances, can only be justified by a conviction, founded on the best grounds, that in any specific change contemplated, taken in all its consequences, the balance of evil will preponderate.

Thirdly, there is one cause in every state which absolutely impels the government to action, and puts an end to the possibility of letting things alone. This is the necessity of taxation; and as taxes cannot, in the nature of things, be imposed without interfering with individual industry and wealth, it becomes a matter of the very highest importance to know how they may take place with the least possible prejudice to the prosperity of the state, and the happiness of individuals.

With regard to this latter subject indeed, it bears on so many points, that the truth or falsehood of the theories on all the principal questions in political economy would occasion, or at least ought to occasion, a practical difference in the mode of raising some of the actual taxes. It is well known that, if the theory of the Economists were true, all taxes should be laid on the land; and it depends entirely upon the general laws which regulate the wages of labour, the profits of stock, the rent of land, exchangeable value, the currencies of different countries, the production and distribution of wealth, &c. &c. whether any existing system of taxation be the best, or whether it might be altered for the better.

It is obviously, therefore, impossible for a government strictly to let things take their natural course; and to recommend such a line of conduct, without limitations and exceptions, could not fail to bring disgrace upon general principles, as totally inapplicable to practice.

It may, however, safely be asserted, that a propensity to govern too much is a certain indication of ignorance and rashness. The ablest physicians are the most sparing in the use of medicine, and the most inclined to trust to the healing power of nature. The statesman, in like manner, who knows the most of his business, will be the most unwilling to interrupt the natural direction of industry and capital. But both are occasionally called upon to interfere, and the more science they respectively possess, the more judiciously will they do it; nor will the acknowledged propriety of interfering but little supersede, in any degree, the use of the most extensive professional knowledge in both cases.

One of the specific objects of the present work is to prepare the general rules of political economy for practical application, by a frequent reference to experience, and by taking as comprehensive a view as I can of all the causes that concur in the production of particular phenomena.

I am sufficiently aware, that in this mode of conducting inquiry, there is a chance of falling into errors of an opposite kind to those which arise from a tendency to simplification. Certain appearances, which are merely co-existent and incidental, may be mistaken for causes; and a theory formed upon this mistake will unite the double disadvantage of being both complex and incorrect. I am inclined to think that Adam Smith occasionally fell into this error, and drew inferences from actual appearances, not warranted by general principles. From the low price of wheat, for instance, during the first half of the last century, he seems to infer that wheat is generally cheaper in rich than in poor countries; and from the small quantity of corn actually imported during that period, even in the scarcest years, he infers generally, that the quantity imported can never be such as to interfere with the home growth. The actual state of things at a subsequent period, and particularly during the last twenty-five years, has sufficiently shewn that these appearances were merely incidental; that a very rich country may have its corn extremely dear, as we should naturally expect; and that importation in England has amounted to more than $\frac{1}{10}$ instead of $\frac{1}{571}$* part of the crop raised in the country; and may, therefore, essentially interfere with the home growth.

Aware, however, of my liability to this error on the one side, and to the error of not referring sufficiently to experience on the other, my aim will be to pursue, as far as I am able, a just mean between the two extremes, and to approach, as near I can, to the great object of my research – the truth.

Many of the doctrines of Adam Smith, which had been considered as settled, have lately been called in question by writers entitled to great attention; but they have often failed, as it appears to me, to make good their objections; and in all such cases I have thought it desirable to examine anew, with reference to such objections, the grounds on which his doctrines are founded.

It has been my wish to avoid giving to my work a controversial air. Yet to free it entirely from controversy, while one of my professed objects is to discuss controverted opinions, and to try their truth by a reference to an enlarged experience, is obviously not possible. There is one modern work, in particular, of very high reputation, some of the fundamental principles of which have appeared to me, after the most mature deliberation, to be erroneous; and I should not have done justice to the ability with which it is written, to the high authority of the writer, and the interests of the science of which it treats, if it had not specifically engaged a considerable portion of my attention. I allude to Mr Ricardo's work, *On the Principles of Political Economy and Taxation.*

I have so very high an opinion of Mr Ricardo's talents as a political economist, and so entire a conviction of his perfect sincerity and love of truth, that I frankly own I have sometimes felt almost staggered by his authority, while I have remained unconvinced by his reasonings. I have thought that I must unaccountably have overlooked some essential points, either in my own view of the subject, or in his; and this kind of doubt has been the principal reason of my delay in publishing the

* *Wealth of Nations,* B. IV. c. ii. p. 190. 6th edit.

present volume. But I shall hardly be suspected of not thinking for myself on these subjects, or of not feeling such a degree of confidence in my own conclusions, after having taken full time to form them, as to be afraid of submitting them to the decision of the public.

To those who are not acquainted with Mr Ricardo's work, and do not properly appreciate the ingenuity and consistency of the system which it maintains and developes with so much ability, I am apprehensive that I shall appear to have dwelt too long upon some of the points on which we differ. But as they are, for the most part, of great importance both theoretically and practically, and as it appeared to me extremely desirable, with a view to the interests of the science, that they should, if possible, be settled, I did not feel myself justified in giving less time to the consideration of them.

I am far from saying that I may not be wrong in the conclusions at which I have arrived, in opposition to those of Mr Ricardo. But I am conscious that I have taken all the means to be right, which patient investigation and a sincere desire to get at the truth can give to the actual powers of my understanding. And with this consciousness, both with respect to the opinions I have opposed, and those which I have attempted to establish, I feel no reluctance in committing the results to the decision of the public.

T. R. MALTHUS.

East India College, }
  Dec. 1, 1819. }

CHAPTER VII, SECTION III

Of Accumulation, or the Saving from Revenue to add to Capital, considered as a Stimulus to the Increase of Wealth.

Those who reject mere population as an adequate stimulus to the increase of wealth, are generally disposed to make every thing depend upon accumulation. It is certainly true that no permanent and continued increase of wealth can take place without a continued increase of capital; and I cannot agree with Lord Lauderdale[10] in thinking that this increase can be effected in any other way than by saving from the stock which might have been destined for immediate consumption, and adding it to that which is to yield a profit; or in other words, by the conversion of revenue into capital.*

But we have yet to inquire what is the state of things which generally disposes a nation to accumulate; and further, what is the state of things which tends to make that accumulation the most effective, and lead to a further and continued increase of capital and wealth.

It is undoubtedly possible by parsimony to devote at once a much larger share than usual of the produce of any country to the maintenance of productive labour; and it is quite true that the labourers so employed are consumers as well as unproductive labourers; and as far as the labourers are concerned, there would be no diminution of consumption or demand. But it has already been shewn that the consumption and demand occasioned by the persons employed in productive labour can never alone furnish a motive to the accumulation and employment of capital; and with regard to the capitalists themselves, together with the landlords and other rich persons, they have, by the supposition, agreed to be parsimonious, and by depriving themselves of their usual conveniences and luxuries to save from their revenue and add to their capital. Under these circumstances, I would ask, how it is possible to suppose that the increased quantity of commodities, obtained by the increased number of productive labourers, should find purchasers, without such a fall of price as would probably sink their value below the costs of production, or, at least, very greatly diminish both the power and the will to save.

---

* See Lord Lauderdale's Chapter on Parsimony, in his Inquiry into the Nature and Origin of Public Wealth, ch. iv. p. 198. 2d. edit. Lord Lauderdale appears to have gone as much too far in deprecating accumulation, as some other writers in recommending it. This tendency to extremes is exactly what I consider as the great source of error in political economy.

It has been thought by some very able writers, that although there may easily be a glut of particular commodities, there cannot possibly be a glut of commodities in general; because, according to their view of the subject, commodities being always exchanged for commodities, one half will furnish a market for the other half, and production being thus the sole source of demand, an excess in the supply of one article merely proves a deficiency in the supply of some other, and a general excess is impossible. M. Say,[11] in his distinguished work on political economy, has indeed gone so far as to state that the consumption of a commodity by taking it out of the market diminishes demand, and the production of a commodity proportionably increases it.

This doctrine, however, to the extent in which it has been applied, appears to me to be utterly unfounded, and completely to contradict the great principles which regulate supply and demand.

It is by no means true, as a matter of fact, that commodities are always exchanged for commodities. The great mass of commodities is exchanged directly for labour, either productive or unproductive; and it is quite obvious that this mass of commodities, compared with the labour with which it is to be exchanged, may fall in value from a glut just as any one commodity falls in value from an excess of supply, compared either with labour or money.

In the case supposed there would evidently be an unusual quantity of commodities of all kinds in the market, owing to the unproductive labourers of the country having been converted, by the accumulation of capital, into productive labourers; while the number of labourers altogether being the same, and the power and will to purchase for consumption among landlords and capitalists being by supposition diminished, commodities would necessarily fall in value, compared with labour, so as to lower profits almost to nothing, and to check for a time further production. But this is precisely what is meant by the term glut, which, in this case, is evidently general not partial.

M. Say, Mr Mill,*[12] and Mr Ricardo, the principal authors of the new doctrines on profits, appear to me to have fallen into some fundamental errors in the view which they have taken of this subject.

In the first place, they have considered commodities as if they were so many mathematical figures, or arithmetical characters, the relations of which were to be compared, instead of articles of consumption, which must of course be referred to the numbers and wants of the consumers.

If commodities were only to be compared and exchanged with each other, then indeed it would be true that, if they were all increased in their proper proportions to any extent, they would continue to bear among themselves the same relative value; but, if we compare them, as we certainly ought to do, with the numbers and wants of the consumers, then a great increase of produce with comparatively stationary numbers and with wants diminished by parsimony, must necessarily occasion a great fall of value estimated in labour, so that the same produce, though it might have *cost* the same quantity of labour as before, would no longer *command* the same quantity; and both the power of accumulation and the motive to accumulate would be strongly checked.

It is asserted that effectual demand is nothing more than the offering of one commodity in exchange for another. But is this all that is necessary to effectual demand? Though each commodity may have cost the same quantity of labour and capital in its production, and they may be exactly equivalent to each other in exchange, yet why may not both be so plentiful as not to command more labour, or but very little more than they have cost; and in this case, would the demand for them be effectual? Would it be such as to encourage their continued production?

* Mr Mill, in a reply to Mr Spence, published in 1808, has laid down very broadly the doctrine that commodities are only purchased by commodities, and that one half of them must always furnish a market for the other half. The same doctrine appears to be adopted in its fullest extent by the author of an able and useful article on the Corn Laws, in the supplement to the Encyclopaedia Britannica.

Unquestionably not. Their relation to each other may not have changed; but their relation to the wants of the society, their relation to bullion, and their relation to domestic and foreign labour, may have experienced a most important change.

It will be readily allowed that a new commodity thrown into the market, which, in proportion to the labour employed upon it, is of higher exchangeable value than usual, is precisely calculated to increase demand; because it implies, not a mere increase of quantity, but a better adaptation of the produce to the tastes, wants and consumption of the society. But to fabricate or procure commodities of this kind is the grand difficulty; and they certainly do not naturally and necessarily follow an accumulation of capital and increase of commodities, most particularly when such accumulation and increase have been occasioned by economy of consumption, or a discouragement to the indulgence of those tastes and wants, which are the very elements of demand.

Mr Ricardo, though he maintains as a general position that capital cannot be redundant, is obliged to make the following concession. He says, 'There is only one case, and that will be temporary, in which the accumulation of capital with a low price of food may be attended with a fall of profits; and that is, when the funds for the maintenance of labour increase much more rapidly than population; – wages will then be high and profits low. If every man were to forego the use of luxuries and be intent only on accumulation, a quantity of necessaries might be produced for which there could not be any immediate consumption. Of commodities so limited in number, there might undoubtedly be an universal glut; and consequently there might neither be demand for an additional quantity of such commodities, nor profits on the employment of more capital. If men ceased to consume, they would cease to produce.' Mr Ricardo then adds, 'This admission does not impugn the general principle.'* In this remark I cannot quite agree with him. As, from the nature of population, an increase of labourers cannot be brought into the market, in consequence of a particular

* *Princ. of Polit. Econ.* ch. xxi. p. 364. 2d edit.

demand, till after the lapse of sixteen or eighteen years, and the conversion of revenue into capital may take place much more rapidly; a country is always liable to an increase of the funds for the maintenance of labour faster than the increase of population. But if, whenever this occurs, there may be a universal glut of commodities, how can it be maintained, as a general position, that capital is never redundant; and that because commodities may retain the same relative values, a glut can only be partial, not general?

Another fundamental error into which the writers above-mentioned and their followers appear to have fallen is, the not taking into consideration the influence of so general and important a principle in human nature, as indolence or the love of ease.

It has been supposed* that, if a certain number of farmers and a certain number of manufacturers had been exchanging their surplus food and clothing with each other, and their powers of production were suddenly so increased that both parties could, with the same labour, produce luxuries in addition to what they had before obtained, there could be no sort of difficulty with regard to demand, as part of the luxuries which the farmer produced would be exchanged against part of the luxuries produced by the manufacturer; and the only result would be, the happy one of both parties being better supplied and having more enjoyments.

But in this intercourse of mutual gratifications, two things are taken for granted, which are the very points in dispute. It is taken for granted that luxuries are always preferred to indolence, and that the profits of each party are consumed as revenue. What would be the effect of a desire to save under such circumstances, shall be considered presently. The effect of a preference of indolence to luxuries would evidently be to occasion a want of demand for the returns of the increased powers of production supposed, and to throw labourers out of employment. The cultivator, being now enabled to obtain the necessaries and conveniences to which he had been accustomed, with less toil and trouble, and his tastes for ribands,

* *Edinburgh Review*, No. LXIV. p. 471.

lace and velvet not being fully formed, might be very likely to indulge himself in indolence, and employ less labour on the land; while the manufacturer, finding his velvets rather heavy of sale, would be led to discontinue their manufacture, and to fall almost necessarily into the same indolent system as the farmer. That an efficient taste for luxuries, that is, such a taste as will properly stimulate industry, instead of being ready to appear at the moment it is required, is a plant of slow growth, the history of human society sufficiently shews; and that it is a most important error to take for granted, that mankind will produce and consume all that they have the power to produce and consume, and will never prefer indolence to the rewards of industry, will sufficiently appear from a slight review of some of the nations with which we are acquainted. But I shall have occasion for a review of this kind in the next section; and to this I refer the reader.

A third very serious error of the writers above referred to, and practically the most important of the three, consists in supposing that accumulation ensures demand; or that the consumption of the labourers employed by those whose object is to save, will create such an effectual demand for commodities as to encourage a continued increase of produce.

Mr Ricardo observes, that 'If 10,000*l.* were given to a man having 100,000*l.* per annum, he would not lock it up in a chest, but would either increase his expenses by 10,000*l.*, employ it himself productively, or lend it to some other person for that purpose; in either case demand would be increased, although it would be for different objects. If he increased his expenses, his effectual demand might probably be for buildings, furniture, or some such enjoyment. If he employed his 10,000*l.* productively, his effectual demand would be for food, clothing, and raw materials, which might set new labourers to work. But still it would be *demand*.'*

Upon this principle it is supposed that if the richer portion of society were to forego their accustomed conveniences and luxuries with a view to accumulation, the only effect would

* *Princ. of Polit. Econ.* chap. xxi. p. 361. 2d edit.

be a direction of nearly the whole capital of the country to the production of necessaries, which would lead to a great increase of cultivation and population. But, without supposing an entire change in the usual motives to accumulation, this could not possibly happen. The usual motives for accumulation are, I conceive, either the future wealth and enjoyment of the individual who accumulates, or of those to whom he means to leave his property. And with these motives it could never answer to the possessor of land to employ nearly all the labour which the soil could support in cultivation; as by so doing he would necessarily destroy his neat rent, and render it impossible for him, without subsequently dismissing the greatest part of his workmen and occasioning the most dreadful distress, either to give himself the means of greater enjoyment at a future distant period, or to transmit such means to his posterity.

The very definition of fertile land is, land that will support a much greater number of persons than are necessary to cultivate it; and if the landlord, instead of spending this surplus in conveniences, luxuries and unproductive consumers, were to employ it in setting to work on the land as many labourers as his savings could support, it is quite obvious that, instead of being enriched, he would be impoverished by such a proceeding, both at first and in future. Nothing could justify such a conduct but a different motive for accumulation; that is, a desire to increase the population – not the love of wealth and enjoyment; and till such a change takes place in the passions and propensities of mankind, we may be quite sure that the landlords and cultivators will not go on employing labourers in this way.

What then would happen? As soon as the landlords and cultivators found that they could not realize their increasing produce in some way which would give them a command of wealth in future, they would cease to employ more labour upon the land;* and if the business of that part of the society which

---

* Theoretical writers in Political Economy, from the fear of appearing to attach too much importance to money, have perhaps been too apt to throw it out of their consideration in their reasonings. It is an abstract truth that we want commodities, not money. But, in reality, no commodity for which it is

was not engaged in raising raw produce, consisted merely in preparing the other simple necessaries of life, the number required for this purpose being inconsiderable, the rest of those whom the soil could support would be thrown out of work. Having no means of legally demanding a portion of the raw produce, however plentiful it might be at first, they would gradually decrease in numbers; and the failure of effective demand for the produce of the soil would necessarily diminish cultivation, and throw a still greater number of persons out of employment. This action and reaction would thus go on till the balance of produce and consumption was restored in reference to the new tastes and habits which were established: and it is obvious that without an expenditure which will encourage commerce, manufactures, and unproductive consumers, or an Agrarian law calculated to change the usual motives for accumulation, the possessors of land would have no sufficient stimulus to cultivate well; and a country such as our own, which had been rich and populous, would, with such parsimonious habits, infallibly become poor, and comparatively unpeopled.

The same kind of reasoning will obviously apply to the case noticed before. While the farmers were disposed to consume the luxuries produced by the manufacturers, and the manufacturers those produced by the farmers, all would go on smoothly; but if either one or both of the parties were disposed to save with a view of bettering their condition, and providing for their families in future, the state of things would be very different. The farmer, instead of indulging himself in ribands, lace, and

---

possible to sell our goods at once, can be an adequate substitute for a circulating medium, and enable us in the same manner to provide for children, to purchase an estate, or to command labour and provisions a year or two hence. A circulating medium is absolutely necessary to any considerable saving; and even the manufacturer would get on but slowly, if he were obliged to accumulate in kind all the wages of his workmen. We cannot therefore be surprized at his wanting money rather than other goods; and, in civilized countries, we may be quite sure that if the farmer or manufacturer cannot sell his products so as to give him a profit estimated in money, his industry will immediately slacken. The circulating medium bears so important a part in the distribution of wealth, and the encouragement of industry, that to set it aside in our reasonings may often lead us wrong.

velvets,* would be disposed to be satisfied with more simple clothing, but by this economy he would disable the manufacturer from purchasing the same amount of his produce; and for the returns of so much labour employed upon the land, and all greatly increased in productive power, there would evidently be no market. The manufacturer, in like manner, instead of indulging him self in sugar, grapes and tobacco, might be disposed to save with a view to the future, but would be totally unable to do so, owing to the parsimony of the farmers and the want of demand for manufactures.†

An accumulation, to a certain extent, of common food and common clothing might take place on both sides; but the amount must necessarily be extremely confined. It would be of no sort of use to the farmer to go on cultivating his land with a view merely to give food and clothing to his labourers. He would be doing nothing either for himself or family, if he neither consumed the surplus of what they produced himself, nor could realize it in a shape that might be transmitted to his descendants. If he were a tenant, such additional care and labour would be entirely thrown away; and if he were a landlord, and were determined, without reference to markets, to cultivate his estate in such a way as to make it yield the greatest neat surplus with a view to the future, it is quite certain that the large portion of this surplus which was not required either for his own consumption, or to purchase clothing for himself and his labourers, would be absolutely wasted. If he did not choose to use it in the purchase of luxuries or the maintenance of unproductive labourers, it might as well be thrown into the sea.

---

* *Edinburgh Review*, No. LXIV. p. 471.
† Of all the opinions advanced by able and ingenious men, which I have ever met with, the opinion of M. Say, which states that, *un produit consommé ou détruit est un débouché fermé*: (1. i. ch. 15.) appears to me to be the most directly opposed to just theory, and the most uniformly contradicted by experience. Yet it directly follows from the new doctrine, that commodities are to be considered only in their relation to each other – not to the consumers. What, I would ask, would become of the demand for commodities, if all consumption except bread and water were suspended for the next half year? What an accumulation of commodities! Quels *débouchés!* What a prodigious market would this event occasion!

To save it, that is to use it in employing more labourers upon the land would, as I said before, be to impoverish both himself and his family.

It would be still more useless to the manufacturers to go on producing clothing beyond what was wanted by the agriculturists and themselves. Their numbers indeed would entirely depend upon the demands of the agriculturists, as they would have no means of purchasing subsistence, but in proportion as there was a reciprocal want of their manufactures. The population required to provide simple clothing for such a society with the assistance of good machinery would be inconsiderable, and would absorb but a small portion of the proper surplus of rich and well cultivated land. There would evidently therefore be a general want of demand, both for produce and population; and while it is quite certain that an adequate passion for consumption may fully keep up the proper proportion between supply and demand, whatever may be the powers of production, it appears to be quite as certain that a passion for accumulation must inevitably lead to a supply of commodities beyond what the structure and habits of such a society will permit to be consumed.*

But if this be so, surely it is a most important error to couple the passion for expenditure and the passion for accumulation together, as if they were of the same nature; and to consider the demand for the food and clothing of the labourer, who is to be employed productively, as securing such a general demand for commodities and such a rate of profits for the capital employed in producing them, as will adequately call forth the powers of the soil, and the ingenuity of man in procuring the greatest quantity both of raw and manufactured produce.

Mr Ricardo has very clearly shewn that the rate of profits must diminish, and the progress of accumulation be finally stopped, under the most favourable circumstances, by the

---

* The reader must already know, that I do not share in the apprehensions of Mr Owen[13] about the permanent effects of machinery. But I am decidedly of opinion, that on this point he has the best of the argument with those who think that accumulation ensures effective demand.

increasing difficulty of procuring the food of the labourer. I, in like manner, endeavoured to shew in my Essay on the Principle of Population that, under circumstances the most favourable to cultivation which could possibly be supposed to operate in the actual state of the earth, the wages of the labourer would become more scanty, and the progress of population be finally stopped by the increasing difficulty of procuring the means of subsistence.

But Mr Ricardo has not been satisfied with proving the position just stated. He has not been satisfied with shewing that the difficulty of procuring the food of the labourer is the only *absolutely necessary cause* of the fall of profits, in which I am ready fully and entirely to agree with him: but he has gone on to say, that there is *no other cause* of the fall of profits in the actual state of things that has any degree of permanence. In this latter statement he appears to me to have fallen into precisely the same kind of error as I should have fallen into, if, after having shewn that the unrestricted power of population was beyond comparison greater than the power of the earth to produce food under the most favourable circumstances possible, I had allowed that population could not be redundant unless the powers of the earth to keep up with the progress of population had been tried to the uttermost. But I all along said, that population might be redundant, and greatly redundant, compared with the demand for it and the actual means of supporting it, although it might most properly be considered as deficient, and greatly deficient, compared with the extent of territory, and the powers of such territory to produce additional means of subsistence; that, in such cases, notwithstanding the acknowledged deficiency of population, and the obvious desirableness of having it greatly increased, it was useless and foolish directly to encourage the birth of more children, as the effect of such encouragement, without a demand for labour and the means of paying it properly, could only be increased misery and mortality with little or no final increase of population.

Though Mr Ricardo has taken a very different course, I think that the same kind of reasoning ought to be applied to the rate of profits and the progress of capital. Fully acknowledging that there is hardly a country in the four quarters of the globe where capital is not deficient, and in most of them very greatly deficient, compared with the territory and even the number of people; and fully allowing at the same time the extreme desirableness of an increase of capital, I should say that, where the demand for commodities was not such as to afford fair profits to the producer, and the capitalists were at a loss where and how to employ their capitals to advantage, the saving from revenue to add still more to these capitals would only tend prematurely to diminish the motive to accumulation, and still further to distress the capitalists, with little increase of a wholesome and effective capital.

The first thing wanted in both these cases of deficient capital and deficient population, is an effective demand for commodities, that is, a demand by those who are able and willing to pay an adequate price for them; and though high profits are not followed by an increase of capital, so certainly as high wages are by an increase of population, yet I believe that they are so followed more generally than they appear to be, because, in many countries, as I have before intimated, profits are often thought to be high, owing to the high interest of money, when they are really low; and because, universally, risk in employing capital has precisely the same effect in diminishing the motive to accumulate and the reward of accumulation, as low profits. At the same time it will be allowed that determined extravagance, and a determined indisposition to save, may keep profits permanently high. The most powerful stimulants may, under peculiar circumstances, be resisted; yet still it will not cease to be true that the natural and legitimate encouragement to the increase of capital is that increase of the power and will to save which is held out by high profits; and under circumstances in any degree similar, such increase of power and will to save must almost always be accompanied by a proportionate increase of capital.

One of the most striking instances of the truth of this remark, and a further proof of a singular resemblance in the laws that regulate the increase of capital and of population, is to be found in the rapidity with which the loss of capital is recovered during a war which does not interrupt commerce. The loans to government convert capital into revenue, and increase demand at the same time that they at first diminish the means of supply.* The necessary consequence must be an increase of profits. This naturally increases both the power and the reward of accumulation; and if only the same habits of saving prevail among the capitalists as before, the recovery of the lost stock must be rapid, just for the same kind of reason that the recovery of population is so rapid when, by some cause or other, it has been suddenly destroyed.

It is now fully acknowledged that it would be a gross error in the latter case, to imagine that, without the previous diminution of the population, the same rate of increase would still have taken place; because it is precisely the high wages occasioned by the demand for labour, which produce the effect of so rapid an increase of population. On the same principle it appears to me as gross an error to suppose that, without the previous loss of capital occasioned by the expenditure in question, capital should be as rapidly accumulated; because it is precisely the high profits of stock occasioned by the demand for commodities, and the consequent demand for the means of producing them, which at once give the power and the will to accumulate.

Though it may be allowed therefore that the laws which regulate the increase of capital are not quite so distinct as those which regulate the increase of population, yet they are certainly just of the same kind; and it is equally vain, with a view to the permanent increase of wealth, to continue converting revenue into capital, when there is no adequate demand for the products of such capital, as to continue encouraging marriage and the birth of children without a demand for labour and an increase of the funds for its maintenance.

---

* Capital is withdrawn only from those employments where it can best be spared. It is hardly ever withdrawn from agriculture. Nothing is more common, as I have stated in the Chapter on Rent, than increased profits, not only without any capital being withdrawn from the land, but under a continual addition to it. Mr Ricardo's assumption of constant prices would make it absolutely impossible to account theoretically for things as they are. If capital were considered as not within the pale of demand and supply, the very familiar event of the rapid recovery of capital during a war would be quite inexplicable.

CHAPTER VII, SECTION IV

Of the Fertility of the Soil, considered as a Stimulus to the continued Increase of Wealth.

In speaking of the fertility of the soil as not affording an adequate stimulus to the continued increase of wealth, it must always be recollected that a fertile soil gives at once the greatest natural capability of wealth that a country can possibly possess. When the deficient wealth of such a country is mentioned, it is not intended always to speak positively, but comparatively, that is with reference to its natural capabilities; and so understood, the proposition will be liable to few or no exceptions. Perhaps, indeed, it may be said that no instance has occurred, in modern times, of a large and very fertile country having made full use of its natural resources; while there have been many instances of small and unfertile states having accumulated within their narrow limits, by means of foreign commerce, a degree of wealth very greatly exceeding the proportion which should belong to them, in reference to their physical capabilities.

If a small body of people were possessed of a rich and extensive inland territory, divided into large proportions, and not favourably situated with respect to markets, a very long period might elapse before the state became wealthy and populous, notwithstanding the fertility of the soil and the consequent facility of production. The nature of such a soil would make it yield a profit or rent to the owner in its uncultivated state. He would set a value therefore upon his property, as a source of profit as well as of power and amusement; and though it was capable of yielding much more raw produce than he and his immediate dependents could consume, he would by no means be disposed to allow others to seize on it, and divide it at their pleasure. He would probably let out considerable portions of it for small rents. But the tenant of these portions, if there were no foreign vent for the raw produce, and the commodities which contribute to the conveniences and luxuries of life were but little known, would have but small incitement to call forth the resources of his land, and give encouragement to a rapid increase of population. By employing ten families he might perhaps, owing to the richness of the soil, obtain food for fifty; but he would find no proportionate market for this additional food, and would be soon sensible that he had wasted his time and attention in superintending the labour of so many persons. He would be disposed therefore to employ a smaller number; or if, from motives of humanity, or any other reason, he was induced to keep more than were necessary for the supply of the market, upon the supposition of their being tolerably industrious, he would be quite indifferent to their industry, and his labourers would naturally acquire the most indolent habits. Such habits would naturally be generated both in the masters and servants by such circumstances, and when generated, a considerable time and considerable stimulants are necessary to get rid of them.

It has been said, that those who have food and necessaries at their disposal will not be long in want of workmen, who will put them in possession of some of the objects most useful and desirable to them.* But this appears to be directly contradicted by experience. If the establishment, extension, and refinement of domestic manufactures were so easy a matter, our ancestors would not have remained for many hundred years so ill supplied with them; and been obliged to expend the main part of their raw produce in the support of idle retainers. They might be very ready, when they had the opportunity, to exchange their surplus raw produce for the foreign commodities with which they were acquainted, and which they had learnt to estimate. But it would be a very difficult thing, and very ill suited to their habits and degree of information, to employ their power of commanding labour in setting up manufactures on their own estates. Though the land might be rich, it might not suit the production of the materials most wanted; and the necessary machinery, the necessary skill in using it, and the necessary intelligence and activity of superintendance, would

* Ricardo's Princ. of Polit. Econ. ch. xxi. p. 363. 2d. edit.

all unavoidably be deficient at first, and under the circumstances supposed, must be of very slow growth; so that after
those ruder and more indispensable articles were supplied,
which are always wanted and produced in an early stage of
society, it is natural enough that a great lord should prefer distinguishing himself by a few splendid foreign commodities, if
he could get them, and a great number of retainers, than by a
large quantity of clumsy manufactures, which involved great
trouble of superintendence.

It is certainly true, however, taking as an instance an individual workman, and supposing him to possess a given degree of
industry and skill, that the less time he is employed in procuring food, the more time will he be able to devote to the
procuring of conveniences and luxuries; but to apply this truth
to whole nations, and to infer that the greater is the facility of
procuring food, the more abundantly will the people be supplied with conveniences and luxuries would be one among the
many rash and false conclusions which are often made from
the want of due attention to the change which the application
of a proposition may make in the premises on which it rests. In
the present case, all depends upon the supposition of a given
degree of industry and skill, and the means of employing them.
But if, after the necessaries of life were obtained, the workman
should consider indolence as a greater luxury than those which
he was likely to procure by further labour, the proposition
would at once cease to be true. And as a matter of fact, confirmed by all the accounts we have of nations, in the different
stages of their progress, it must be allowed that this choice
seems to be very general in the early periods of society, and by
no means uncommon in the most improved states.

Few indeed and scanty would be the portion of conveniences
and luxuries found in society, if those who are the main instruments of their production had no stronger motives for their
exertions than the desire of enjoying them. It is the want of
necessaries which mainly stimulates the labouring classes to
produce luxuries; and were this stimulus removed or greatly
weakened, so that the necessaries of life could be obtained with

very little labour, instead of more time being devoted to the production of conveniences, there is every reason to think that less time would be so devoted.

At an early period of cultivation, when only rich soils are worked, as the quantity of corn is the greatest, compared with the quantity of labour required to produce it, we ought always to find a small portion of the population engaged in agriculture, and a large portion engaged in administering to the other wants of the society. And there can be little doubt that this is the state of things which we really should see, were it true, that if the means of maintaining labour be found, there can be no difficulty in making it produce objects of adequate value; or that when food can be obtained with facility, more time will be devoted to the production of conveniences and luxuries. But in examining the state of unimproved countries, what do we really see? – almost invariably, a much larger proportion of the whole people employed on the land than in those countries where the increase of population has occasioned the necessity of resorting to poor soils; and less time instead of more time devoted to the production of conveniences and luxuries.

Of the great landed nations of Europe, and indeed of the world, England, with only one or two exceptions, is supposed to have pushed its cultivation the farthest; and though the natural qualities of its whole soil by no means stand very high in the scale of comparative richness, there is a smaller proportion of the people employed in agriculture, and a greater proportion employed in the production of conveniences and luxuries, or living on monied incomes, than in any other agricultural country of the world. According to a calculation of Susmilch,[14] in which he enumerates the different proportions of people in different states, who live in towns, and are not employed in agriculture, the highest is that of seven to three, or seven people living in the country to three living in the towns:* whereas in

---

* Susmilch, vol. iii. p. 60. Essay on Population, vol. i. p. 459. edit. 5th. In foreign states very few persons live in the country who are not engaged in agriculture; but it is not so in England.

England, the proportion of those engaged in agriculture, compared with the rest of the population, is less than as two to three.*

This is a very extraordinary fact, and affords a striking proof how very dangerous it is, in political economy, to draw conclusions from the physical quality of the materials which are acted upon, without reference to the moral as well as physical qualities of the agents.

It is undoubtedly a physical quality of very rich land, if worked by people possessing a given degree of industry and skill, to yield a large quantity of produce, compared with the number of hands employed; but, if the facility of production which rich land gives has the effect, under certain circumstances, of preventing the growth of industry and skill, the land may become practically less productive, compared with the number of persons employed upon it, than if it were not distinguished for its richness.

Upon the same principle, the man who can procure the necessary food for his family, by two days labour in the week, has the physical power of working much longer to procure conveniences and luxuries, than the man who must employ four days in procuring food; but if the facility of getting food creates habits of indolence, this indolence may make him prefer the luxury of doing little or nothing, to the luxury of possessing conveniences and comforts; and in this case, he may devote less time to the working for conveniences and comforts, and be more scantily provided with them than if he had been obliged to employ more industry in procuring food.

Among the crowd of countries which tend more or less to illustrate and confirm by their present state the truth of these positions, none perhaps will do it more strikingly than the Spanish dominions in America, of which M. Humboldt has lately given so valuable an account.[16]

These accounts strikingly shew the indolence and improvidence which prevail among the people. Such habits must necessarily act as formidable obstacles in the way of a rapid

* Population Abstracts, 1811.[15]

increase of wealth and population. Where they have been once fully established, they are not likely to change, except gradually and slowly under a course of powerful and effective stimulants. And while the extreme inequality of landed property continues, and no sufficient vent is found for the raw produce in foreign commerce, these stimulants will be furnished very slowly and inadequately.

Except in the neighbourhood of the mines and near the great towns, the effective demand for produce is not such as to induce the great proprietors to bring their immense tracts of land properly into cultivation: and the population, which, as we have seen, presses hard against the limits of subsistence, evidently exceeds in general the demand for labour, or the number of persons which the country can employ with regularity and constancy in the actual state of its agriculture and manufactures.

In the midst of an abundance of fertile land, it appears that the natives are often very scantily supplied with it. They would gladly cultivate portions of the extensive districts held by the great proprietors, and could not fail of thus deriving an ample subsistence for themselves and families; but in the actual state of the demand for produce in many parts of the country, and in the actual state of the ignorance and indolence of the natives, such tenants might not be able to pay a rent equal to what the land would yield in its uncultivated state, and in this case they would seldom be allowed to intrude upon such domains; and thus lands which might be made capable of supporting thousands of people, may be left to support a few hundreds of cattle.

Altogether the state of New Spain, as described by Humboldt, clearly shews –

1st. That the power of supporting labour may exist to a much greater extent than the will.

2dly. That the time employed in working for conveniences and luxuries is not always great in proportion as the time employed in working for food is small.

3dly. That the deficient wealth of a fertile country may be more owing to want of demand than want of capital.

And, in general, that fertility of soil alone is not an adequate stimulus to the continued increase of wealth.

It is not necessary, however, to go so far as the Spanish dominions in America, to illustrate these propositions. The state of the mother-country itself, and of most of the countries of Europe, would furnish the same conclusions. We need not indeed go farther than Ireland[17] to see a confirmation of them to a very considerable extent.

The cultivation of the potato, and its adoption as the general food of the lower classes of the people in Ireland, has rendered the land and labour necessary to maintain a family, unusually small, compared with most of the countries of Europe. The consequence of this facility of production, unaccompanied by such a train of fortunate circumstances as would give it full effect in the increase of wealth, is a state of things resembling, in many respects, countries less advanced in civilization and improvement.

The prominent feature of Ireland is, the power which it possesses and actually exercises, of supporting a much greater population than it can employ, and the natural and necessary effect of this state of things, is the very general prevalence of habits of indolence. The landed proprietors and principal tenants being possessed of food and necessaries, or at least of the ready means of procuring them, have found workmen in abundance at their command; but these workmen not finding sufficient employment in the farms on which they had settled, have rarely been able to put their landlords in possession of the objects 'most useful and most desirable' to them. Sometimes, indeed, from the competition for land occasioned by an overflowing population, very high rents have been given for small portions of ground fit for the growth of potatoes; but as the power of paying such rents must depend, in a considerable degree, upon the power of getting work, the number of families upon an estate, who can pay high money rents, must have an obvious limit. This limit, there is reason to believe, has been often found in the inability of the Irish cottar[18] to pay the rent which he had contracted for; and it is generally understood that the most intelligent Irish landlords, influenced both by motives of humanity and interest, are now endeavouring to check the progress of that redundant population upon their estates, which, while it generates an excessive degree of poverty and misery as well as indolence, seldom makes up to the employer, in the lowness of wages, for the additional number of hands which he is obliged to hire, or call upon for their appointed service in labour. He is now generally aware that a smaller number of more industrious labourers would enable him to raise a larger produce for the consumption of towns and manufacturers, and at the same time that they would thus contribute more largely to the general wealth of the country, would be in a more happy condition themselves, and enable him to derive a larger and more certain rent from his estates. It may fairly be said therefore, that the possessors of food and necessaries in Ireland have not been able to obtain the objects most useful and desirable to them in return.

The indolence of the country-labourers in Ireland has been universally remarked. And whether this arises from there being really little for them to do in the actual state of things, or from a natural tendency to idleness, not to be overcome by ordinary stimulants; it is equally true that the large portion of time of which they have the command, beyond what is employed in providing themselves with necessaries, does not certainly produce the effect of making them abound in conveniences and luxuries. The poor clothing and worse lodging of the Irish peasant are as well known as the spare time which it might be expected would be the means of furnishing him amply with all kinds of conveniences.

In defence, however, of the Irish peasant, it may be truly said, that in the state of society in which he has been placed, he has not had a fair trial; he has not been subjected to the ordinary stimulants which produce industrious habits. In almost every part of the island, particularly in the south and west, the population of the country districts is greater than the actual business to be done on the land can employ. If the people, therefore, were ever so industriously inclined, it is not possible for them all to get regular employment in the occupations which belong to the soil. In the more hilly parts of the country which are devoted chiefly to pasture, this impossibility is more particularly striking. A small farm among the Kerry mountains may support perhaps a large family, among whom are a number of grown-up sons; but the business to be done upon the farm is a mere trifle. The greatest part of it falls to the share of the women. What remains for the men cannot occupy them for a number of hours equal to a single day in the week; and the consequence is, they are generally seen loitering about, as if time was absolutely of no value to them.

They might, one should suppose, with all this leisure, employ themselves in building better houses, or at least in improving them, and keeping them neat and clean. But with regard to the first, some difficulties may occur in procuring materials; and with regard to the second, it appears from experience, that the object is either not understood, or not considered as worth the trouble it would cost.

They might also, one should suppose, grow or purchase the raw materials of clothing, and work them up at home; and this in fact is really done to a certain extent. Most of the linen and woollen they wear is prepared by themselves. But the raw materials, when not of home growth, cannot be purchased without great difficulty, on account of the low money prices of labour; and in preparing them for wear, the temptations to indolence will generally be too powerful for human weakness, when the question is merely about a work which may be deferred or neglected, with no other effect than that of being obliged to wear old clothes a little longer, in a country where custom is certainly in their favour.

If the Irish peasant could find such a market for the result of his in-door occupations as would give him constant employment at a fair money price, his habits might soon change; but it may be doubted whether any large body of people in any country ever acquired regular and industrious habits, where they were unable to get regular and constant work, and when, to keep themselves constantly and beneficially employed, it was necessary to exercise a great degree of providence, energy, and self-command.

It may be said, perhaps, that it is capital alone which is wanted in Ireland, and that if this want were supplied, all her people might be easily employed. That one of the great wants of Ireland is capital will be readily allowed; but I conceive it would be a very great mistake to suppose that the importation of a large quantity of capital, if it could be effected, would at once accomplish the object required, and create a quantity of wealth proportioned to the labour which seems ready to be employed in its production. The amount of capital which could be laid out in Ireland in preparing goods for foreign sale, must evidently depend upon the state of foreign markets; and the amount that could be employed in domestic manufactures, must as evidently depend upon the domestic demand. An attempt to force a foreign market by means of capital, must necessarily occasion a premature fall of profits, and might, after great losses, be quite ineffectual; and with regard to the domestic demand, while the habits of the great mass of the people are such as they are at present, it must be quite inadequate to take off the products of any considerable mass of new capital. In a country, where the necessary food is obtained with so little labour, and the population is still equal or nearly equal to the produce, it is perhaps impossible that the time not devoted to the production of food should create a proportionate quantity of wealth, without a very decided taste for conveniences and luxuries among the lower classes of society, and such a power of purchasing as would occasion an effective demand for them. But it is well known, that the taste of the Irish peasant for articles of this description is yet to be formed. His wants are few, and these wants he is in the habit of supplying principally at home. Owing to the cheapness of the potato, which forms the principal food of the lower classes of the people, his money wages are low; and the portion which remains, after providing absolute necessaries, will go but a very little way in the purchase of conveniences. All these circumstances are most unfavourable to the increase of wealth derived from manufactures destined for home consumption. But the tastes and habits of a large body of people are extremely slow in changing; and in the mean time the application of capital in larger quantities than was suited to the progress of the change, would certainly fail to yield such profits as would encourage its continued accumulation and application in the same way. In general it may be said that demand is quite as necessary to the increase of capital as the increase of capital is to demand. They mutually act upon and encourage each other, and neither of them can proceed with vigour if the other be left far behind.

In the actual state of Ireland, I am inclined to believe, that the check which the progress of her manufactures has received, has been owing to a want of demand rather than a want of capital. Her peculiar distress upon the termination of the late war[19] had unquestionably this origin, whatever might have been the subsequent destruction of capital. And the great checks to her manufactures formerly were the unjust and impolitic restrictions imposed by England which prevented, or circumscribed the demand for them. When, however, a brisk demand for any manufacture has existed, few instances I believe have occurred of its being allowed to languish through the want of capital; though there is reason to think that advances of capital have been sometimes made, which have failed to create an adequate market.

The state of Ireland in respect to the time and labour necessary to the production of her food is such, that her capabilities for manufacturing and commercial wealth are prodigious. If an improved system of agriculture were to raise the food and raw materials required for the population with the smallest quantity of labour necessary to do it in the best manner, and the remainder of the people, instead of loitering about upon the land, were engaged in manufactures and commerce carried on in great and flourishing towns, Ireland would be beyond comparison richer than England. This is what is wanted to give full scope to her great natural resources; and to attain this state of things an immense capital is undoubtedly required; but it can only be employed to advantage as it is gradually called for; and a premature supply of it would be much less beneficial and less permanent in its effects, than such a change in the tastes and habits of the lower classes of people, and such an alteration in the mode of paying their labour, as would give them both the will and the power to purchase domestic manufactures and foreign commodities.

The state of Ireland then may be said to lead to nearly the same conclusions as that of New Spain, and to shew –

That the power of supporting labour may often exist to a much greater extent than the will;

That the necessity of employing only a small portion of time in producing food does not always occasion the employment of a greater portion of time in procuring conveniences and luxuries;

That the deficiency of wealth in a fertile country may be more owing to want of demand than to want of capital;

And, in general, that the fertility of the soil alone is not an adequate stimulus to the permanent increase of wealth.

Notes

An Essay on the Principle of Population

1   The friend in question was Malthus's father, Daniel.
2   William Godwin (1756–1836) was a radical thinker whose fame rested on *An Enquiry Concerning Political Justice* (1793), a book that has been seen as originating modern anarchism. *An Enquiry* expresses the quintessentially Enlightened belief that reason can overcome prejudice to allow individuals to build a better society. From its second edition of 1796 onwards, *An Enquiry* discussed the possibility that human life could be infinitely extended and that human sexual appetites would dim to refute the idea that the principle of population could prevent the progress of reason Godwin envisaged. Malthus set out to refute these points in the *Essay*. *The Enquirer: Reflections on Education, Manners and Literature* (1797) was a set of shorter essays by Godwin on a range of topics. The Malthus library records his ownership of the second edition of *An Enquiry* and of *The Enquirer*.
3   The later editions of the *Essay* (1803, 1806, 1807 and 1826) were much longer precisely because Malthus collected a greater number of facts.
4   The dating of the Preface to 7 June 1798 is significant as this coincides precisely with the peak of fears that Britain would be invaded by Napoleon and of the insurrectionary events taking place in Ireland. Napoleon was known to have a large fleet at sea, but it was not known that its destination was Egypt. On 7 June itself, the town of Wexford fell to Irish forces rebelling against English rule; this was to many a presage of 'the long dreaded day, when the French Revolution would spread to Ireland' (Thomas Pakenham, *The Year of Liberty: The Story of*

the Great Irish Rebellion of 1798 [London: Phoenix ed. 1992]), p. 180.

5   'Cunning; skilful; dexterous' Johnson, *Dictionary*, sense 3.

6   'One of a hot imagination, or violent passions' Johnson, *Dictionary*, sense 2.

7   'To return any argument, censure, or incivility' Johnson, *Dictionary*, sense 2.

8   *Philosophy* meaning here 'Reasoning, argumentation' Johnson, *Dictionary*, sense 4.

9   David Hume (1711–76), philosopher and man of letters, at the heart of the Scottish Enlightenment. Where today Hume is remembered mainly for his philosophical works, in Malthus's age it was his historical writings and his essays that secured his reputation. Of particular importance to Malthus, and alluded to here, is his essay 'Of the Populousness of Ancient Nations' (1752). Malthus referred to the 1764 edition but by his death his library recorded ownership of an edition from 1800.

10   Adam Smith (1723–90), political economist and philosopher, is mainly remembered today for *The Wealth of Nations* (1776), which is the work to which Malthus alludes here and with which he engages later in the *Essay*. Smith is framed as the founder of modern economics, and this is certainly how Malthus depicts him here and throughout his career. The Malthus library only records an 1828 edition of Smith, but he must have owned or had regular access to this text throughout his life.

11   Robert Wallace (1697–1771) was a more minor Scottish thinker who wrote *A Dissertation on the Numbers of Mankind in Ancient and Modern Times* (1753), which criticized Hume's views on population, arguing against him that the population of Europe was greater in antiquity than in the present day. Malthus owned a copy of this book.

12   Jean Antoine Nicolas de Caritat, Marquis de Condorcet (1743–94), philosopher, mathematician and politician whose posthumous masterpiece, *Equisse d'un Tableau Historique des Progrès de l'Esprit Humain*, was translated into English in 1795 as *Outlines of an Historical View of the Progress of the Human Mind*. *Outlines* argues that the progress of reason will allow human lifespans to increase with 'no assignable limit' and that, in such a context, people will voluntarily limit births when this is needed, which would only be in the remote future. All these propositions Malthus would attack in the *Essay*. Malthus's library does not record his ownership of a copy of the *Outlines*.

13   'Mental entrance into anything abstruse', 'acuteness; sagacity'
      Johnson, *Dictionary*, senses 2 and 3.

14   'Position assumed without proof' Johnson, *Dictionary*. The
      logical style of reasoning Malthus deploys here would have been
      enforced by his studies at Cambridge University.

15   The eighteenth century saw the development of 'stadial theories'
      of social development, arguments, that is, about the ways in
      which societies move from being hunter-gatherers, through pas-
      toral and agricultural stages to the emergent industrial societies
      of which Britain was the most advanced example. Malthus
      would deploy these theories to structure chapters Three to Six of
      the *Essay*.

16   Malthus exemplifies these ratios in chapter Two, but in his terms
      a 'geometrical' ratio is where numbers increase by a fixed mul-
      tiple, whilst an 'arithmetic' ratio is where numbers increase by a
      fixed amount.

17   Malthus draws here on the influential findings of Benjamin
      Franklin in *Observations Concerning the Increase of Mankind,
      Peopling of Countries, etc* (1751). Malthus owned the 1779 edi-
      tion of Franklin's *Political, Miscellaneous and Philosophical
      Pieces*.

18   'Course of action; uninterrupted procedure' Johnson, *Diction-
      ary*, sense 3.

19   'In a cross direction' Johnson, *Dictionary*.

20   ... *farmers and capitalists*: i.e. farmers own land and capitalists
      own money/stock, in contradistinction to labourers owning only
      their own labour.

21   'Union for some certain purpose; association; league' Johnson,
      Dictionary, sense 1.

22   'Rough; savage; coarse of manners; uncivil; brutal' Johnson,
      Dictionary, sense 1.

23   The Khoikhoi people of Southern Africa; they were routinely
      described by travellers as the most primitive of societies and
      were thus modelled by theorists of the stages of social
      development.

24   A general term for slaves or subjugated people, derived from the
      category deployed in ancient Sparta.

25   Nomadic peoples of the area north of the Black Sea, immortal-
      ized for European thinkers by Herodotus. It is hard not to read
      in this paragraph Malthus's indebtedness to Gibbon's *Decline
      and Fall of the Roman Empire*, which he had read a decade earl-
      ier as a student in Cambridge. Later editions of the *Essay* reveal

his debt to Gibbon explicitly. Malthus owned an edition of Gibbon.

26   'Dreadful; horrible; astonishingly terrible' Johnson, *Dictionary*.

27   The quotation is from John Milton, *Paradise Lost*, XII 646. Malthus owned the 1775 edition of *Paradise Lost*.

28   Alaric (370–410), Attila the Hun (d. 453) and Genghis Khan (1162–1227) were the best known exemplars of the migratory violence of pastoral societies that Malthus addresses here.

29   There was in fact a considerable debate in the generation before Malthus as to whether the population of Europe had increased or decreased since antiquity. Montesquieu had influentially argued for a dramatic population decline of up to 90 per cent in his *Persian Letters*, a view supported by Robert Wallace (see above, note 11 to p. 14). This was the position Hume had denied in 'Of the Populousness of Ancient Nations' (1752). Britain in Malthus's age saw large-scale driving of cattle and sheep from Wales and Scotland to England as the national economy became increasingly integrated around London. Malthus owned a 1748 edition of the *Persian Letters* in the original French.

30   For Hume's essay, see above, note 9 to p. 14.

31   Smith discusses China in *The Wealth of Nations*, Book I, chapter Eight.

32   'Familiar; closely acquainted' Johnson, *Dictionary*, sense 3.

33   'Communication' Johnson, *Dictionary*, sense 2.

34   'Parish for support' refers to the system of Poor Relief that was arranged at parish level as established by the provisions of the Poor Law Relief Act of 1601, which Malthus criticizes later in the *Essay*.

35   *Bills of mortality*: the registers of deaths kept in London which allowed for the calculation of rates of death.

36   Malthus wrote the *Essay* whilst living in the Weald area of Surrey, an area of considerable poverty at this time. It is speculated by Patricia James, Malthus's biographer, that this section is a reflection of his first-hand experience.

37   'A writ conferring some exclusive right or privilege' Johnson, *Dictionary*.

38   The term is not in Johnson's *Dictionary*, but resonates with his definition of 'to manufacture' as 'to form by workmanship'. Malthus appears to have in mind any form of employment that involves workmanship not on the land, that is, local crafts and proto-industries. He is not, in 1798, envisaging large-scale factories of the sort we associate with mid nineteenth-century Britain.

39 Under the Settlement Act of 1662, a claimant for Poor Relief had to prove they were settled in a parish by birth, marriage or employment to be eligible for relief. Malthus sees this as inhibiting migration and thereby, as with Poor Relief more generally, creating the poor it maintains, in this case by discouraging them from seeking employment elsewhere.

40 William Pitt the Younger introduced a bill to modify Poor Relief to the House of Commons in 1797 but it was easily defeated. Pitt's proposals included one whereby every poor man with more than two children who was not self supporting, and every widow with more than one child, would be eligible for a weekly allowance for each extra child. It was this that led to Malthus's critical comments here.

41 'Something mitigating; something alleviating' Johnson, *Dictionary*.

42 Malthus consistently opposed the provisions of the Poor Relief Act of 1601, the only exception being the positive comments in his 1800 *Investigation of the Cause of the Present High Price of Provisions* (see page 184–5 in this edition). For this reason he was closely associated in the public imagination with the New Poor Law of 1834, which brought in the workhouse system that Dickens would castigate. Whilst Malthus influenced those who framed this legislation through his works, he had no direct input into the process.

43 In other words, Malthus argues that manufacturing and the urban trades limit their supply of qualified labour through the need for qualifications and admission to select societies, and that this inflates the price of urban labour vis-à-vis agricultural labour, which lacks such restrictions on labour supply.

44 The British in Malthus's age routinely rehearsed the so-called 'black legend' of the infamy and iniquity of Spanish imperial governance, normally in explicit or implied contradistinction to the allegedly benevolent operation of the British Empire.

45 Antonio de Ulloa (1716–95), author of *A Voyage to South America*, which was translated into English in 1758. The Malthus library catalogue records that he owned the 1752 French translation.

46 *The Wealth of Nations*, Book IV, chapter Seven, section b.

47 The rule that the eldest inherits the entirety of their parents' estate. Malthus also draws his evidence here from Smith, *The Wealth of Nations*, Book IV, chapter Seven, section b.

48 Richard Price, *Observations on Reversionary Payments*. This was one of the most influential treatises of the age about

population, politics and poverty. Price (1723–91) was a radical Welsh dissenting minister with a high level of mathematical skills who pioneered social insurance schemes, his aim being to secure the lot of the poor by such schemes. Malthus refers to the fourth edition of 1783 in two volumes (as is made clear in the footnote to page 51), a copy of which was in his library. Styles is John Styles who wrote *A Discourse of Christian Union* (1761).

49   Malthus was consistent in his dislike of the emergent conditions in British towns of his era from his own brief stay at Gilbert Wakefield's academy in Warrington in the early 1780s until his death.

50   Malthus probably refers to the devastating impact of the Thirty Years War (1618–48) in this area in particular but it was more generally a cockpit of European conflict in the early modern era.

51   A state of the Holy Roman Empire in the Rhineland. This area was also devastated in the Thirty Years War, seeing up to a 50 per cent loss of population by deaths and emigration. Louis XIV invaded the Palatinate in the 1670s and '80s, most notably in the Nine Years War (1688–97), again leading to major depopulation of the area.

52   The Great Plague of London is estimated to have killed around 100,000 people, or up to 15 per cent of London's population.

53   The Lisbon Earthquake of 1 November 1755 was an 8.5–9 magnitude earthquake with aftershocks, resultant fires and a tsunami. Estimates of the numbers killed vary wildly, but this was a cause célèbre in the eighteenth century, with Voltaire in *Candide* seeing it as proof that this Earth was not a divinely ordained best of all possible worlds. Lima had experienced a similarly massive earthquake and tsunami in 1746.

54   Johann Peter Süssmilch (1707–67), German demographer who assiduously collected population data in his *Die Göttliche Ordnung* (*The Divine order in the circumstances of the human sex, birth, death and reproduction* [1741 and other editions]). Price used the 3rd edition of Süssmilch (1765) in his *Observations on Reversionary Payments* and the details excerpted by Malthus can be found in the second volume (pp. 314–15).

55   Thomas Short (1690–1772), author of *New Observations, Natural, Moral, Civil, Political, and Medical, on City, Town and Country Bills of Mortality* (1750).

56   That the population of England and Wales had declined in the century since the Glorious Revolution of 1688 was a key contention in Price's *Observations*.

57 Gregory King (1648–1712), pioneering demographer.

58 Here and at several other points in the *Essay*, Malthus blends a quintessentially Enlightened belief in the power of human reason with a sense of the universe as mechanical in its operation which derives from a Newtonian worldview. For Malthus, as becomes apparent again in the final two chapters of the *Essay*, God exists, but works via laws that can be scrutinized and understood by reason. This stance was conventional enough for someone educated at Cambridge and under the influence of William Paley's moral philosophy, but it would offend some of Malthus's more orthodox clerical critics.

59 It appears that Malthus draws on Adam Smith's account in *The Wealth of Nations*, volume I Book VIII, which itself draws on Jean-Baptiste Du Halde's *Description of China*, which was widely cited in the original French and in an English translation by Samuel Johnson.

60 *Hindustan*, i.e. India.

61 For Pitt and his Poor Bill, see above, note 40 to page 47.

62 Refers to *The Wealth of Nations*, Book 1, chapter Eleven, section b, which in fact discusses this issue for Europe as a whole, not for England specifically.

63 Condorcet had been a member of the General Assembly of the French Revolution but then fell from favour during the Terror. Whilst his *Equisse* was begun at a much earlier stage, it was said that he was revising it at the time when he was finally captured. Condorcet then died in prison, prior to any formal judicial hearing. This section makes Malthus's hostility to the French Revolution most transparent.

64 The *Equisse* is divided into ten 'epochs', the last of which addresses the future improvements to be expected in human societies. It is this section that is the target of Malthus's criticism.

65 'Trifling, futile, insignificant' Johnson, *Dictionary*.

66 '*killing frost*' is from Shakespeare, *Henry VIII*, Act III, Scene II, line 355.

67 *Concubinage* is 'the act of living with a woman not married', Johnson, *Dictionary*. Malthus seems here to mean that in Condorcet's future scenarios marriage may be one of those 'ridiculous prejudices of superstition' that has been overthrown. If so, and as he says elsewhere, for Malthus prostitution or promiscuous concubinage may lead to fewer births most probably through sexual disease. *Something else as unnatural* is a delicate

euphemism for contraception, something Malthus also refers to with similar obliqueness in the 1803 *Essay* as 'improper arts', and which, in accord with the standard Christian injunctions of his age, he regarded with repugnance.

68   This section makes plain the degree to which Malthus's conception of the scientific study of society was modelled on Newton's achievements.

69   Biblical, from 1 Corinthians, 15: 51–2.

70   The quotation is from Alexander Pope, *An Essay on Man* (1732–4), 1, 18. Malthus's library contained Pope's *Works*.

71   Refers to the *Tatler*, a hugely successful periodical edited by Richard Steele and to which Pope, Swift and Addison all contributed. In *Tatler* 75 (1709) Isaac Bickerstaff, the fictional author of the essays, suggests that the family has engaged in selective breeding down the centuries, with Maud the Milkmaid having 'spoiled our Blood, but mended our Constitutions'. Malthus possessed four separate editions of the *Tatler* in his library.

72   The quotations are from Prospero's speech in *The Tempest*, Act IV, Scene I, lines 151–3.

73   A clear expression of Malthus's lifelong hostility to urban centres. This is also a close echo of Richard Price's favoured image of a happy future for the British Isles.

74   For Styles, see note 48, above, on p. 51.

75   Another example of Malthus's belief in the existence of Newtonian laws of nature governing society and accessible to rational scrutiny.

76   *Commerce between the sexes*, i.e. sexual relationships.

77   Malthus here follows the conventionally accepted Christian chronology of the earth as being of the order of 6,000 years old. Concurrently, James Hutton's researches were starting to develop geological evidence of a far longer history for the earth.

78   The moral philosopher William Paley who was Archdeacon of Carlisle and whose doctrine in *Principles of Moral and Political Philosophy* (1785) Malthus here summarizes.

79   Probably an attorney's clerk named Foster Powell, whom some called 'the Horsforth Pedestrian', who walked from London to York and then back again several times between 1773 and 1792, a distance of 400 miles that he covered in six days.

80   From Hamlet's soliloquy, Act III, Scene 1, line 75.

81   The fable of the tortoise and the hare is from Aesop.

82   Mr Brothers is Richard Brothers (1757–1824), the self-declared apostle of a new religion, who issued a series of published

prophecies, was arrested for treason for prophesying the king's death and was declared insane in 1795.

83 *Revelation . . . natural religion*, i.e. the arguments from Scripture and from the laws of nature, which were deemed to prove the truth of the Christian religion.

84 Another example of Malthus's belief in a Newtonian social science and in the importance of applied knowledge not abstract speculations in the study of societies.

85 'A small dagger' Johnson, *Dictionary*.

86 A structure in philosophical argument in which a major proposition and a minor proposition combine to make a logically necessary conclusion. Where the propositions do not inevitably lead to the conclusion, one of them must be flawed.

87 'Earth; soil; ground in which anything grows' Johnson, *Dictionary*, sense 2.

88 Not in Johnson's *Dictionary*, but defined by the *Oxford English Dictionary* as: 'the whorl of leaves (sepals), either separate or grown together, and usually green, forming the outer envelope in which the flower is enclosed while yet in the bud'.

89 Malthus refers to Book II, chapter Three in Smith's *The Wealth of Nations*.

90 Just as Malthus was no admirer of urban centres (above, note 73 to page 81), so he was ambivalent about manufacturing, seeing agriculture throughout his life as the bedrock of a stable society. He reverts to this topic at greater length in chapters Sixteen and Seventeen.

91 'Such a confused apprehension as does not leave reason its full force' Johnson, *Dictionary*, sense 1.

92 Probably a reference to Book IV, chapter Nine of *The Wealth of Nations*, which attacks the French *economistes*, who argued that agriculture was the sole ground for a real increase in wealth and population, a doctrine with which Malthus had more sympathy than Smith.

93 Smith defines wealth thus in *The Wealth of Nations*, Book 1, chapter Eleven, section n.

94 'Provision of conveniencies' Johnson, *Dictionary*, sense 1.

95 That is, the so-called Glorious Revolution of 1688.

96 Price, in his *Observations*, argued for a decline in the population of England and Wales since the Glorious Revolution. John Howlett (1731–1804) controverted Price's position and argued for an increasing population in *An Examination of Dr Price's Essay on the Population of England and Wales* (1781).

Malthus's library at his death contained two works by Howlett, but not the one discussed in the text here. Current work in historical demography suggests that the population of England and Wales in the 1680s was just over 5 million, where as the population by the 1790s when Malthus wrote was 8¼ millions. See E. A. Wrigley et al., *English Population History from Family Reconstitution, 1580–1837* (Cambridge, 1997), appendix 9, p. 614.

97   The school of French students of political economy often known as the Physiocrats led by Quesnay and Turgot, for whom the sole source of true wealth was the land.

98   The parish laws are the Poor Laws again, which restricted the movement of people away from their parish as they would not then be eligible for support. Corporation laws appears to refer not to the Test and Corporation Act (1661), which restricted those who could take up civic posts by the need for allegiance to the Anglican Church, but more likely to the various acts of the seventeenth and eighteenth centuries that created monopolies in certain trades and allowed corporations and guilds to restrict entry to those trades.

99   Smith makes this observation in Book 1, chapter Nine of *The Wealth of Nations*. Malthus closely follows Smith's discussion in this section of the *Essay*.

100 The eighteenth century is often seen to herald the rise of a consumer society and contemporary observers such as Malthus were highly ambivalent about its moral and economic consequences.

101 Price discusses this in the 'Supplement' to volume 2 of his *Observations*.

102 In Greek mythology, Sisyphus is condemned in Hades to roll a stone to the top of a hill, which will then come back down such that he has to do the same task for all eternity.

103 The final two chapters of the *Essay*, where Malthus argues for a Christian interpretation of the principle of population, suggesting that the pain and suffering the principle necessitates are not inconsistent with a good and wise God, were highly controversial upon publication and Malthus removed them from all subsequent editions.

104 The quotation is from Alexander Pope's *Essay on Man*, 1: 16.

105 Biblical, from Isaiah, 55: 9.

106 Biblical, from Job, 11: 7.

107 Malthus adopts a strongly rationalist/natural religion approach to Christianity here and it is this that offended orthodox critics

for its apparent elevation of reason over Scripture. He then goes on to see our earthly existence as designed to form our minds, not, as in more conventional Christian arguments, as a state of trial or probation. Contrary to later critics who view Malthus as 'conservative', this section was seen as radical for its religious implications.

108 'Dullness, obtuseness, bluntness' Johnson, *Dictionary*.

109 Necessity the mother of invention: in twentieth-century debates between neo-Malthusians and their critics, the argument that necessity would lead human invention to circumvent the resource scarcity issues created by population growth as developed by Ester Boserup and Julian Simon was deemed a rebuttal of Malthus. It is worth noting here, however, that Malthus himself invoked the same emphasis on population pressure as a spur to human creativity, which could improve society and stave off the rigours of the principle of population he adumbrated.

110 I cannot find a precise passage in Locke to this effect, but parallel comments are offered at several points in the *Essay Concerning Human Understanding*, notably in Book II chapters Seven to Eight and Twenty to Twenty-one.

111 Malthus here argues for the virtue to be found in the 'middling sorts' of which he was a member as opposed to the labouring or aristocratic classes. His parallel between the middle class and the temperate zones draws on ideas of environmental determinism, which argued that different climatic/environmental zones created different human characteristics, the middle or temperate zones being the best suited to optimal mental and civilizational attainment. These ideas were most closely associated in this period with Montesquieu's *Spirit of the Laws*.

112 This is the closest to a 'pragmatic utopianism' that Malthus comes in the *Essay* in response to the visions of Godwin and Condorcet.

113 Malthus was himself a younger brother!

114 Shakespeare, *Antony and Cleopatra*, Act II, Scene ii, lines 243–4.

115 Biblical, from Ecclesiastes, 1: 9.

116 'A fish which while alive, if touched . . . benumbs the hand that so touches it' Johnson, *Dictionary*.

117 Alexander Pope, *Essay on Man*, 1: 95–6.

The Travel Diaries of Thomas Robert Malthus:
The Scandinavian Journal

Immediately after completing the *Essay* in 1798, Malthus asked his father to acquire more books for him about travel and demography and set off with friends from his Cambridge days to travel to Scandinavia and Russia, a journey during which he gathered considerable evidence about regional demography, economics and resource issues. Both strands of activity were clearly designed to contribute to a longer, more nuanced and more substantiated version of the *Essay*, which would appear in 1803. The sorts of complexity that would figure in Malthus's later writings are neatly prefigured in the following lightly edited extract from his travel diaries, as Malthus reached his furthest northerly point in Trondheim in 1799.

1   Count Gerhard Moltke, governor of Trondheim.
2   Note that Malthus remains a keen opponent of the French Revolution and its impact on the aspirations of the poorer classes in his comments here. Drontheim is Trondheim.
3   Malthus here starts to address issues of 'food security', which would come to the fore fifteen years later in his arguments about the worth of the Corn Laws (see later extract).
4   The laws of inheritance called Odels Right are explained in the following paragraph.
5   Christiania, i.e. modern Oslo.
6   Roraas, i.e. Roras.

An Investigation of the Cause of the
Present High Price of Provisions

Malthus's first publication on his return to England was 'An Investigation', a short tract that has been praised for its prescience as an economic analysis of the linkage of price and food shortage by the Nobel Laureate Amartya Sen. Malthus is keen to dispel the idea that high prices are being created intentionally by those who own food stocks or by the commercial middlemen he sees as essential to the operation of a modern economy and draws on his recent experience in Scandinavia to elucidate his argument.

1   'One that anticipates the market; one that purchases before others to raise the price' Johnson, *Dictionary*. (*Regrater* is defined in the *Dictionary* as a synonym of forestaller.)

2   Lloyd Kenyon, 1st Baron Kenyon (1732–1802), who was Lord Chief Justice 1788–1802.

3   *Parish allowances*, i.e. the amount of subsidized relief offered to the poor based on the high price of provisions.

4   A quartern is a traditional English unit of weight equal to 1/4 stone, 3.5 pounds or about 1.5876 kilogrammes; a quartern loaf is made from a quartern of flour.

5   Smith discusses this in *The Wealth of Nations* Book I, chapter Seven.

6   *Toties quoties*, i.e. repeatedly.

7   A load was sometimes a standardized unit, but it varied with the commodity being carried. A typical size was 40 bushels (roughly 1.4 cubic metres).

8   The Justices of the Peace, who ran the poor relief system at the parish level.

9   Tantalus was condemned for offering the gods a feast of his own son Pelops. His punishment was to stand in water but that it would recede from his lips whenever he sought to drink of it.

10 The Dutch East India Company (Vereenigde Oost-Indische Compagnie, VOC), founded in 1602, whose trading charter had finally expired permanently the year prior to this essay.

11 Those merchants who trade in corn.

12 *In another place*, i.e. in the 1798 *Essay*.

13 It is worth noting Malthus's flexibility here; the laws he was most vehemently opposed to, the Elizabethan Poor Laws, have functioned, he believes, to stave off starvation, albeit at the cost of more than proportionately elevated prices.

14 The Bank of England came off the Gold Standard in 1797 and only returned to it in 1821.

15 Country banks could issue their own notes throughout Malthus's lifetime. The Bank of England's notes only became the 'legal tender' of Britain in 1833 and the last private bank only ceased issuing notes in 1921.

16 Of medieval origin, the Assize of Bread and Ale regulated the price, weight and quality of bread until statutory reforms in 1822 and 1836. As such, the abolition Malthus advocated would come shortly after his essay.

17 An Act of 1797 that added detail to the Assize of Bread stipulated that within London weekly reports of the quantities of wheat

traded and their price were delivered to meal weighers by the cornfactors who traded them and by the bakers who bought them. The intention was to prevent speculative stockpiling of wheat.

18 William Henry Cavendish-Bentinck, 3rd Duke of Portland (1738–1809), at this time Home Secretary in Pitt's government and a staunch opponent of state intervention to address food shortages. Portland did allow state intervention to bolster the price of grain and alleviate distress in 1795 and again in 1800 as Malthus's tract was published. The publication Malthus alludes to appears to be in fact addressed to the Lord Lieutenant of Chester, viz. *Copy of a letter from the Duke of Portland, to the Lord Lieutenant of the county of Chester, and of His Lordship's letter, directing the same to be laid before the magistrates for the said county, at their general quarter-sessions, on the 14th Jan. 1800, for the purpose of alleviating the distresses of the poor, from the effects of the late unfavourable harvest, by the substitution of soup and other food, in lieu of bread corn; and copy of several suggestions transmitted by the Duke of Portland to the Lord Lieutenant, on the same subject: printed pursuant to an order made at the said quarter sessions* (Chester: J Fletcher, 1800).

Two Selections from the 1803 Edition of the Essay

As advertised at the end of his 1800 *Investigation of the Cause of the Present High Price of Provisions*, Malthus was working on a longer, more empirically substantiated version of his *Essay*. When it emerged in 1803, he rightly noted that, whilst it retained its title from 1798 'in its present shape it may be considered as a new work'. The 55,000-word *Essay* of 1798 had nearly quadrupled in size by 1803 and its argument shifted to see the power of preventive checks to population increase, this acting 'to soften some of the harshest conclusions of the first essay'. And yet the 1803 *Essay*, despite being over 200,000 words long and 'softer', gained infamy and is primarily remembered for its harshest paragraph, about 'nature's mighty feast', which is reproduced here and seemed to epitomize Malthus as the hard-hearted enemy of the poor. This paragraph, which Malthus deleted in all subsequent editions, was seized upon by Romantic poets and then by Marx and Engels. More representative of where Malthus's thinking was moving is the second selection here, which addresses questions of food security in an increasingly industrial and commercialized society. These concerns would preoccupy him over the next twenty years as subsequent selections will demonstrate.

Book IV chapter vi: Nature's Mighty Feast

1   English discourse of the eighteenth century routinely saw 'stand-
     ing armies' – regular, levied military forces – as inimical to
     liberty, which latter demanded the use of temporary militias
     comprised of the people. The roots of this discourse are in repub-
     licanism as demonstrated in J. G. A. Pocock's classic work, *The
     Machiavellian Moment* (1975).

2   As a note in later editions explained, Malthus here refers to the
     high price of provisions in 1800–1801, which had been the sub-
     ject of his 'Investigation'.

3   Hume discusses the euthanasia of the constitution at the close of
     his essay 'Whether the British Government Inclines more to Abso-
     lute Monarchy, or to a Republic' in his *Essays, Moral, Political
     and Literary*. Malthus's library contained a copy of this work.

4   Career: see note 18 *Essay*, p. 21.

5   *vox populi . . . vox Dei*: a maxim – the voice of the people is the
     voice of God – common in populist political discourse from the
     fifteenth century on whose meaning Malthus here inverts.

6   *existing circumstances*, i.e. people were sceptical of claims that
     current circumstances necessitated the suspension of liberties,
     viewing this instead as a convenient fiction of Pitt the Younger's
     government as it moved in an authoritarian direction.

7   Latin, meaning 'on the threshold', more generally, 'initially'. So,
     Malthus says we should not be sceptical merely because an indi-
     vidual relies on the idea of existing circumstances to justify a
     change of view.

8   Thomas Paine's *The Rights of Man* (1791) was the most influen-
     tial defence of the French Revolution and, because of its cheap
     price, the most widely distributed amongst the poorer classes.
     The critique Malthus makes of Paine here recapitulates that
     made against Condorcet and Godwin in the 1798 *Essay*, adding
     only that Paine's experience in North America during the War of
     Independence was not transferrable to Europe due to the more
     immediate resource pressures there.

9   This paragraph acquired a considerable notoriety for its appar-
     ent callousness that would dog the rest of Malthus's career.

10   Guillaume Raynal (1713–96), whose philosophical history of
     European colonization, *Histoire philosophique des deux Indes*
     (1770), encoded a strong message both opposing empire and
     endorsing libertarian government, in good part thanks to the
     considerable input Denis Diderot had in its construction.

Book III, chapter x

1   For the *economistes*, see note 92 to page 128 of 1798 *Essay*.

2   Malthus here shows an awareness that the character of the Brit-
    ish economy had changed in his lifetime in the direction of
    commerce and manufactures, something now often labelled as
    the 'Industrial Revolution'. Here and in his work on the Corn
    Laws and economic depression (see 'Observations on the Effects
    of the Corn Laws' and 'Selections from Principles of Political
    Economy', below) Malthus was a keen analyst of the socio-
    economic pitfalls associated with these changes.

3   Again, the late scarcities are those of 1800 reflected on in
    Malthus's 'Investigation'.

4   Malthus refers to the warfare that ensued after the French Revo-
    lution. As he wrote the 1803 *Essay*, the Treaty of Amiens of
    1802 had brought a temporary cessation to the hostilities,
    thereby opening up the possibility of Britain losing its trading
    monopoly that Malthus detected. The resumption of warfare in
    the Napoleonic Wars came in 1803.

5   Primary produce or raw materials that have not been worked up.

6   'Inferiour in order' Johnson, *Dictionary*, sense 1, here meaning
    'dependent'.

7   *body politic . . . members*: i.e. limbs. Malthus here deployed the
    venerable trope of the state as a body or person, where it is the
    task of the statesman to ensure that person's health.

8   Government intervention in the operation of the economic system.

Observations of the Effects of the Corn Laws (1814)

This was the first of two essays Malthus wrote regarding the Corn
Laws, the subsidies intended to ensure British grain supplies. There
was, in the face of scarcity and high prices, considerable debate at this
time between advocates of the Corn Laws and those seeking their abolition in favour of a free trade in corn. As might be anticipated from the
previous selection, Malthus saw in these debates the confirmation of his
view that corn supplies could not be treated as just another good, and
that the strictures developed by Adam Smith's political economy were,
therefore, not applicable here as they could compromise food security
and thereby might compromise peaceable libertarian government.

1   The Corn Laws excluded the importation of corn to Britain until
    the price reached a certain threshold, the aim being to ensure the

continued agricultural vibrancy of the British economy. The revision Malthus alludes to was enacted in 1815 and set the threshold price before importation was allowed at 80 shillings per quarter, this being a price corn never attained in Malthus's lifetime, meaning that restrictions on imports were in fact enacted without intermission.

2   Smith discusses the Corn Laws in Book IV, chapter Five of *The Wealth of Nations*, in his 'Digression concerning the Corn Trade and Corn Laws'. There was a bounty or financial inducement to the exportation of corn enacted in 1688, which Smith discusses here.

3   Malthus is referring to the section in his editions of the *Essay* from 1803 onwards 'Of Bounties on the Exportation of Corn' (Book II, I chapter Ten in 1803 and chapter Eleven in later editions).

4   Smith makes this argument in *The Wealth of Nations*, Book IV, chapter Five 'Of Bounties'.

5   Frederick Eden (1766–1809) wrote *The State of the Poor* (1797), a path-breaking analysis of the economic condition of the labouring classes.

6   These two paragraphs are a good example of Malthus seeing that adjustments between supply and demand and between price signals and responses will display lags such that economic equilibrium will be a rare phenomenon. As we shall see in the final selections, Malthus continued these enquiries in his analysis of economic depression and effective demand in his *Principles of Political Economy*.

7   Owners of capital.

8   Malthus, drawing on Adam Smith, distinguishes 'demand' in the sense of something wanted from 'effectual demand', which is the same want supported by the ability to pay for its satisfaction. This would become an important concept for Malthus's analysis in *Principles of Political Economy*.

9   A quarter was 2 stones in weight. J. J. Oddy, *European commerce, showing new and secure channels of trade with the continent of Europe* (1805).

10   *Governments acting from passion*: refers to the events of the Napoleonic Wars, as Malthus confirms two paragraphs later.

11   1812 saw Britain engaged both in the Napoleonic Wars and in the consequent conflict with the United States. This latter saw a blockade, which reduced the importation of American foodstuffs into Britain. The resultant distress fuelled the Luddites, who in addition to destroying machines also threatened food

merchants. Malthus fears that a repeat of these events, in a society with a growing population and declining agricultural sector, could seriously threaten national security in the future.

12   Amendments were made to the bounty on corn exportation and the tariff on corn importation by Parliamentary act in 1804. Malthus returns to the 1804 act towards the end of this essay.

13   The anxieties Malthus displays here with regard to manufacturing's impact on social stability and individual morals repeat his concerns in the 1798 *Essay*. The positive side of manufacturing, rehearsed in the next paragraph, similarly recapitulates themes from the *Essay*.

14   *Fluxions*: differential calculus and the analysis of rates of change in quantities. Malthus would have been exposed to this through his mathematical and Newtonian education in Cambridge. The topic Malthus opens up here would be taken further in economics in the nineteenth century in the so-called 'marginalist revolution'. What Malthus seems to argue is that the growth of a manufacturing sector is good, but if the rate of growth is too large with respect to agrarian growth, it becomes socially and economically problematic.

15   Malthus returns here to a theme already aired in the selection offered from the 1803 *Essay*.

16   That is, if Britain returns to the Gold Standard, something which did not occur until 1821. In this and the next two short paragraphs, Malthus considers whether and to what extent the detail of the Corn Laws may need to change. As those laws set a price per quarter at which importation faced duties, the changing nominal price of corn had to be watched carefully if the laws were to encourage domestic agriculture effectively. Going back on to the Gold Standard could cause an alteration in the nominal price of corn, which would also require legislative adjustments to the Corn Laws.

17   The repose Malthus mentions is the cessation of the Napoleonic Wars that came in 1815. The historical parallel Malthus draws is to the end of the War of Spanish Succession (1701–14) a century earlier.

18   By the time of this essay, the results of the censuses of 1801 (the first ever in Britain) and 1811 were available, allowing Malthus some confidence in the current population of Britain but far less with regard to change since the mid eighteenth century.

19   Malthus is contending that the rise of a middle class has led to a greater demand for meat in the diet, this in turn changing the relative demand for arable and pastoral land in favour of the latter and, therefore, against the production of corn.

Selections from Principles of Political Economy (1820)

While Malthus continued to make amendments to his *Essay* until the final edition of 1826, his major new work in the second half of his career was *Principles of Political Economy* (1820). Having attended to economic debates about the poor laws, food shortages, bullion and the Corn Laws for the past two decades, Malthus was convinced of the complexity of questions in political economy, of the intricacies of making general statements in social science. Paradoxically, if Malthus is normally remembered for the simple 'laws' of the first edition of the *Essay*, by the end of his life his credo as a scholar was a reverse one of attending to complexity and contingencies. This credo is spelled out in the first selection here, his 'Introduction' to the *Principles*. And the importance of this is exemplified by the other selection included here, where Malthus discusses the idea that an economy can experience what Keynes came to call 'underconsumption' or, viewed the other way around, a structural glut of goods coupled with unemployment. Malthus was drawn to these questions both in challenging the orthodoxy developed by his good friend David Ricardo (against many of whose ideas the *Principles* is directed), which he viewed as a theoretical structure inadequately attentive to empirical complexity in its argument that supply and demand will automatically reach an equilibrium, and because of the economic depression Britain experienced in the Napoleonic Wars. Malthus goes on to evidence this from Alexander von Humboldt's work in South America and his own experience of Ireland. Both selections have been lightly edited to shorten them.

1   The mercantile system, now often called 'mercantilism', was a diffuse set of doctrines in economic policy prior to the emergence of classical political economy with Smith, Malthus and Ricardo. Mercantilism emphasized each state's need to maximize its bullion reserves through limiting imports and encouraging exports. Mercantilism therefore viewed free trade as reducing an individual state's wealth, where Smith would see it as maximizing total wealth.

2   'Economists' are the French school of the *economistes*, mentioned in note 92 to page 128 of the *Essay*.

3   Malthus clearly believes that the events of the decades since the French Revolution have been a testing ground in which the adequacy of the theories of both the *economistes* and Adam Smith

can be assessed, but, as he goes on to state on page 245–6, a considered judgement on these questions has yet to be ventured.

4 Malthus suggests that there are two groups who write about political economy: theoretically minded economists and practical students of a specific trade or sector of the economy.

5 Malthus has the work of David Ricardo in mind in particular in discussing this 'contrary extreme'. Much of this introduction, some of it explicitly so towards the conclusion, is a polite riposte to Ricardo and the perceived influence of his *On the Principles of Political Economy and Taxation* (1817).

6 The Malthus of the 1798 *Essay* was far more directly in the thrall of Newtonianism as a model for social science than is the Malthus of *Principles* in 1820.

7 The so-called 'chemical revolution' of the later eighteenth century transformed the basis of chemistry through an awareness of the law of the conservation of matter and the oxygen theory of combustion. As such, chemistry underwent a profound theoretical change under Lavoisier at the same time as political economy did under Adam Smith.

8 As well as writing about population and the Corn Laws as we have seen, Malthus had written two pamphlets in 1811 addressing currency questions: 'Depreciation of Paper Currency' and 'The High Price of Bullion', both in the *Edinburgh Review*. The *Quarterly Review* article Malthus cites was published in the 1816 edition and penned by Malthus's long-time adversary, the Romantic poet Robert Southey. The article reviewed a number of titles, including one on population by John Weyland.

9 *Cui bono*: who benefits? Malthus defends the importance of research in political economy even where it leads merely to a better understanding of the economic system and not to any immediate economic benefit.

10 James Maitland, 8th Earl of Lauderdale (1759–1839), Whig and political economist.

11 Jean-Baptiste Say (1767–1832), author of *Traité d'économie politique* (1803).

12 James Mill, father of John Stuart Mill. The 1808 reply mentioned is *Commerce Defended. An Answer to the Arguments by which Mr Spence, Mr Cobbett, and Others, have attempted to Prove that Commerce is not a source of National Wealth*. Mr Spence is Thomas Spence (1750–1814), who advocated a common ownership of land and its removal from private hands

to ensure a just distribution of wealth as part of a radical political platform that also included universal suffrage.

13   Mr Owen is the utopian, social reformer and industrialist Robert Owen (1771–1858).

14   For Süssmilch, see above, note 54 to page 54 of the *Essay*.

15   The Population Abstracts are the published versions of the findings of the second British census of that year, issued in 1812 under the title *Abstracts of the Answers and Returns Made pursuant to an Act, passed in the Fifty-first Year of His Majesty King George III. Intituled, 'An Act for taking an Account of the Population 'of Great Britain, and the Increase or 'Diminution thereof.'* Preliminary Observations.

16   Malthus's long quotations from Alexander von Humboldt's *Essai politique sur le royaume de la Nouvelle-Espagne* (1808–11) are omitted here, with only his conclusions included. Alexander von Humboldt (1769–1859) was the most celebrated scientist of his age in good part thanks to the multiple volumes he wrote about his scientific travels to South America (1799–1804). Humboldt described Malthus's work as 'one of the most profound works in political economy which has ever appeared' in the same work Malthus cites here (*Political Essay on the New Kingdom of Spain* [New York: AMS Press, 1966]), I 107.

17   Malthus visited Ireland in 1817, but his interest in its demographic and socio-economic conditions long predated this, being clearly evidenced in two essays 'On the State of Ireland' he published in the *Edinburgh Review* in 1808 and 1809.

18   Cottars or cottiers were tenants who rented land and often paid for it by labour rather than cash. As the rent payable increased if the land improved, cottars were structurally discouraged from improving the productivity of the land.

19   The late war is again the Napoleonic Wars.